NAVIGATING THE BOOK OF REVELATION

NAVIGATING THE BOOK OF REVELATION
Special Studies on Important Issues

Kenneth L. Gentry, Jr., Th.D.
Director, GoodBirth Ministries

Fountain Inn, South Carolina 29644

Navigating the Book of Revelation: Special Studies on Important Issues
by Kenneth L. Gentry, Jr., Th.D.
Director, GoodBirth Ministries
Second edition © Copyright 2010 by Gentry Family Trust udt April 2, 1999
First edition © Copyright 2009 by Gentry Family Trust udt April 2, 1999

GoodBirth Ministries
P.O. Box 1722, Fountain Inn, SC 29644
www.GoodBirthMinistries.com
Email: GoodBirthMin@cs.com

GoodBirth Ministries, Inc., is a 501 (c) (3) corporation located in Fountain Inn, South Carolina. As a religious educational ministry, we are committed to sponsoring, subsidizing, and advancing serious Christian scholarship and education in order to:

(1) Assist individual Christians, local congregations, and other bodies of believers in understanding, applying, and promoting a full-orbed Christian worldview, so that Christians might be committed to the call of Scripture that "whether, then, you eat or drink or whatever you do, do all to the glory of God" (1 Cor. 10:31); and

(2) Defend against and challenge the various expressions of unbelief in our modern culture, by demonstrating "that the weapons of our warfare are not of the flesh, but divinely powerful for the destruction of fortresses" with a view to "destroying speculations and every lofty thing raised up against the knowledge of God by taking every thought captive to the obedience of Christ" (2 Cor. 10:4–5).

Printed in the United States of America

ISBN: 978-0-9843220-3-9

Cover Art: Brian Godawa (brian@godawa.com)

Dedicated to my

Revelation Commentary Project Donors

Thanking them for their financial support
and spiritual encouragement

TABLE OF CONTENTS

ABBREVIATIONS

ABD   *The Anchor Bible Dictionary*. David Noel Freedman, ed. 6 vols. New York: Doubleday, 1992.

Ant.   *The Antiquities of the Jews* by Flavius Josephus

Ap.   *Against Apion* by Flavius Josephus

BAGD   F. Wilbur Gingrich and Frederick W. Danker, *A Greek -English Lexicon of the New Testament and Other Early Christian Literature*. 2d. ed.: Chicago: University of Chicago Press, 1979.

BBC   *The Broadman Bible Commentary*. Clifton J. Allen, ed. 12 vols. Nashville: Broadman, 1970-73.

BEB   *Baker Encyclopedia of the Bible*. Ed. by Walter E. Elwell. Grand Rapids: Baker, 1988.

DBI   *Dictionary of Biblical Imagery*. Leland Ryken, James C. Wilhoit, Tremper Longman III, eds. Downers Grove, Ill: InterVarsity, 1998.

DNTB   *Dictionary of New Testament Background*. Craig A. Evans and Stanley E. Porter, eds. Downer's Grove, Ill.: Inter Varsity, 2000.

J.W.   *The Jewish War* by Flavius Josephus

LCL   *Loeb's Classical Library*

Life   *The Life of Flavius* by Flavius Josephus

TDNT   *Theological Dictionary of the New Testament*. Edited by Gerhard Kittel and Gehard Friedrich. Trans. by Geoffery W. Bromiley. 10 vols. Grand Rapids: Eerdmans, 1964-76.

ZPEB   *The Zondervan Pictorial Encyclopedia of the Bible*. 5 vols. Merrill C. Tenney, ed. Grand Rapids: Zondervan, 1976.

PREFACE

I first became deeply interested in Revelation studies while a seminary student at Reformed Theological Seminary from 1975 to 1977. While there I took a theology-changing — and ultimately, life-altering — course titled "History and Eschatology" taught by a new instructor, Greg L. Bahnsen (who shortly thereafter received his Ph.D. in philosophy at the University of Southern California). Bahnsen surprised, intrigued, and challenged me with his commitment to the early date for Revelation and his preterist approach to it. Though at first I resisted his argument, I was eventually overwhelmed by his exegetical, historical, and logical argumentation. From that time forward, my interest in Revelation began to grow increasingly stronger.

In 1985 I began working on my Th.D. at Whitefield Theological Seminary. My interest in Revelation was now quite high, leading me to research the question of the date of its composition. The result was my 468 page dissertation, titled: "The Date of Revelation: An Exegetical and Historical Argument for Its Pre-A.D. 70 Composition." After receiving my Th.D. on December 10, 1988, I submitted my dissertation to Dr. Gary North at the Institute for Christian Economics for publication. He published it in 1989 under the title: *Before Jerusalem Fell: Dating the Book of Revelation*. It has remained in print since its first publication, being released by three different publishers.

Since then I have published a number of articles and books on Revelation. Books involving studies on Revelation that I have either written or contributed to include: *The Beast of Revelation* (1989, 1997), *He Shall Have Dominion* (1990, 1997, 2009), *Perilous Times* (1999), *The Standard Bearer* (2002), *Nourishment from the Word* (2008), and *The Book of Revelation Made Easy* (2008). My earlier studies resulted in my being invited by Zondervan to contribute to one of their Counter Point series books on Revelation: *Four Views on the Book Revelation* (1998).

Since 2005 I have been researching a commentary on the Book of Revelation, tentatively titled *The Divorce of Israel: A Redemptive-Historical Interpretation of Revelation*. By God's grace and with the encouragement and financial support of many friends, GoodBirth Ministries was established in 2005 as a religious educational ministry committed to sponsoring, subsidizing, and advancing serious

Christian scholarship and education. The main function of Good-Birth thus far has been to raise funds to allow me time to research a full-length, in-depth, academically-oriented commentary on Revelation. I am deeply grateful to all who have supported this difficult project. I am also thankful for the assistance and encouragement of GoodBirth Ministries' board: Bill Boney, Kevin Clauson, and Lyle Frazer. Without these contributors and Board members I could not have hoped to engage such an intensive project.

Though I had John's enthusiasm at the beginning of my research, I began to wonder if the completion of my book would "shortly come to pass." Indeed, for awhile I began to doubt whether I could ever hope that "the time is at hand" for its publication. When I began the research in earnest in 2005 I believed that forty-two months or 1260 days or three and one-half years would be sufficient for the project. My hope to finish my research seemed so biblical. But then I realized that after these Revelation time-frames I had to face another: the thousand years!

Nevertheless, I am now past the thousand years of Revelation 20 and into the early verses of Revelation 21, headed toward John's glorious conclusion. Once I have completed the main research and rough draft (later this year, hopefully by December 31, 2009), I will return to Revelation 1 and begin filling out the earlier chapters (which are disproportionately smaller than chapters 10–20) — I tended to dig deeper and research more widely in ancient Jewish documents as I went further into Revelation. Then I will polish up the final project. I am aiming to have the commentary ready for publication by the end of 2010 — barring the Rapture or any other discontinuous event.

GoodBirth Ministries' Board thought it might be helpful to release a forerunner to the commentary — not only as a means for raising much needed additional funds, but also for thanking those who have funded my Revelation research (showing some fruit for their investment). They believe also that it might whet the appetite of other parties interested in Revelation studies.[1] Thus, in the present work I collect some of the special studies from within the commentary; most of these chapters represent *summaries* of Excursuses contained in the commentary.[2] They highlight some critical issues

---

[1] I would also point out that my research has already led to the publication of *The Book of Revelation Made Easy*, as well as this book *Navigating the Book of Revelation*. Once the full (1000 page?) commentary is complete I will produce a 250 page version for pastors and a 100 page version for high schoolers.

[2] When an actual "Excursus" from the fuller commentary is given, the reader should realize that it is a *condensed* version of that material. My commentary Excur-

faced in presenting, defending, and promoting a redemptive-historical, preteristic approach to Revelation. By the very nature of the case, a fuller appreciation of the issues presented within requires the full commentary. Nevertheless, I trust that these studies might encourage further inquiry into and understanding of this viewpoint. My reader should also be aware that some of these chapters will overlap and repeat certain pieces of evidence. This is necessary to filling out each of the arguments more fully.

Though the bulk of the research within assumes familiarity with the general preterist argument for Revelation, I have included some early chapters to bring the uninitiated reader up-to-speed (chs. 1–3). If you are familiar with preterism in general, you may skip these opening chapters and begin with the more detailed chapters (chs. 4ff). The latter chapters are studies of important issues for fleshing out redemptive-historical preterism. They assume a strong understanding of the Revelation and its focus on God's judgment of Israel in A.D. 70.

I would like to thank my good friend, Brian Godawa, for his cover design for this project. He explains the cover as portraying Christ's white horse in the clouds above, the scarlet dragon or beast in the abyss below, and the water in the middle as a dark sea of trouble. This not only matches the sea in Revelation but also reflects the navigation metaphor in the title. Also the fact of a three way split of photos with the title in the middle between the horse and dragon/beast, reinforces the metaphor of navigating between the two sides. Brian's artistic skills and insights have always impressed me.

I must also express my deep appreciation to Lisa Downing who helped with proofreading during the final stages of the preparation of the manuscript for publication. Her volunteer work has been enormously helpful, not only in this project, but in the church that I pastor. She is a committed, diligent Christian who loves the Lord and his Word.

I would also like to acknowledge the immensely helpful work of Jimmy Smith at the Greenville Public Library for his excellent Inter-Library Loan assistance. Many of the references within came to me through his help.

Kenneth L. Gentry, Jr., Th.D
Director, GoodBirth Ministries
www.GoodBirthMinistries.com
Thanksgiving, 2009

---

suses will be more fully argued and footnoted.

Part 1
GENERAL INTRODUCTION TO PRETERISM

1

A.D. 70 IN REDEMPTIVE HISTORY

When you see Jerusalem surrounded by armies, then recognize that her desolation is at hand. Then let those who are in Judea flee to the mountains, and let those who are in the midst of the city depart, and let not those who are in the country enter the city; because these are days of vengeance, in order that all things which are written may be fulfilled. (Luke 21:20–22)

Introduction

As I open this series of studies, it is absolutely essential that we bear in mind the enormous significance of A.D. 70 on redemptive-history and the biblical record. In this first chapter I will provide introductory orientation to this matter. The importance of A.D. 70 will be the controlling presupposition of all that follows.

The presentation below provides only a small sample of evidence demonstrating the significance of A.D. 70, which is too often overlooked by Christians. Our deficient understanding of the purpose and consequences of A.D. 70 diminishes our understanding not only of early Christian history, but of the New Testament record itself.

The Anticipation of A.D. 70

My approach to Revelation is known generally as "preterism." The preterist analysis holds that when John prophesies the events within, they are fast approaching in the first century and would occur not long after he finishes Revelation. My form of preterism holds that the vast bulk of Revelation focuses on the events leading up to and including the fall of Jerusalem and the destruction of the temple in A.D. 70. This view is called "preterism," which derives from the Latin *preteritus*, which means "gone by, past." Thus, the prophecies of Revelation lie in our past.

I call my form of preterism "redemptive-historical preterism." The significance of this approach is not simply that the events John prophesies are past, but that they are *enormously significant* redemptive-historical events that are past. Indeed, they are events that are crucial to the progress of God's redemptive work in history. As the old covenant closes the new covenant is fully and permanently established with the final removal of the Jewish temple. The A.D. 70 events are not just "big" events that are greatly interesting for the study of ancient history; they are big *redemptive-historical* events fundamentally important to the study of God's Word.

As a *key* moment in the progress of God's redemptive work in history, Jerusalem's catastrophic destruction is anticipated everywhere in the New Testament. To miss the significance of A.D. 70 is not just to miss the meaning of an important historical event, but to misunderstand much of the New Testament message. In this chapter I will survey Matthew's Gospel as a sample of the many New Testament statements anticipating A.D. 70. As we shall see, this Gospel is an excellent specimen of the enormity of that fateful year. I could do this with each of the Gospels, Acts, and many of the New Testament epistles for the shadow of A.D. 70 falls over virtually the entire New Testament. Space constraints forbid such an undertaking. I plan on producing a separate book providing a fuller account.[1]

Matthew's Gospel is very Hebraic in style, argument, and purpose. He distinctively uses fulfillment statements followed by an Old Testament reference for proving his point (e.g., Mt 1:22; 2:15, 17, 23; 4:14; 8:17; 12:17; 13:14, 35; 21:4; 26:54-56; 27:9). Matthew shows that Jesus is "the Christ, the Son of the living God" (Mt 16:16) who has come to bring in "the kingdom of heaven" (Mt 16:18-19) through his suffering and death at Jerusalem under the hands of Israel's "elders and chief priests and scribes" (Mt 16:21). Christ promises his disciples that though they may resist his death (Mt 16:22-23), a consequence of it will be that his kingdom will demonstrate itself in power in the events of A.D. 70: "there are some of those who are standing here who shall not taste death until they see the Son of Man coming in His kingdom" (Mt 16:28). Mark's version emphasizes the powerful implications of the matter: "And He was saying to them, 'Truly I say to you, there are some of those who are standing here who shall not taste death until they see the kingdom of God after it has come with power" (Mk 9:1).

Let us see how Matthew relentlessly presses the significance of A.D. 70. Some of his evidence is subtle and must be interpreted in light of the more obvious statements, but much of it is quite obvious. We will see that the evidence greatly intensifies when the Lord

---

[1] For a thorough presentation, see : J. Stuart Russell, The Parousia: A Study of the New Testament Doctrine of Our Lord's Second Coming (Grand Rapids: rep. Baker, 1983 [1887]). Though he presses the evidence too far, his work is quite valuable. For additional materials on the significance of A.D. 70 see: Peter W. L. Walker, *Jesus and the Holy City: New Testament Perspectives on Jerusalem* (Grand Rapids: Eerdmans, 1996) and N. T. Wright, *The New Testament and the People of God* (Minneapolis: Fortress, 1992).

enters Jerusalem during Passion Week. Matthew records a long prophetic discourse, presents several rejection and judgment parables,
shows Christ engaging in prophetic theater, and presents him
weeping over Jerusalem — all of which point to the coming holocaust.

Early Matthean Evidence

In Matthew 1 the Apostle traces the genealogy of Christ to Abraham, the father of the Jews (Mt 1:1, 17). In fact, the very opening
words of his Gospel are: "The book of the genealogy of Jesus Christ,
the son of David, the son of Abraham." Matthew does this in order
to present Jesus as the Jewish Messiah who has come to fulfill the
promises to the fathers. But though Matthew opens with the
genealogical evidence that Jesus is the Messiah, immediately in
Matthew 2 he begins painting a gloomy picture of the Jewish
condition. In this he begins subtly showing Israel's resistance to
Christ's coming, signifying the very thing that John laments in the
opening of his Gospel: " He came to His own, and those who were
His own did not receive Him" (Jn 1:11).

Matthew notes that after Jesus' birth, men from *the east* come to
worship him — but that all *Jerusalem* is "troubled" (Mt 2:3). In presenting matters thus, Matthew differs greatly from Luke, who shows
the Jewish shepherds (and other lowly individuals outside the realm
of power) excited about the news.

Thus, early on in his commentary Matthew prepares his Jewish
audience for the Messiah's rejection by the Jews and his acceptance
by the Gentiles. Indeed, this foreshadows Jesus' lament over Jerusalem toward the end of his ministry in Matthew 23:37–38 (see
below). His Gospel will gradually unfold an intensifying message of
God's coming judgment upon Jerusalem and Israel as a consequence
of their rejecting Christ.

In Matthew 3:9–12 Christ's forerunner John the Baptist rebukes
the Jews for proudly touting Abraham as their father. (In Revelation
Jesus declares that the Jews vacuously "say they are Jews, and are
not, but lie," Rev 3:9; cp. 2:9.[2]) Then just before Christ's ministry begins, John warns that "the axe is already laid at the root of the trees"
(Mt 3:10). He notes that "He who is coming" has a "winnowing fork
is in His hand, and He will thoroughly clear His threshing floor; and
He will gather His wheat into the barn, but He will burn up the
chaff with unquenchable fire" (Mt 3:12). This provides the fore-glow
of Jerusalem's flames to erupt in A.D. 70.

---

[2] See: Philip L. Mayo, *"Those Who Call Themselves Jews": The Church and Judaism
in the Apocalypse of John* (Eugene, Ore.: Pickwick, 2006).

Christ's Early Ministry

As Christ opens his formal ministry, he leaves Nazareth and goes to Capernaum (Mt 4:13) so that Isaiah's prophecy might be fulfilled: "The land of Zebulun and the land of Naphtali, by the way of the sea, beyond the Jordan, *Galilee of the Gentiles* — the people who were sitting in darkness saw a great light" (Mt 4:15-16a). Significantly, the Lord begins proclaiming his message in "Galilee of the *Gentiles*." Hints of his future turning to the Gentiles arise alongside of the adumbrations of Israel's A.D. 70 judgment.

Following this, the Lord's first major sermon (the Sermon on the Mount, Mt 5-7), declares blessings on his followers. He warns, though, that they will be persecuted by the Jewish leaders because of their allegiance to him — for the Jews also persecuted the prophets before them (Mt 5:10-12). Thereupon he denounces the scribes and Pharisees as false teachers who mislead the people (Mt 5:20, cf. vv 21-48). They are hypocrites (Mt 6:5) who do no better than the Gentiles (Mt 6:7). They are "false prophets" (Mt 7:15) who will be cut down and thrown into the fire (Mt 7:19).

In Matthew 8 we read the surprising account of the believing Gentile who exercises more faith than anyone in Israel (Mt 8:10). As a result of this man's faith we hear once again of people coming from the east — and west: this time Jesus teaches that they will sit with Abraham, Isaac, and Jacob (the rightful place of the Jews), while the Jews themselves ("the sons of the kingdom") are cast out in suffering at the A.D. 70 holocaust (Mt 8:11-12). Once again, Matthew anticipates Jerusalem's destruction.

As a result of the coming expansion of God's people by those coming from east and west, in Matthew 9:16-17 Jesus teaches that the constraints of Judaism and the old covenant are like old wineskins that would burst were his message to continue within them. So then, God provides new wineskins for the coming of the new covenant: the new covenant Church, which is the "Israel of God" (Gal 6:16; cp. Ro 9:6; Gal 3:7, 29; Php 3:3).

Shortly thereafter in Matthew 10:5-6 Jesus expressly limits his personal ministry to Israel as a witness to her (cp. Mt 15:24). But in Matthew 10:16-17 he notes that despite such favor, the synagogues will punish his followers. As a result, in Matthew 10:23 he promises that he will return to judge the Jews before the apostles have finished going through all of Israel (A.D. 70): "But whenever they persecute you in this city, flee to the next; for truly I say to you, you shall not finish going through the cities of Israel, until the Son of Man comes [i.e., in judgment]." In Matthew 10:34-36 he warns that he has not come to bring peace on the earth (literally, "the Land," i.e., Israel), but a sword which will divide homes — because of the

[handwritten margin note: fore-shadowing]

[handwritten note at bottom: cp = compare / cf = confer]

Jewish opposition (see the experience of the blind man in Jn 9:1, 16–23; cp. Lk 6:22; Jn 12:42; 16:2; Ac 9:1–2; 22:4–5; 26:9–11).

Later in Matthew 11:14 Jesus declares that John the Baptist fulfills the prophecy of Elijah's return. When we read the Old Testament backdrop to this in Malachi 3–4, we discover that he will proclaim judgment in Israel before the great and terrible day of the Lord (Mal 4:5–6; cp. Mal 3:1–3; John mentions the day of Lord in Rev 6:17; 16:14). In Matthew 11:20–24 Jesus rebukes cities in Israel and warns of their judgment, comparing them unfavorably to wicked Old Testament cities (in Rev 11:8 Jerusalem is called Egypt, and in 17:3–19:2 Jerusalem is called Babylon). In Matthew 12:39 he speaks of the Jews of his day as an "evil and adulterous generation." This imagery appears in John's Revelation as he presents Jerusalem as a great "harlot" (Rev 17:3ff), as did the Old Testament prophets (Isa 1:21; Jer 2:20; 3:1, 6, 8; Eze 16:9, 15–17, 26; Hos 2:5; 4:10, 12–15).[3] In Matthew 12:41–42 the Lord once again rebukes and warns cities in Israel of coming judgment.

In Matthew 12:43–45 Jesus warns of the seven-fold demonization of Israel in "this generation" (in Rev 2:9 and 3:9 John calls the synagogue a "synagogue of Satan"; Rev 9 speaks of the flood of demons coming upon Israel; in Rev 13:11ff the High Priest speaks as the dragon, i.e., Satan). In Matthew 13:58 he performs no miracles in Nazareth due to their lack of faith. In Matthew 15:7–14 he cites Isaiah against the rabbis in Israel for neglecting God's Word and teaching falsely.

In Matthew 16:4 the Lord once again speaks of Israel as an evil and adulterous generation, keeping up the drumbeat of Israel's sinful condition and conduct. In Matthew 16:21 Jesus teaches his disciples that their chief priests, representatives of the temple and the worship of God, will kill him (in Rev 11:8 Jerusalem appears as the place "where also their Lord was crucified"; in Rev 17:4–6 the harlot is dressed in the clothing of the High Priest and drunk on the blood of the saints; see Ch. 12 below). In Matthew 16:28 he notes that some of his followers will live to see his kingdom coming with power (this nearness is John's expectation in Revelation as well; Rev 1:1, 3; 22:6, 10).

Christ's Later Ministry

In Matthew 17:10–13 Jesus calls John the Baptist "Elijah," who is not recognized as such and is killed — just as the Jewish leaders will kill him. Matthew 17:17 once again calls first century Israel an "evil generation." In Matthew 19:28 Jesus teaches that the Son of Man will

---

[3] See Ch. 11 below.

come and the apostles will sit on thrones to judge the twelve tribes of Israel (this is the message of Rev 1:7, as I demonstrate in *The Book of Revelation Made Easy* [2009]). In Matthew 20:18–19 Christ once again prophesies that the chief priests — the religious rulers of Israel and the representatives of the nation before God[4] — will condemn him to death.

In Matthew 21:12 Jesus casts out the moneychangers and overturns their tables. By this he engages in prophetic theater, showing the coming overthrow of the temple[5] (in Rev 18:3, 11ff the enormous wealth of the temple is lost due to its destruction). In Matthew 21:19–21 he curses the fig tree and speaks of the mountain being thrown in the sea, both of which serve as signs of judgment on Israel. The "mountain" probably refers to the temple mount because he was approaching the temple[6] (John speaks of the burning mountain being thrown into the sea, signifying the temple, Rev 8:8). In Matthew 21:33–43, 45 the parable of the landowner shows the kingdom will be taken from the Jews and they will be crushed (John's general message in Revelation is the divorce of Israel and God's marriage to the new covenant Church, see later discussion in Ch. 4). In Matthew 22:2–7 their city will be burned (in Rev 17:6 Jerusalem is stripped and burned).

As we enter Matthew 23, we hear Jesus uttering seven woes upon the scribes and Pharisees (Mt 23:13–16, 23, 29). He charges that they vainly swear by the temple (Mt 23:16–22), which will soon be destroyed. By clinging to the temple, they follow the same pattern as their sinful Old Testament forbears: they trust that the temple will ensure their blessing. But Jeremiah warned the Jews then: "Do not trust in deceptive words, saying, 'This is the temple of the Lord, the temple of the Lord, the temple of the Lord'" (Jer 7:4).

---

[4] The High Priest wears upon his holy garments onyx stones engraved with "the names of the sons of Israel" (Ex 28:9–11, 21, 29–30; cp. Heb 2:17).

[5] Prophetic theater is a non verbal communication, a *verbum visible* which involves prophets acting out their warnings. We see examples in Isa 20; Jer 13:1-11; 19; 27:1-15; 32; 43:8-13; Eze 4:1-3; 4:4-8; 4:9-17; 5:1-54; 12:1-16; 12:17-20; 37:15-28. That John in Revelation would employ prophetic theater in a written work he would never perform is "astonishing," indicating his intent not only for "emphasis," but "as a striking attempt to signal his prophetic identity" (F. D. Mazzaferri, *The Genre of the Book of Revelation from a Source-critical Perspective* [Berlin: de Gruyter, 1989], 329).

[6] Morna D. Hooker, *Gospel according to St. Mark* (BNTC) (Peabody, Mass.: Hendrickson, 1991), 269; N. T. Wright, *Jesus and the Victory of God* (Minneapolis: Fortress, 1996), 422; G. K. Beale, *The Book of Revelation* (NIGTC) (Grand Rapids: Eerdmans, 1999), 183.

In Matthew 23:34–35 the Lord warns that God will judge first century Israel for the righteous blood shed in the land (John applies this statement in Rev 18:24). In Matthew 23:36–38 Jesus laments Jerusalem's coming destruction and declares her temple desolate (John declares Jerusalem "desolate" in Rev 17:16). In Matthew 24:2–3 he leaves the temple and prophesies its destruction (this prophecy is recorded in Lk 21:24 in the very form picked up by John in Rev 11:2). In Matthew 24:16 he notes that his followers must flee Judea because in 24:34 "this generation" will experience judgment (John calls the saints out of Jerusalem, Rev 18:4). Matthew 24 is one of the five major discourses— and the final, climactic one — structuring Matthew's Gospel, and it deals at length with Jerusalem's destruction (Mt 24:30 and Rev 1:7 are the only places in the New Testament that merge Da 7:13 and Zec 12:10 — and both of these contexts involve near term indicators [Mt 24:34; Rev 1:1, 3] and references to the temple [Mt 24:2; Rev 11:1–2]).

In Matthew 26:2–5 the chief priests and the High Priest counsel Jesus' death. In vv 14–16 the chief priests pay Judas to betray Christ to them. In vv 17–31 Jesus institutes the Lord's Supper in the context of the Passover, warning that he will soon be struck down and they will be scattered (v 31). (In Revelation Jesus appears as the slain Passover Lamb: Rev 5:6, 8, 12–13; 6:1, 16; 7:9–10, 14, 17; 12:11; 14:1, 4, 10; 15:3; 17:4; 19:7, 9; 21:9, 14; 22:3.) In v 47 the High Priest has Jesus arrested (in Rev 18:2 Jerusalem appears as Babylon and as a prison).

In Matthew 26:57 he is tried before the High Priest, who in v 59 brings false witnesses (in Revelation the second beast is the false prophet who deceives, Rev 13:14; 19:20). In vv 63–64 Jesus warns that the High Priestly aristocracy before whom he stands will witness his coming in cloud judgment upon Israel (this judgment appears in Rev 1:7; 17:14):

> And the high priest said to Him, "I adjure You by the living God, that You tell us whether You are the Christ, the Son of God." Jesus said to him, "You have said it yourself; nevertheless I tell you, hereafter you shall see the Son of Man sitting at the right hand of Power, and coming on the clouds of heaven."

This cloud-coming language reflects that of God's judgment on Egypt in the Old Testament (Isa 19:1).

In Matthew 27:1 the High Priest plots to kill Jesus. In Matthew 27:20 the High Priest persuades the crowds to turn against him, after which in v 25 the people call his blood down upon themselves (in Revelation Christ's followers actually win the victory over Israel because of his blood, Rev 7:14; 12:11). In vv 41–43 the High Priest and the leaders of Israel mock him on the cross. In v 51 the temple veil is torn, signifying the temple's soon coming destruction and the opening of the Holy of holies without any need of an earthly priest (in Rev 11:19 God's temple in heaven is opened after the temple is destroyed by the Gentiles, 11:2). In vv 62–66 the chief priests and the Pharisees vainly seek to insure that his grave is sealed and protected from his disciples (in Rev 1:18 Jesus actually has the keys to the grave and death and he is alive for evermore).

In Matthew 28:11–15 the chief priests and elders of Israel pay off the Roman soldiers to say the disciples stole his body, though he had actually arisen from the dead just as he prophesied (Mt 16:21; 17:23; 26:32). This story was "widely spread among the Jews" (Mt 28:15b). Though Matthew opens his Gospel with Christ's Jewish genealogy, and though he alone of the Gospel writers declares Christ intentionally restricts his own ministry to Israel (Mt 10:6; 15:24), and though he repeatedly shows the Old Testament prophecies fulfilled in Christ's life, he ends his Gospel in Matthew 28:19 with the Great Commission designed for "all the nations" (John declares that "all the nations will come and worship before Thee," Rev 15:4; cp. Rev 21: 24, 26; 22:2).

The Significance of A.D. 70

Too often we tend to view Jerusalem's destruction as a horrible human tragedy befalling a helpless people under the crushing oppression of a mighty empire. But when we understand the event from the context of both Scripture's unfolding of *redemptive* history *and* from the religious history of the Jews, we gain a far deeper insight into its significance.

Many historians view Jerusalem's destruction as one of the most revolutionary events in Judaism's history. They note the centrality of the temple to Israel's self-understanding and to *biblical* Judaism's purpose. Philo observes of his own people: "their holy temple is the most predominant, and vehement, and universal feeling throughout the whole nation" (*Embassy* 31 [§212]). Thus, we must understand that "Jews were a nation dedicated to religion and ruled by priests. The essence of their nation lay in the Temple in Jerusalem."[7]

Consequently, after A.D. 70 "no longer did Judaism have a sacred center, a temple, a priesthood, and a sacrificial cult."[8] Price observes that "the Jews had staked their lives and their Temple, which was to some dearer than life, on political freedom. The destruction

---

[7] Martin Goodman, *The Ruling Class of Judaea: The Origins of the Jewish Revolt Against Rome A.D. 66–70* (Cambridge: Cambridge University Press, 1987), 30.

[8] Shaye J. D. Cohen, "The Destruction: From Scripture to Midrash." *Prooftexts* 2 (1982): 18–39.

of the Temple and dissolution of the short-lived state [A.D. 67–70] completely refocused Jewish religion."[9] DeYoung comments that "this judgment marks the end of Jerusalem's validity in the history of redemption."[10] Such is the enormous religious significance of Jerusalem's fall after her centrality in biblical religion for more than 1000 years.

In that the first Christians tend to focus on and gravitate to Jerusalem,[11] her fall in A.D. 70 makes a significant impact on nascent Christianity. Thus, Christian theologians offer important observations on A.D. 70 and its impact *upon the Church*. Reymond observes that: "after the destruction of Jerusalem in A.D. 70 . . . the church was no longer viewed as existing within the national life of Israel."[12] Vos, in fact, speaks of A.D. 70 as "the complete overthrow of the theocracy, and the rearing from the foundation up of a new structure in which the Son would receive full vindication and supreme honor."[13]

In fact, A.D. 70 is an enormously significant event for *both* Judaism *and* Christianity. Berlin and Overman note that

> the Revolt had a profound and enduring impact on the development and shape of Judaism and Christianity. . . . It is safe to say that had there not been a Jewish revolt in Judea in 66–70 C.E., Christianity and Judaism, as we know them today, would not exist. . . . Many have argued that the destruction of the temple in Jerusalem in 70 C.E. constitutes the seminal event in the formation of both early Christianity and Rabbinic Judaism.[14]

After Jerusalem's fall, *biblical* Judaism ceases and *rabbinic* Judaism begins to take its place in Israel. No longer will Israel be governed by the God-revealed and God-ordained Mosaic levitical code with its centralized sacrificial worship.

Brandon explains that "the Jewish overthrow of A.D. 70 emancipated the infant faith from its Jewish cradle, thus making possible

---

[9] J. J. Price, *Jerusalem Under Siege: The Collapse of the Jewish State 66–70 C.E.* (New York: Brill, 1992), 175.

[10] James C. DeYoung, *Jerusalem in the New Testament: The Significance of the City in the History of Redemption and in Eschatology* (Kampen: J. H. Kok, 1960), 98.

[11] See particularly Lk 24:4, 52; Ac 1:4, 8, 12; 8:1, 14, 25; 11:22; 15:2, 4; 16:4; Ga 1:17–18, 21.

[12] Robert L. Reymond, *A New Systematic Theology* (Nashville: Nelson, 1998), 837.

[13] Geerhardus Vos, *The Self-Disclosure of Jesus: The Modern Debate about the Messianic Consciousness* (Grand Rapids: Eerdmans, 1954 [rep.]), 162.

[14] Andrea M. Berlin and J. Andrew Overman, *The First Jewish Revolt: Archaeology, History, and Ideology* (London: Routledge, 2002), 5–6.

its career as a world-religion. . . . The destruction of Jerusalem gave other cities decisive parts in the life of the Church, especially Rome. The Jewish catastrophe of A.D 70 probably [was] the next most crucial event for Christianity after the Resurrection experiences."[15] Frend writes that:

> the fall of Jerusalem left a permanent mark on the development of the Church. First and foremost, it meant a violent shift of centre, in which the Church was gradually to lose Palestine, the homeland of Jesus and his disciples, and with Palestine Aramaic-speaking Judaism, including the opportunity of spreading eastwards beyond the Roman Empire into Persia and to the second great centre of Jewry at Babylon.[16]

Speaking in terms of the redemptive-historical drama, the consequences of A.D. 70 are so significant that "the destruction of Jerusalem and of its temple marked not the end of *the* world, but the end of *a* world. It indicated the final separation of Judaism from Christianity, of the synagogue from the Church . . . which thereby opens up principally to the Gentiles."[17] When God removes the temple, the holy faith is universalized. It is no longer sequestered in a particular land, focused on a local shrine, and maintained by a singular people (Mt 21:43; Jn 4:20-23; Heb 8:13). Thus, Christianity may not be physically destroyed, extinguishing or even incapacitating the true religion. This is the significance of the "times of the Gentiles" being "fulfilled" (Luke 21:24). The Gentiles may no longer render God's worship inoperative. As a result Christianity differs from biblical Judaism in that "the temple . . . was constantly threatened by heathen powers."[18] We see this danger under Nebuchadnezzar's destruction of the first temple (2Ki 24-25), and the desecration of the second temple under Antiochus Epiphanes (Macc 1), Pompey (*Ant.* 14:4:3), and, Pilate (Lk 13:1), as well as Vespasian and Titus's final devastation of the temple in A.D. 70 (*J.W.* 6-7).

---

[15] S. G. F. Brandon, *The Fall of Jerusalem and the Christian Church: A Study of the Effects of the Jewish Overthrow of A.D. 70 on Christianity* (London: S. P. C. K., 1957), xix.

[16] W. H. C. Frend, *Martyrdom and Persecution in the Early Church: A Study of a Conflict from the Maccabees to Donatus* (Garden City: Anchor, 1967), 133.

[17] André Feuilett, *Johannine Studies*, trans. Thomas E. Crane (Staten Island, N.Y.: Alba, 1964), 229-30.

[18] Lloyd Gaston, *No Stone On Another: Studies in the Significance of the Fall of Jerusalem in the Synoptic Gospels* (Leiden: Brill, 1970), 116.

Conclusion

If we are aware of the redemptive-historical significance of the temple's destruction in A.D. 70, we will be able to discern precursors to that event in Christ's teaching and actions as found in the Gospel record. I have used Matthew's Gospel to show how we can see the case against Israel being built up in the New Testament record. We could conduct the same sort of survey throughout the Gospel record and Acts — and several of the Epistles. The destruction of the temple is not simply an event of past history, it is an event establishing the final phase of redemptive-history: the new covenant phase of the Church (Lk 22:20; 1Co 11:25; 2Co 3:6). Truly, the new covenant has burst the constraints of Israel (Mt 9:16–17).

2

THE DATE OF REVELATION

Here is the mind which has wisdom. The seven heads are seven mountains on which the woman sits, and they are seven kings; five have fallen, one is, the other has not yet come; and when he comes, he must remain a little while. (Rev 17:9–10)

Introduction

An important presupposition for my presentations in this work and in my forthcoming commentary is the proper dating of Revelation. I believe Revelation was written *prior* to the destruction of Jerusalem in A.D. 70. The chapters below should be read with this perspective in mind. This matter was the subject of my doctoral dissertation at Whitefield Theological Seminary. For a fuller treatment of this matter see my dissertation:

Kenneth L. Gentry, Jr., *Before Jerusalem Fell: Dating the Book of Revelation* (3d. ed.: Fountain Inn, S.C.: Victorious Hope, 1998).

Throughout the chapters below, I will be arguing that the Book of Revelation (primarily, though not exclusively) focuses on Jerusalem's destruction in A.D. 70.[1] I will be providing evidence for a Judaic focus on the temple and priesthood in Revelation. The temple disappears with Titus' final siege in A.D. 70, while the priesthood fades out as no longer relevant. Theoretically John could be writing an *explanatory* drama *after* the events, thereby explaining to Christians what has become of Jerusalem.[2] Yet, I believe he is actually writing a *prophetic* drama *before* the events, thereby warning Christians of the soon-coming removal of the city that had been the focus even of first century Christianity. Thus, establishing Revela-

---

[1] Even when it brings in the Roman Empire as a source of evil, it does so largely to show Israel's linkage to it and influence on it. In Rev 13:1–10 John presents Rome as the sea beast, an oppressor of Christianity (cf. Rev 13:5, 7). In Rev 13:11 he presents the land beast (which is Jerusalem's religious establishment, see Ch. 9 below) as the servant of Rome. In Rev 17 the beast is a stage prop holding up the Jerusalem-harlot, who sits on (controls) the beast (Rev 17:3, 6). See Chs. 10 and 11.

[2] As per Eugenio Corsini, *The Apocalypse: The Perennial Revelation of Jesus Christ* (Wilmington, Del.: Michael Glazier, 1983).

tion's date is significant for my approach — much like an early date for Daniel is significant for its proper interpretation.[3]

The Practical Issues

Although this topic may initially appear to be purely academic, it raises extremely practical issues. Resolving the question of Revelation's compositional date is one of the most — if not *the* most — important issues facing the interpreter. We may see its significance both regarding the *interpretive* and the *practical* questions revolving around the book in the following:

First, interpretively, Revelation's date exercises a tremendous influence upon its proper understanding. The current majority of biblical scholars is in fundamental disagreement with the majority of the scholars from one hundred years ago. The current opinion — the late-date view — holds that John writes Revelation while in exile during the closing days of the reign of Domitian Caesar, about A.D. 95 or 96. This contradicts the nineteenth century view — the early-date view — which held that John writes Revelation prior to the destruction of Jerusalem and the temple in A.D. 70. This position was held by such worthies as John Lightfoot, Moses Stuart, B. F. Westcott, F. J. A. Hort, Alfred Edersheim, Philip Schaff, Milton Terry, and others.[4]

Early-date advocates generally understand Revelation's prophecies to be dealing with the tremendous spiritual, social, political, and cultural upheaval leading up to and culminating in the destruction of the temple and Jerusalem in the ill-fated Jewish War of A.D. 67–70.[5] This war effectively serves as the birth-pangs delivering

---

[3] Indeed, dating issues are significant virtually throughout the Scriptures. Rather than accept the Pentateuch as a later, composite work, evangelicals argue for its earlier Mosaic authorship. Rather than accept the multiple authorship of Isaiah (deutero-, trito-), evangelicals argue for its unity and earlier date. Witness the debates over the dates and genuineness of the Pauline epistles. The preterist is not embarrassed by a "unique" do-or-die problem regarding dating, despite such assertions as for example by Mark L. Hitchcock, "A Defense of the Domitianic Date of the Book of Revelation," Ph.D. dissertation, Dallas: Dallas Theological Seminary, 2005), 3–4.

[4] For a fuller presentation of early-date advocates see: Gentry, *Before Jerusalem Fell* (3d. ed.: Fountain Inn, S.C.: Victorious Hope, 1998), 30–38.

[5] Many early date advocates see Revelation as providing even more space to the Roman Empire and its judgment (Rev 13–19). My view is that John's primary focus is on the collapse of biblical Judaism and its temple system. The references to God's judgment on the Romans appears to be limited to Nero's death and the Roman civil wars of A.D. 68–69.

Christianity from her mother's womb (Israel), thereby effecting an irremediable separation between these two great monotheistic, Bible-birthed religions. These first-century issues also include the first Roman persecution of Christianity under Nero Caesar (A.D. 64–68), the catastrophic Roman Civil Wars (A.D. 68–69), and the extinction of the Julio-Claudian line of emperors when Nero dies (A.D. 68). Thus, the events Revelation prophesies highlight the catastrophes leading to the final *foundation stone* securing the Messianic kingdom in history.

Though yet a minority view today a growing number of scholars is returning to a date prior to A.D. 70. These diverse scholars include liberals (C. C. Torrey, Rudolf Bultmann, J. M. Ford, and John A. T. Robinson[6]), evangelicals (C. F. D. Moule, F. F. Bruce, R. B. Moberly; E. Earle Ellis, Roland Worth, Stephen Smalley, and Ian Boxall[7]), and reformed conservatives(Cornelis Vanderwaal, Jay Adams, David Chilton, and R. C. Sproul.)[8] Boxall observes that "this date was favoured by nineteenth-century scholars, such as Westcott, Lightfoot and Hort, and is undergoing something of a revival in scholarly circles."[9]

The late-date view, on the other hand, allows for an almost infinite variety of interpretations. The three other basic schools of interpretation (other than preterism) prefer a late-date of composition: historicism, idealism, and futurism (see discussion of interpretive schools in Ch. 3 below). Most of the supposed alternative possibilities relate to events lying in John's distant future, events

---

[6] Charles C. Torrey, *The Apocalypse of John* (New Haven: Yale, 1958). J. Massyngberde Ford, *Revelation* (Garden City, N.Y.: Anchor, 1975). John A. T. Robinson, *Redating the New Testament* (Philadelphia: Westminster, 1976). For Bultmann, see statement by C. H. Dodd in Robinson, *Redating the New Testament*, 359.

[7] C. F. D. Moule, *The Birth of the New Testament* (3rd ed., San Francisco: Harper and Row, 1982), 174. F. F. Bruce, *New Testament History* (Garden City, N.Y.: Doubleday, 1969), 411. R. B. Moberly, "When Was Revelation Conceived?," *Biblica* 73 (1992): 376–93. E. Earle Ellis, *The Making of the New Testament Documents* (Boston: Brill, 1999), 210. Stephen S. Smalley, *The Revelation to John: A Commentary on the Greek Text of the Apocalypse* (Downers Grove, Ill.: InterVarsity, 2005), 352. Roland H. Worth, Jr., *Seven Cities of the Apocalypse and Roman Culture* (New York: Paulist, 1999), 90, 136. Ian Boxall, *The Revelation of Saint John* (BNTC) (Peabody, Mass.: Hendrikson, 2006), 8.

[8] Jay E. Adams, *The Time is at Hand* (Phillipsburg, NJ: Presbyterian and Reformed, 1966). Cornelis Vanderwaal, *Search the Scriptures*, vol.10 (Ontario: Paideia, 1979). David Chilton, *The Days of Vengeance: An Exposition of the Book of Revelation* (Fort Worth: Dominion, 1987). R. C. Sproul, *The Last Days according to Jesus* (Grand Rapids: Baker, 1998).

[9] Boxall, *Revelation*, 8.

betokening the end of world history. As such, Revelation would be speaking of the *conclusion* of the kingdom, or of the Church Age, if you will.

Thus, the date one assigns Revelation has the potential for placing the majority of its prophecies, particularly its judgment scenes, either at the *beginning* of Christian history or at its *end*. Thus, the dating issue may literally turn Revelation on its head. Since Revelation is a book in the canon of Scripture, and since *all* Scripture is inspired of God and "profitable" (2Ti 3:16), we must strive to rightly interpret it, which requires that we properly understand its setting — a most practical reality for the evangelical Christian. As I note above, we see this same "problem" in dating Daniel: the majority scholarly view places Daniel rather late (in the Maccabean era of the second century B.C.), whereas conservative commentators place it much earlier (during the Babylonian exile in the sixth century B.C.).

Second, practically, the dating of Revelation has a great bearing on our current outlook and prospects, on our biblical eschatology, and our Christian worldview. Our understanding of Revelation has great social and cultural issues hanging in the balance:

> Does Revelation speak of a looming great tribulation, which soon will bring upon the scene of history irresistible worldwide chaos and upheaval? Or did it inform the *first century* Christians of grave and trying times *they* would face, which would demonstrate that Christianity could weather the most furious storms, thereby bracing them for the long haul?

> Should we brace ourselves for the worst and, as Hal Lindsey urged us almost a half-century ago, "live like people who don't expect to be around much longer"? Or may we look to the future as lying before a conquering Church, which has *already* endured the great tribulation and now seeks victory in the world over the long haul?

Of course we must determine the particular date for Revelation on the historical and exegetical *evidence,* not upon our psychological *predisposition,* our sociological *longing,* or our theological *pre-commitments.* So let us now consider the evidence for Revelation's dating. The view that I will be defending is that Revelation was written by the Apostle John in about A.D. 65 or 66, just after the outbreak of the Neronic persecution (November, A.D. 64) and just prior to the eruption of both the Jewish War (A.D. 67) and the Roman Civil Wars (A.D. 68).

The Internal Evidence

I will first engage the internal indicators of time that we discover in Revelation, that is, the evidence from Revelation's *self-witness*. In that I hold to the full inspiration and inerrancy of Scripture, I am convinced that these are the most fundamental evidences. Later I will consider the external evidence, the material arising from Church tradition. In that I am a Protestant I hold that the latter evidence bears a lesser weight. Generally, the late-date advocates begin with the evidence from tradition, and the early-date advocates with the evidence from self-witness. I am convinced that the late-date reliance upon external indicators is methodologically flawed in this book (Revelation) containing so many historical and cultural indicators.

As I begin let me point out what should be obvious: the issue cannot finally be resolved in the small amount of space available. Indeed, I wrote my doctoral dissertation of over 450 pages on the subject. Nevertheless, I will lay before the reader some compelling introductory evidence which I trust will at least provide the *prima facie* plausibility for the early date. I will focus on three internal evidences for the early date.

The Temple in Revelation 11

In Revelation 11:1, 2 John experiences something as he is receiving the vision:

> There was given me a reed like unto a rod: and the angel stood, saying, Rise, and measure the temple of God, and the altar, and them that worship therein. But the court which is without the temple leave out, and measure it not; for it is given unto the Gentiles: and the holy city shall they tread under foot forty and two months.

Here we find a temple standing in "the holy city." It seems indisputable that a Christian Jew, such as John, would have in mind historical Jerusalem when he speaks of "the holy city." This is so for two basic reasons: (1) The biblical context. Jerusalem is frequently called such in Scripture: Isaiah 48:2; 52:1; Nehemiah 11:1–18; Matthew 4:5; 27:53. (2) Revelation's context. Revelation 11:8 informs us that this is the city where "also our Lord was crucified." The place of our Lord's crucifixion is historical Jerusalem, according to the clear testimony of Scripture (e.g., Lk 9:22; 13:32; 17:11; 19:28).

Now what temple stood in Jerusalem? Obviously the Jewish temple ordained by God, wherein the Jewish sacrifices were offered — the first century temple known as Herod's temple because of his expanding and embellishing it. John must be alluding to that historical structure for three reasons:

First, it is located in Jerusalem (Mk 11:11, 15, 27; Lk 4:9; Ac 22:17), as the text clearly states. The audience could have thought of nothing else than Jerusalem's famous temple, which was noted for its magnificence in the writings even of Roman historian Tacitus. Tacitus states that the Jewish temple "was famous beyond all other works of men," a "temple of immense wealth."[10] Ancient accounts of the temple portray its striking beauty, accounts such as those we find in Josephus and the Jewish Mishnah.[11]

The first century Jewish philosopher Philo (25 B.C. – A.D. 40) says its was "beautiful beyond all possible description," and that "the buildings of it are of most exceeding beauty and magnificence, so as to be universal objects of admiration to all who behold them, and especially to all foreigners who travel to those parts, and who comparing them with their own public edifices, marvel both at the beauty and sumptuousness of this one."[12] The ancient Jewish rabbis exult in the temple: "He that never saw the temple of Herod never saw a fine building" (Baba Bathra).

Second, John prophesies that the temple he has in mind will be under assault for a period of forty-two months. The "forty-two months" (Rev 11:2) or "1260 days" (Rev 11:3) happens to parallel the period of the Jewish War with Rome from the time of its formal engagement by Nero until the temple is destroyed by Titus. Nero commissions his most capable general Flavius Vespasian to engage Israel in war in February, A.D. 67; Vespasian actually enters the Promised Land and engages in battle that Spring: "When Vespasian arrived the following Spring [A.D. 67] to take charge of operations, he steadily reduced Galilee [and] Peraea. . . . Titus [Vespasian's son] began the siege of Jerusalem in April, 70. . . . By the end of August the Temple area was occupied and the holy house burned down."[13] From Spring A.D. 67 to August/September A.D. 70 is a period right around forty-two months. The time-frame correspondence is tolerably precise.

Third, the structure of Revelation 11:1, 2 parallels and seems to be built upon Jesus's statement in his Olivet Discourse as found in Luke 21:24. In Luke 21:1–5, the disciples are in Jerusalem and specifically point out the temple when inquiring about its future. Jesus tells them that it will soon be destroyed stone by stone (Lk 21:6).

---

[10] Tacitus, *Fragments of the Histories* 2; *History* 5:8.

[11] Josephus, *Antiquities* 15:11:3, 5; *Wars* 5:5. *Middoth* 1:1–5:4 in Herbert Danby, transl., *The Mishnah* (New York: Oxford University Press, 1933), 589–97.

[12] Philo, *The Special Laws: I*, 1:72, 73.

[13] Bruce, *New Testament History*, 381–82.

Finally in Luke 21:24 he speaks in terms that seem clearly to form the foundation for Revelation 11:2:

> Revelation 11:2: "The court which is without the temple leave out, and measure it not; for it is given unto the *Gentiles* [*ethnesin*] and the *holy city* shall they *tread under foot* forty and two months."

> Luke 21:24: "*Jerusalem* will be *trampled underfoot* by the *Gentiles* [*ethnōn*] until the times of the Gentiles be fulfilled."

Revelation 11 incorporates the reference to the Gentiles, the trampling under foot, and the city of Jerusalem ("Jerusalem"/"holy city"). The two passages speak of the same event: the looming destruction of Jerusalem. And the Olivet Discourse ties the destruction of the temple to "this generation" to whom Christ spoke (Lk 21:32; cp. Mt 24:34; Mk 13:30), while John declares that his prophecies "must shortly take place" (Rev 1:1) because "the time is at hand" (Rev 1:3).

We know as a matter of clear historical and archaeological record that the temple is destroyed in August/September, A.D. 70:

> The recent excavations have provided striking evidence of Titus's destruction.... In the destruction of these buildings, walls were razed, paving stones torn up, and the drain clogged with material firmly dated to the last part of the century by the pottery. In the drain were human skulls and other bones, washed down from the ruined city higher up the slope.

> Even more dramatic were the finds in Site N, the area in which the fine street of Herod Agrippa was uncovered. Reference has already been made to the collapse of the staircase leading east from the street. The tumble of stones was remarkable even for Jerusalem where tumbles of stones are a phenomenon all too common in excavations. The magnitude of the disaster perhaps made a special impact owing to the excellence of the destroyed buildings as shown by the magnificently-dressed stones, and the period of the collapse was very precisely pinpointed by the discovery at its base of a hoard of coins of the First Revolt, hidden by defenders who could not recover them before the city was overwhelmed by Titus. Even more indicative of the complete desolation of this area that had formed part of the city of Herod Agrippa was the state of the ruins.... It was two centuries or more before human activity began once more to make its mark in the whole area of ancient Jerusalem.[14]

---

[14] Kathleen M. Kenyon, *Jerusalem: Excavating 3000 Years of History* (New York: McGraw-Hill, 1967), 185ff.

This historical fact is a *major* apologetic point early Christians drive home, as we may discover in Barnabas 16 (*ca.* A.D. 75–100). We see this also in the *Epistle of Ignatius to the Magnesians* 10: "It is absurd to speak of Jesus Christ with the tongue, and to cherish in the mind a Judaism which has now come to an end." Other Church fathers follow suit: Justin Martyr, *Apology* 32 (A.D. 147); Melito of Sardis, *Fragments* (A.D. 160–180); and many others.

But when John writes, the temple in the holy city is still standing, awaiting its fast approaching doom (Rev 11:1–2). If John writes this twenty-five years *after* the temple's fall it would be horribly anachronous. Such requires a suppressed premise of an unmentioned temple rebuilding, while John overlooks the very recent catastrophic destruction of that famous temple he, all Jews, and the rest of the Roman Empire know very well. The reference to the temple is hard architectural evidence (no pun intended) that gets us back into an era pre-A.D. 70.

The Seven Kings in Revelation 17

In Revelation 17:9–10 John records a vision of a seven-headed Beast. In this vision we discover remarkable evidence that John is writing Revelation *before* the death of Nero (June 9, A.D. 68), well before the temple's destruction in August/September, A.D. 70:

> Here is the mind which hath wisdom. The seven heads are seven mountains, on which the woman sitteth. And there are seven kings: five are fallen, and one is, and the other is not yet come; and when he cometh, he must continue a short space.

Perhaps no point is more obvious in Revelation than this: Rome is here symbolized by the seven mountains. After all, Rome is the one city in history universally recognized for its seven hills: the Palatine, Aventine, Caelian, Esquiline, Viminal, Quirinal, and Capitoline hills. The Roman writers Suetonius and Plutarch refer to the first century festival in Rome called Septimontium, i.e., the feast of "the seven hilled city." The Coin of Vespasian (emperor A.D. 69–79) pictures the goddess Roma as a woman sitting on seven hills. Ancient pagan writers often mention the famed seven hills of Rome, writers such as Ovid, Claudian, Statius, Pliny, Virgil, Horace, Propertius, Martial, and Cicero, as well as by Christian writers, such as Tertullian and Jerome. Indeed, "there is scarce a poet that speaks of Rome but observes it."[15]

---

[15] John Gill, *An Exposition of the New Testament* (Streamwood, Ill.: Primitive Baptist Library, 1976 [rep. 1809]), 3:824.

John writes to be understood (Rev 1:3) and specifically points out here that the wise one who follows the interpretive angel's declaration *will* understand: "*Here is the mind which has wisdom*. The seven heads are seven mountains on which the woman sits" (Rev 17:9). On both the early-date and late-date views, Revelation's recipients live under the rule of Rome, which is universally distinguished by its seven hills. How could the recipients, living in the seven historical churches of Asia Minor and under Roman imperial rule, understand anything else but this geographical feature?

We learn further that the seven heads also represent a *political* situation in which five kings have fallen, the sixth is, and the seventh is yet to come and will remain but for a little while. Remarkably we must note that Nero is the sixth emperor of Rome. Flavius Josephus, the Jewish contemporary of John, points out that Julius Caesar was the first emperor of Rome and that he was followed in succession by Augustus, Tiberius, Caius (a.k.a. Caligula), Claudius, and Nero (*Antiquities* 18; 19). We learn this also from other near contemporaries of John, including the Jewish *4 Ezra* (chs 11 and 12), and the *Sibylline Oracles* (books 5 and 8); the Christian *Barnabas* (ch 4). The biographer Suetonius confirms this matter just a little later in his famous work, *Lives of the Twelve Caesars* — which begins the list of the Caesars up to his own time with Julius Caesar. We also see this chronology in the Roman writer Dio Cassius (*Roman History* 5). The text of Revelation states that of the seven kings "five have fallen." These emperors are dead, when John writes.

But Revelation 17:10 goes on to say "one is." That is, since the first five are dead, the sixth one is *then reigning* even as John writes. That would be Nero Caesar, who assumes imperial power upon the death of Claudius in October, A.D. 54, and remains emperor until his death on June 9, A.D. 68.

John continues: "The other is not yet come; and when he cometh, he must continue a short space." As the Roman Civil Wars break out in rebellion against Nero, he commits suicide on June 9, A.D. 68. When John writes, the seventh king/emperor has "not yet come." That would be Galba, who assumes power in June, A.D. 68. But he only continues a "short space": his reign lasts but seven months, until January 15, A.D. 69. In fact, he is the shortest reigning emperor to that time.

Now some evangelical commentators, such as John Walvoord, attempt to circumvent this political evidence by pointing out that it: (1) is taken from a highly figurative vision and (2) is introduced by a call for "the mind which has wisdom," thereby indicating the *difficulty* of the interpretation.[16] But this is twisting the text to say what it does not intend.

Upon seeing the symbolic vision itself, John is in fact perplexed: he "wondered with great wonder" (Rev 17:1, 7a). But an interpretive angel appears with the promise that he would show John the proper understanding (Rev 17:7): "Why do you wonder? I shall tell you the mystery." Revelation 17:9 and 10 is the *explication* of the vision. It is not given to make the matter more difficult. The inherent difficulty requiring wisdom lay in the fact that the seven heads involve a *double* referent: geographical and political. The angel functions here much like the angel in Revelation 7:13, 14 — to *interpret* the revelational data, not to confound the already perplexed apostle.

Thus, we see that while John writes, the sixth king, Nero, is still alive; the seventh, Galba, is looming in the near future. John does not write Revelation after June, A.D. 68, according to the internal political evidence.

The Jews in Revelation

The final evidence I will present for Revelation's self-witness focuses on the relationship of Christianity and Judaism in Revelation. And although there are several aspects of this evidence, I will just briefly introduce it. We may illustratively refer to two important passages and their implications:

First, when John writes Revelation, by all appearances Christianity is in its early, formative, "Jewish" stage. Initially Christians tend to mingle with the Jews (since the apostles and most Christians are Jews), considering themselves members of the "true Israel." We must remember that Jews trust in and boast about their descent from Abraham[17] and that circumcision is the distinguishing covenantal mark of the Jews.[18]

Yet early Christianity applies to itself terms historically associated with Israel and her privileges. Paul writes that Christians are "the seed of Abraham" (Ro 4:13–17; Gal 3:6–9, 29), "the circumcision" (Ro 2:28–29; Php 3:3; Col 2:11), the "temple of God" (1Co 3:16; 6:19; 2Co 6:16; Eph 2:21ff). In fact, he rebukes the racial Jew

---

[16] John F. Walvoord, *The Revelation of Jesus Christ* (Chicago: Moody, 1966), 250.

[17] We read often of "the God of Abraham" (Ge 28:13; 31:42, 53; Ex 3:6, 15–16; 4:5; 1Ki. 18:36; 1Ch 29:18; 2Ch 30:6; Ps 47:9; Mt 22:32; Mk 12:36; Lk 20:37; Ac 3:13; 7:32). The Jews expect blessings in terms of their Abrahamic descent (Mt 3:9; 8:11; Lk 3:8; 13:16, 28; 16:23–30; 19:9; Jn 8:39, 53; Ro 11:1; 2Co 11:22).

[18] Circumcision is *the* special sign of God's covenant with Abraham and Israel (Ge 17:10, 13). Circumcision is mentioned eighty-six times in the Scriptures; the uncircumcised are mentioned sixty-one times.

who is not committed to Jesus Christ: "He is not a Jew who is one outwardly; neither is circumcision that which is outward in the flesh" (Ro 2:28). Peter follows Paul's practice, designating Christians as "stones" being built into a "spiritual house" (1Pe 2:5) and applying Old Testament designations of Israel to the Church. Christians are "a chosen generation, a royal priesthood, an holy nation" (1Pe 2:9-10; cp. Ex 19:5-6; Dt 7:6; 14:2; 26:18). Both Peter and Paul call Christians "a people for God's possession" (Eph 1:14; Tit 2:14; 1Pe 2:10), a familiar Old Testament designation for Israel.[19]

After the destruction of the temple, however, the tendency for Christians to inter-mingle with the Jews ceases. This tendency is beginning to break down by the time of the writing of Hebrews in the mid-60s. There we hear warnings of judgments upon Jewish Christian who apostatize back into Judaism (Heb 2:1-6; 6:1-4; 10:26-36). Shortly after the Jewish War Gamaliel II in A.D. 80 inserts in the Jewish daily prayer (*Shemone Esre*) a curse on the Christians: "Let the Nazarene [sc. Christian] and the Menim perish utterly."[20] Interestingly, the Christian writer Barnabas in the A.D. 80s makes a radical "us/them" division between Israel and the Church (*Barnabas* 13:1).

Now what does this have to do with Revelation? In this very Hebraic book in Revelation 2:9 (see also 3:9) John is still applying Jewish terms to Christians — and denying them to Jews: There we read of Jesus' word to the churches of the day: "I know your tribulation and your poverty (but you are rich), and the blasphemy by those who *say they are Jews and are not*, but are a synagogue of Satan." In the early Christians' minds, the non-Christian Jews emptily call themselves "Jews"; they are not true Jews. This suggests a date prior to the final separation of Israel and Christianity. This separation is beginning in its earliest stages with the Neronic persecution (when Rome first recognizes a legal distinction between Judaism and Christianity); it is finalized with the temple's destruction (when the Christians turn their backs on the temple).

Second, at the time John writes, Jewish/Christian relations are beginning a fundamental and irreversible change. Revelation 3:9 reads: "Behold, I will cause those of the synagogue of Satan, who say that they are Jews, and are not, but lie — behold, I will make them to come and bow down at your feet, and to know that I have loved you."

---

[19] Ex 19:5; 34:9; Dt 4:20; 7:6; 14:2; 26:18; Ps 135:4.

[20] See: Torrey, *The Apocalypse*, 82; H. Daniel-Rops, *The Church of Apostles and Martyrs*, trans. by Audrey Butler (London: Dent, 1963), 48.

John here points to the approaching humiliation of the Jews, noting that God will — in the *near future,* Rev 1:1, 3; cp. 1Th 2:14–16; Heb. 8:13 — vindicate his Church against them. In effect, he will make the Jews to lie down at the Christians' feet. This refers to the destruction of Israel and the temple, which Christ prophesies (Mt 23:35 — 24:2). After that horrible event Christians begin using the temple's destruction as an apologetic for and vindication of Christianity (as we saw above). Justin Martyr's *First Apology* 32 is an excellent illustration of this tendency:

> And the prophecy, "He shall be the expectation of the nations," signified that there would be some of all nations who should look for Him to come again. And this indeed you can see for yourselves, and be convinced of by fact. For of all races of men there are some who look for Him who was crucified in Judea, and after whose crucifixion the land was straightway surrendered to you as spoil of war. And the prophecy, "binding His foal to the vine, and washing His robe in the blood of the grape," was a significant symbol of the things that were to happen to Christ, and of what He was to do. For the foal of an ass stood bound to a vine at the entrance of a village, and He ordered His acquaintances to bring it to Him then; and when it was brought, He mounted and sat upon it, and entered Jerusalem, where was the vast temple of the Jews which was afterwards destroyed by you.[21]

Although other arguments regarding the Jewish character of Revelation (its Hebraic grammar, Jewish symbols, numerous Old Testament allusions, reference to the twelve tribes, allusions to the priesthood, and so forth) exist, the point is clear enough: When John writes Revelation, Christianity is not yet wholly divorced from Israel. After A.D. 70 the separation is full and permanent. This is strong socio-cultural evidence for a pre-A.D. 70 composition.

Conclusion

Thus, we see from the the Book of Revelation itself the clear and compelling architectural evidence of the standing temple (Rev 11:1–2), the political evidence regarding the first seven Roman Caesars (Rev 17:9–10), and the socio-cultural evidence of the Israel/ Church relations (Rev 2:9; 3:9) that John must be composing Revelation prior to the destruction of the temple in August, A.D. 70 — and even prior to the death of Nero Caesar in June of A.D. 68. It

---

[21] Cited in Alexander Roberts and James Donaldson, eds., *The Ante-Nicene Fathers* (Grand Rapids: Eerdmans, n.d. [rep 1885]), 1:173.

seems the Neronic persecution is already under way (Rev 1:9; 13:5, 7), hence my preferred date of A.D. 65–66.

Interestingly, such evidences from the text lead liberal scholars to formulate a patchwork, higher critical view of Revelation's text. They see certain of these (and other) elements as originating in earlier documents, but then being incorporated later and even anachronistically in Revelation. For those who hold to a conservative view of inspiration, the unity and integrity of the text of Revelation forbids such a treatment — and demands a pre-A.D. 70 composition.

The External Evidence

As I briefly provide some evidence from Church history and tradition, I will begin with the positive indicators for an early date. After that I will review the contrary evidence, which is so influential in the late date argument.

The Positive Evidence for the Early Date

1. *The Shepherd of Hermas.* The Shepherd of Hermas is little known among evangelical laymen today. In the first three centuries of the Christian era, however, it was so influential that Irenaeus, Origen, Jerome and many others deem it canonical.[22] It even appears in the Codex Sinaiticus, one of the best preserved ancient copies of the whole Bible.[23]

Virtually all scholars agree that The Shepherd of Hermas draws upon Revelation as the source of its imagery — even late-date advocates like H. B. Swete, R. H. Charles, and Robert Mounce.[24] This demands that Revelation be written, copied, and circulated *prior* to the composition of The Shepherd.

A good deal of debate exists regarding The Shepherd's compositional date; thus this line of evidence cannot serve as conclusive. Nevertheless, the strong possibility exists that Hermas writes it in the A.D. 80s. In fact, Philip Schaff decisively supports an early date for The Shepherd, even allowing that it most probably was written

---

[22] Jerome, *On the Lives of Illustrious Men* 10. Irenaeus *Against Heresies* 4:20:2. Origen in his commentary on Romans 16:14.

[23] J. B. Lightfoot and J. R. Harmer, *The Apostolic Fathers* (Grand Rapids: Baker, rep. [1891]), 294.

[24] R. H. Charles, *The Revelation of St. John* (ICC) (Edinburgh: T & T Clark, 1920), 1:xcvii; Henry Barclay Swete, *Commentary on Revelation* (Grand Rapids: Kregel, 1977 [rep. 1906]), cx. Robert H. Mounce, *The Book of Revelation* (NICNT) (Grand Rapids: Eerdmans, 1977), 37.

by the very Hermas mentioned in Romans.[25] J. B. Lightfoot cites several writers supporting the earlier date: Cotelier, Cave, Lardner, Gallandi, Lumper, Lachmann, Sprinzl.[26] More recently still, Lawson,[27] Goodspeed,[28] and others concur in the view that it was written in the A.D. 90s. The two leading evidentiary avenues are: (1) It is written by a Hermas, who seems to be the one Paul refers to in Romans 16:14. (2) Many Church fathers view it as canonical, suggesting its composition around the time of the apostles, or shortly after. If this date, as John A. T. Robinson[29] and others argue, is correct, then Revelation, upon which The Shepherd depends, would be earlier — well before A.D. 95 and almost certainly pre-A.D. 70.

2. *Papias* (A.D. 60–130). Papias, a disciple of John, writes that James and John suffer martyrdom together at the hands of the Jews.[30] We know that James dies before the destruction of the temple (Eusebius, *Eccl. Hist.* 2:23:14; cp. 4:22; *Recog.* 1:66–70), and even late-date advocate H. B. Swete admits that Papias must feel at the very least that John dies no later than the destruction of the temple.[31] This would make Revelation, if written by John, to be earlier still.

3. *The Muratorian Canon* (*ca.* A.D. 170). The Muratorian Canon is the earliest surviving list of canonical books. In this very important manuscript we read the following statement comparing the writings of Paul and John:

> The blessed Apostle Paul, following the rule of his predecessor John, writes to no more than seven churches by name.[32]

Consequently, according to the author's logic, Paul's last writing to a local church could not precede John's writing of Revelation, for here we read that Paul *follows* John in writing to seven churches. As a result of this logic, we may surmise that this writer holds a date of

---

[25] Philip Schaff, *History of the Christian Church* (Grand Rapids: Eerdmans, rep. n.d. [1910]), 2:688ff.

[26] Lightfoot and Harmer, *Apostolic Fathers*, 294.

[27] John Lawson, *A Theological and Historical Introduction to the Apostolic Fathers* (New York: Macmillan, 1961), 225.

[28] Edgar J. Goodspeed, *The Apostolic Fathers* (New York: Harper, 1950), 97; and *A History of Early Christian Literature* (Chicago: University of Chicago, 1942), 47–48.

[29] Robinson, *Redating the New Testament*, 319–320.

[30] See: Henry Barclay Swete, *Commentary on Revelation* (Grand Rapids: Kregel, rep. 1977 [1906]), clxxix–clxxx ; and Lightfoot and Harmer, *Apostolic Fathers*, 519, 531.

[31] Swete, *Revelation*, clxxix–clxxx.

[32] Roberts and Schaff, *The Ante-Nicene Fathers*, 5:603. The seven churches addressed by Paul would be Rome, Corinth, Galatia, Ephesus, Philippi, Colossae, and Thessalonica.

Revelation's composition *earlier* than A.D. 67 or 68 for Revelation, in that Paul is beheaded in A.D. 67–68 before Nero dies (in June 68).[33]

4. *Clement of Alexandria* (A.D. 150–215). Clement of Alexandria does not specifically mention the name of the emperor who banishes John. But he does believe Revelation is inspired revelation from God and is written by the apostle John.[34] And he dogmatically states in his *Miscellanies* 7:17: "The teaching of our Lord at His advent, beginning with Augustus and Tiberius, was completed in the middle of the times of Tiberius. And that of the apostles, embracing the ministry of Paul, ends with Nero." Thus, he becomes a witness for the early date of Revelation.

We see that contrary to the impression many commentators leave, not *all* of the external evidence favors the late date. Now I will consider:

The Negative Evidence Against the Early Date

I will cite the two leading witnesses for the late date: Irenaeus and Origen.

Irenaeus (A.D. 130–202)

Undoubtedly the most commonly used and strongest external objection to Revelation's early date is Irenaeus' famous statement (*ca.* A.D. 180) in book 5 of his *Against Heresies*. This statement is very early and seems clear and to the point. It occurs at the end of a section in which he is dealing with the identification of Revelation's "666," which Irenaeus applies to the Antichrist:

> We will not, however, incur the risk of pronouncing positively as to the name of Antichrist; for if it were necessary that his name should be distinctly revealed in this present time, it would have been announced by him who beheld the apocalyptic vision. For that was seen no very long time since, but almost in our day, towards the end of Domitian's reign.[35]

Thus, upon reading this statement it appears that Irenaeus believes John wrote Revelation "towards the end of Domitian's reign." Nevertheless, several problems reduce the usefulness of this statement for late date advocacy.

---

[33] A. T. Robertson, "Paul" in James Orr and John Nuelson, eds., *International Standard Bible Encyclopedia* (Grand Rapids: Eerdmans, 1929), 3:2287; Richard Longenecker, *The Ministry and Message of Paul* (Grand Rapids: Zondervan, 1971), 86.

[34] Clement, *Who is the Rich Man?* 42 and *Miscellanies*, 6:13.

[35] Cited by Eusebius in *Eccl. Hist.* 3:18:2 (see also 5:8:6). See: A. Cleveland Coxe, *The Apostolic Fathers* in Roberts and Donaldson, eds., *Ante-Nicene Fathers*, 1:559–60.

First, the translation problem. The statement "that was seen" (or "it was seen") grammatically may refer either to one of two antecedents. It may refer either to "the apocalyptic vision" (i.e., Revelation) or to *"him who beheld* the apocalyptic vision" (i.e., John). Greek is an inflected language, containing the pronominal idea in the verb suffix. Here we may legitimately translate the verb either: *"it* was seen" or "he was seen." According to David Aune in his recent, massive commentary, New Testament commentator J. Stolt

> following Wettstein, *Novum Testamentum Gracecum* (2:746), has argued that 'the one who saw the Apocalypse' is the logical subject of *eorathe* and has proposed that what Irenaeus had in mind was to comment on *how long* the author of Revelation had lived, not on *when* he had written Revelation. This is in fact a view argued by various scholars since Wettstein.[36]

The verb ending leaves the question open; Irenaeus does not provide conclusive external evidence.

Second, the contextual indication. Irenaeus' argument regards the identity of the person represented by "666":

> We will not, however, incur the risk of pronouncing positively as to the name of Antichrist; for if it were necessary that his name should be distinctly revealed in this present time, it would have been announced by him who beheld the apocalyptic vision. For that or he was seen no very long time since, but almost in our day, towards the end of Domitian's reign.

This context seems to demand that Irenaeus refers to *John*, whom he believes to have lived almost to his (Irenaeus') own time. When Irenaeus says: "it would have been announced by him" it would most logically follow that his next statement should be translated: "for *he* was seen no very long time since, but almost in our day." In other words, Irenaeus appears to be arguing: If John, who wrote Revelation with its mysterious 666, had wanted us to know who 666 represented, he would have told us personally, for he lived a long time after writing it, almost in my own time.

Third, as Schaff notes, a major point of Irenaeus' work is to demonstrate the living continuity of the Church.[37] He endeavors to show that the truths of Christianity pass on orally from one generation to another. This purpose in his writing suggests that his concern

---

[36] David Aune, *Revelation* (WBC) (Dallas: Word, 1997), 1:lix.
[37] Schaff, *History of the Christian Church*, 2:753. Cp. Bruce, *New Testament History*, 405.

here would be with whether or not *John* talks about it among those to whom he ministers, rather than on *when* John writes.

Fourth, he is referring to the date of the *writing of Revelation* and not the *date to which John the author lived,* then we have an unusual situation. Earlier in the same chapter Irenaeus speaks of "ancient copies" of Revelation (*Heresies* 5:30:1). Would he argue in one paragraph about the *ancient* copies of the book and then a few paragraphs later about the book's original composition *near* to his own time? Surely the book is written earlier — in "ancient" times — even though John himself is presumed to have lived almost into Irenaeus' day.

Fifth, assuming the common translation of Irenaeus' statement, we must note that a major element of his proof is his reference to eyewitnesses. But Irenaeus uses eyewitnesses in another place to prove that Jesus lives to be almost fifty years old:

> For how had He disciples, if He did not teach? And how did He teach, if He had not a Master's age? For He came to Baptism as one Who had not yet fulfilled thirty years, but was beginning to be about thirty years old; (for so Luke, who hath signified His years, hath set it down; Now Jesus, when He came to Baptism, began to be about thirty years old:) and He preached for one year only after His Baptism: completing His thirtieth year He suffered, while He was still young, and not yet come to riper age. But the age of 30 years is the first of a young man's mind, and that it reaches even to the fortieth year, everyone will allow: but after the fortieth and fiftieth year, it begins to verge towards elder age: which our Lord was of when He taught, as the Gospel and all the Elders witness, who in Asia conferred with John the Lord's disciple, to the effect that John had delivered these things unto them: for he abode with them until the times of Trajan. And some of them saw not only John, but others also of the Apostles, and had this same account from them, and witness to the aforesaid relation. Whom ought we rather to believe? These, being such as they are, or Ptolemy, who never beheld the Apostles, nor ever in his dreams attained to any vestige of an Apostle?[38]

So in the final analysis, his use of eyewitnesses is not always trustworthy, to say the least.

Thus, a re-interpretation of Irenaeus, the major witness for the late date, would appear in order. At the very least the strength of his witness should be lessened due to these very real problems facing the interpreter of Irenaeus.

---

[38] Irenaeus, *Against Heresies* 2:22:5.

Origen (A.D. 185–254)

Origen writes early in the third century. Late-date advocates almost universally cite him as evidence. His relevant statement appears in his commentary on Matthew:

> The king of the Romans, as tradition teaches, condemned John, who bore testimony, on account of the word of truth, to the isle of Patmos. John, moreover, teaches us things respecting his testimony, without saying who condemned him when he utters these things in the Apocalypse. He seems also to have seen the Apocalypse in the island.

It should strike the unprejudiced mind that this writer — considered one of the leading witnesses for the late date — does not even name the emperor who banishes John. The name of Domitian is merely *assumed* here, and for two basic reasons: (1) Banishment was more frequently used by Domitian. (2) Irenaeus, a few years earlier, apparently teaches that Revelation was received by John in Domitian's day. But the first reason is a mere probability statement and the second relies on a debatable interpretation of Irenaeus. The reference to Origen is less than convincing.

Conclusion

When we consider all the evidence pro and con regarding Revelation's compositional date we discover that we may make a compelling case for a pre-70 date. In that Revelation is something of an "occasional epistle" ministering to people under dire circumstances (e.g., Rev 1:9; 6:9–10), we would expect that the internal indicators would betray his date. And as we see, they do. John almost certainly writes Revelation around A.D. 65–66.

3

INTERPRETIVE APPROACHES TO REVELATION

Write therefore the things which you have seen, and the things which are, and the things which shall take place after these things. (Rev 1:19)

Introduction

In this book — and in my larger commentary — I will be operating from the perspective known historically as "preterism." As I note in Chapter 1 above I now call my view "redemptive-historical preterism" to emphasize the story of Scripture rather than merely the mundane history of the era. Redemptive-history deals with the unfolding of God's redemptive plan in world history. If my reader is unfamiliar with this approach he will be confused when I begin presenting my exegesis of key passages. A researcher's interpretive approach should be stated early in his work so that his reader will be able to follow his line of evidence and evaluate it as he moves through the material.

The vast majority of evangelical Christians today know only one approach to Revelation: futurism. They are almost wholly unfamiliar with other options available. But if we adopt a wrong approach, then the reader of Revelation will simply overlook contrary evidence that does not fit his interpretive expectations. The classic example of this is the total overlooking of John's temporal statements regarding his prophecies' nearness — though these are cited at the very beginning of the work, at Revelation 1:1, 3.

Interpretive Schools

Historically four basic schools of interpretation have governed Revelation studies. These are broad categories of interpretation, with each school having representatives ranging from conservative evangelicals to radical liberals. I would also note that many commentators meld various aspects the several interpretive approaches into something of an eclectic approach. But historically we find these four basic schools of thought: historicist, idealist, futurist, and preterist. Let us briefly consider them individually.

The Historicist School

The historicist school is also called the "continuous historical" or "world-historical" approach. It sees the prophetic drama in Revelation as providing a panorama of Church history from the apostolic era all the way up to Christ's Second Advent and the consummation. Historical continuity is the main focus of this approach in forecasting history's unfolding to the end. Some historicists have called Revelation an "almanac of Church history."

The historicist applies Revelation's many judgment scenes to various national wars, cultural revolutions, and religious movements, such as the rising of Roman Catholicism, the Inquisition, the outbreak of the Protestant Reformation, the French Revolution, and World Wars I and II. The various evil figures in Revelation are also applied to important historical persons, such as various Popes, Charlemagne, Napoleon, Mussolini, or Hitler.

According to Alan Johnson, Joachim of Floris (d. 1202) popularizes this view in the twelfth century, though traces of it appear earlier in the Ante-Nicene fathers.[1] Many of the Reformers employ this approach against the Roman Catholic Church. Some famous adherents to the historicist view include Sir Isaac Newton, Jonathan Edwards, Joseph Mede, E. B. Elliott, Henry Alford, Charles H. Spurgeon, and more recently, Francis Nigel Lee. It is very popular today in the Adventist movement, though not widely held among evangelicals.

Historicism's strength. This view has certain strengths that make it appealing in the history of exegesis. A few of those include:

First, historicism's apparent contextual plausibility: Revelation 1–3 clearly open with events in John's day, including his own imprisonment (Rev 1:9) and the letters to the seven historical churches (Rev 2–3). And it seems to many that Revelation 21–22 deals with the last days of history and even beyond. As a result this leaves the quite plausible suggestion that chapters 4–20 must cover the history in between. Hence, we have the basic framework of historicism.

Second, historicism appealingly offers a divinely-revealed guide to history. On this analysis Revelation dramatically demonstrates that God controls the end from the beginning (Isa 46:10; Eph 1:11). Since Christianity is an historical religion concerned with God's providence in history, historicism provides an important contribution to the Christian's biblically-based worldview and historical outlook by offering a divinely-revealed outline of history.

Third, historicism insures Revelation's relevance. After all, if it maps history's flow until the end, and if the end has not yet transpired, it speaks of our own day. This maintains the significance of Revelation for the Church in all ages.

---

[1] Alan F. Johnson, in *The Expositor's Bible Commentary*, ed. Frank E. Gaebelein (Grand Rapids: Zondervan/Regency, 1981), 12: 409.

Historicism's weaknesses. Unfortunately, this view is beset with catastrophic problems.

First, historicism's most glaring deficiency lies in the fact that John writes Revelation to a first century Church under siege. Yet in this view John is writing to them about distantly future, detailed events of which they could have absolutely no understanding. And this despite John's concern for his contemporary audience (Rev 1:9) and his promise of a special blessing to them if they heed the things within (Rev 1:3).

Second, historicism downplays the time-frame indicators that frame the book. John specifically declares in his opening and closing that Revelation's events are near at hand (Rev 1:1, 3; 6:10; 22:6, 10). Yet historicism sees most of Revelation as distantly future to John's day.

Third, almost without fail historicism assumes that Revelation's contemporary interpreters live in the final days of history — no matter in which century they read it. Inevitably its adherents believe that Revelation leads up to *their* own time, underscoring its present-day significance. Commenting on recurring problems in eschatological debate in general, Brethren historian F. Roy Coad states a problem that applies particularly well to historicism: "almost invariably interpretation has been vitiated by the reluctance or incapacity of commentators to visualise their own age as other than the end time."[2] John Hendrik de Vries complains of historicism that "this method of interpretation leads to results which reflect the time in which the expositor lives."[3]

Fourth, another problem with historicism is its self-refuting nature. A consequence of the preceding tendency is that historicism's exegesis remains in a constant state of flux, requiring frequent revision. As history grows longer, older varieties of this interpretive school experience a great number of failed expectations. For instance, historicist Mede (1586–1639) notes in his commentary: "While I write news is brought of a Prince from the North (meaning Gustavus Adophus) gaining victories over the Emperor in defence of the German afflicted Protestants."[4] No one would be able to sell

---

[2] F. Roy Coad, "Prophetic Developments: A Christian Brethren Research Fellowship Occasional Paper" (Pinner, England: 1966), 10.

[3] In Abraham Kuyper, *The Revelation of St. John*, trans. By John Hendrik de Vries (Grand Rapids: Eerdmans, 1935), iii.

[4] From Edward B. Elliott, *Horae Apocalypticae* (London: Seeley, Jackson & Halliday 1845), 474. Cited in Henry Barclay Swete, *Commentary on Revelation* (Grand Rapids: Kregel, rep. 1977 [1906]), ccxiv (fn 1).

his commentary today, for no one fears that Gustavus Adophus is any kind of relevant threat.

Fifth, historicism is subject to unchecked subjectivity. Brady makes a helpful observation regarding the perception of historicist exegesis, a perception that is widely held by others and which explains the reason so few scholars hold this position today:

> Revelation was at the mercy of an almost complete subjectivism, for the symbols could be made to represent just whatever feature of notoriety the expositor desired to extract from the records of the Church's history.[5]

He cites Thorndike: "the imputation of Antichrist is a saddle for all horses."[6]

Sixth, as a result, harmony among its proponents is almost wholly lacking. It may be an interpretive school, but its adherents appear to be in different classes. We may complain that wherever you have five historicist commentaries on Revelation, you will find six views of Revelation.

Seventh, a final problem that seems built into historicism is its focus on the Western world. One wonders if historicists in India or Africa might have a wholly different conception of Revelation.

Historicism is a wholly unworkable system, which explains why we find so few of its proponents in theological discussion today. Zondervan's *Four Views on the Book of Revelation* did not even include an historicist in its presentation.

The Idealist School

The idealist school is also known as the "timeless-symbolic" or "supra-historical" approach to Revelation. This school denies that John is painting any objective, concrete, historical portrait at all. Rather, idealists suggest that he is providing a non-historical, allegorical summation of various significant redemptive truths or historical principles. Revelation is, if you will, presenting an abstract behind-the-scenes look at the world. That is, it offers a look at the philosophical/spiritual issues involved in history, rather than at historical characters and events themselves.

Idealist interpreter William Milligan explains: "We are not to look in the Apocalypse for special events, but for an exhibition of the

---

[5] David Brady, *The Contribution of British Writers between 1560 and 1830 to the Interpretation of Revelation 13.16–18: (The Number of the Beast): A Study in the History of Exegesis* (Tübingen: Mohr, 1983), 298.

[6] Herbert Thorndike, *Theological Works* (Oxford: Oxford University Press, 1844 –56), 1:742.

principles which govern the history both of the world and the Church."[7] It provides "the action of great principles and not special events."[8] Thus, Revelation is virtually a theological poem regarding historical struggle, providing a philosophy of history from a Christian perspective. Thus, this view is sometimes called the "poetic-symbolic." The symbols in Revelation reveal God in his sovereign control over men and nations, overriding man's warring resistance and rebellious sin.

This view is the most recent of the major approaches to Revelation. Advocates of idealism include William Milligan, William Hendricksen, Paul S. Minear, and R. J. Rushdoony.

Idealism's strengths. Idealism also has its appealing possibilities; it is not held for no reason at all.

First, everyone immediately recognizes that John is dealing with symbolism throughout the work. The idealistic scheme lends itself well to a symbolic presentation.

Second, idealism avoids misguided historical applications that will embarrass the position and require emendation later. Idealism deals with eternal truths, not temporal events. Therefore, it cannot be impacted by any historical event — short of history ending with God losing.

Third, idealism also is amendable to the other approaches. For in a certain sense this view could be true at the same time as any one of the other views. After all, history *is* in fact the outworking of divinely established principles.

Fourth, idealism is practical in that it encourages Christians caught up in history's struggle. It presents Revelation as God's dramatic promise that ultimately the forces of good will overwhelm the forces of evil.

Idealism's weaknesses. Idealism's weaknesses, though, are debilitating, destroying idealism as a free-standing system of interpretation.

First, contrary to idealism, Revelation appears to be quite concerned with concrete historical realities. After all, John specifically declares that he is dealing with "the things which must shortly take place" (Rev 1:1). In fact, Christ directs John: "Write therefore the things which you have seen, and the things which are, and the things which shall take place after these things" (Rev 1:19; cp. 4:1;

---

[7] William Milligan, *Revelation*, 154. Cited in Robert H. Mounce, *The Book of Revelation* (NICNT) (Grand Rapids: Eerdmans, 1977), 43.

[8] Milligan, *Revelation* 153, cited in D. A. Carson, Douglas J. Moo, and Leon Morris, *An Introduction to the New Testament* (Grand Rapids: Zondervan, 1992), 483.

22:6). But the idealist wholly overlooks particular historical events despite Revelation's appearance.

Second, Revelation is long and complex, but it would seem an idealist scheme should have been presented in a shorter space. And especially should it avoid any sustained appearance of historical reality. Parables do not need to be that long and complex.

Third, most importantly, it downplays the time-frame indicators that frame in the book. John specifically declares in his opening and closing that Revelation's events are near at hand (Rev 1:1, 3; 6:10; 22:6, 10).

The Futurist School

The most widely prevalent interpretive approach to Revelation among evangelicals since the early 1900s is the futurist view. This view is also known as the "end-historical" or the "pure eschatological view." The futurist understands the prophecies beginning at Revelation 4:1 as portraying the remote future from John's time: "After these things I looked, and behold, a door standing open in heaven. And the first voice which I heard was like a trumpet speaking with me, saying, 'Come up here, and I will show you things which must take place after this.'" This view sees Revelation as focusing primarily on the *ultimate* historical issues that the world and the Church will face just prior to Christ's Return.

It is difficult to class some of the very early premillennialists as futurists, despite the claims made by present-day premillennialists. The reason for this is because the several early Church fathers who are premillennial believe that they are living in the very end times. Consequently, from our perspective centuries later, we could take either an historicist or preterist sense. Futurism is almost entirely eclipsed from about the fifth century until over a thousand years later. It is revived by Franciscus Ribera, a Spanish Jesuit scholar, in the sixteenth century.

Futurism is very popular in America due to the widespread influence of dispensationalism. Evangelical proponents of futurism include: George Eldon Ladd, John Walvoord, Charles Ryrie, Robert L. Thomas, and Craig Blomberg. Evangelical and Reformed theologian and amillennialist Abraham Kuyper also holds this view. Kuyper claims that:

> The Apocalypse of St. John treats exclusively of what will come to pass when the ordinary course of things shall be broken up, and the

concluding period of both the life of the church and the life of the world is ushered in.[9]

Futurism's strengths. Futurism maintains a formidable presence in current evangelical discussions. Its strengths are as follows:

First, futurists argue that their view allows a more literal approach to Revelation's prophecies because they appear to be catastrophic and worldwide in effect: "the futuristic position allows a more literal interpretation of the specific prophecies of the book."[10] They argue that this makes the book easier to interpret.

Second, futurism provides an appropriate capstone to biblical revelation. As the New Testament canon closes, Revelation provides us with an outlook of what to expect at the conclusion to world history and the final fulfillment of all prophecy.

Third, futurism maintains a continuing relevance in that the events of Revelation could begin breaking out at any moment. In the dispensational branch of futurism, since we do not know the day or the hour of Christ's return, we must always expect it, and hence the events of Revelation which will follow it. Anyone looking at the events of Revelation should be motivated to commit his life to Christ in order to avoid the horrible catastrophes that will come.

Futurism's weaknesses. The weaknesses of this approach render its initial plausibility null and void.

First, futurism almost totally removes the relevance of Revelation from John's original audience, and at a time of their great suffering. John is writing to a persecuted Church about things they must heed (Rev 1:3, 9; 6:9–11). Yet futurism claims that the events lay off (as we now see) in the distant future.

Second, futurism requires the current-day reader of Revelation to re-interpret its phenomena (which meant something in John's day) to make them fit in modern times. This includes such matters as sword-fighting, military horsemen, walled cities, and so forth. This becomes especially problematic for many futurists because of their pre-commitment to literalism.

Third, the futurist must wholly overlook Revelation's claims of the nearness of the events, despite their introducing and concluding the whole work (Rev 1:1, 3; 22:6, 10).

Fourth, futurism often involves exegetical subjectivity. After all, new technologies will arise that will require a re-interpretation of Revelation's imagery. For instance, Hal Lindsey's Cobra helicopter

---

[9] Abraham Kuyper, *The Revelation of St. John*, trans. by John Hendrik de Vries (Grand Rapids: Eerdmans, 1935), 18.

[10] John F. Walvoord, *The Revelation of Jesus Christ* (Chicago: Moody, 1966), 21

interpretation of Revelation 9 could eventually give way to the newer, remote-controlled drone warfare technology.

The Preterist School

Finally, we have the preterist view, also known as the "contemporary imminent" or "contemporary historical" or "imminent historical" viewpoint. Basically this school understands the great majority of the prophecies of Revelation 4–22 as dealing with issues and events beginning in John's own day. Thus, his prophetic concerns lay in the near future when he issues them, but from our perspective they lie in our distant past. Hence, the designation "preterism," from the Latin word *praeteritus* meaning "gone by," i.e., past.

According to R. H. Charles, traces of this view may be found in some early Church fathers, such as Irenaeus, Hippolytus, and Victorinus (despite some of them being premillennial). But it really becomes prevalent much later, when the Jesuit Luis De Alcasar systematizes it in the early seventeenth century. Many liberals hold this view, though stripped of the supernaturalism of evangelical preterism. Evangelical preterists include Moses Stuart, Milton Terry, Philip Schaff, David Clark, Jay Adams, Greg Bahnsen, David Chilton, and Cornelis Vanderwaal.

Preterists hold that John is warning the first century Christians regarding events that will soon befall them. Indeed, as he writes they are already facing the initial outbreak of those catastrophes (e.g., Rev 1:9; 2:2, 9, 13; 3:3, 9–10). Evangelical preterists generally divide into two approaches. The majority view (Adams and Bahnsen) holds that Revelation prophesies two soon-coming catastrophes: the destruction of Jerusalem (Rev 6–11) and the fall of the Roman Empire (Rev 13–19). The minority view (Terry and Chilton) see John's focus on the destruction of the temple and Jerusalem, as the conclusion of the old covenant and the establishment of the new covenant.

Preterism's strengths. Preterism remains a strong evangelical option due to the following strengths.

First, preterism retains Revelation's relevance for John's original audience, which is undergoing a crisis of persecution and oppression (Rev 1:9; 3:9–10). Just as the Old Testament prophets warn Israel of soon-coming events in the Babylonian conquest, so John warns the developing first century Christians of catastrophic events that they and their children will experience.

Second, the preterist analysis takes seriously the time-frame indicators in Revelation. They take to heart these warnings of nearness occurring in Revelation's introduction and the conclusion (Rev 1:1,

3; 22:6, 10). In fact, these verses provide the very impetus to preterism.

Third, preterism provides a dramatic explanation of major redemptive-historical matters: the demise of Judaism and the temple system and the universalizing of the Christian faith. As we saw in Chapter 1, Christ (and the apostles) give much attention to the temple's removal from history. Revelation provides one focused and highly dramatized presentation of this major shift into redemptive history's final condition.

Fourth, upon the preterist analysis, Christ's victory over his young Church's first century enemies provides evidence for his protective care of the Church as she heads into the future to face whatever later circumstances she must. Thus, the historical realities covered by Revelation's prophecies serve as a pattern showing that Christ will protect his Church in all ages, since he does so in its first century infancy.

Preterism's weaknesses. Non-preterist scholars detect certain elements in the system that they believe render it inoperable.

First, preterism's focus on the first century seems to limit its usefulness to us today. But this complaint is just as true regarding most Old Testament books and much of the contemporary focus of the New Testament epistles. Besides the fourth point of preterism's strength (cited above) more than makes up for this perceived problem.

Second, preterism's focus on first-century events must apply apparent end-time prophecies to those events. But this problem is mitigated by realizing that John is using apocalyptic language, which is fundamentally dramatic and symbolic.

Third, preterism's interpretation of Revelation makes apparently worldwide events apply to local matters. But again, this characterizes apocalyptic language. Hyperbolic images serve to drive home ethical warnings — just as they do in the Old Testament prophets (see Isa 13 and 34).

Fourth, the preterist interpretation does not sell millions of books. But this is a problem preterists have learned to live with.[11]

Conclusion

Although virtually an infinite number of varieties exist within each of these schools, it is helpful to be aware of their basic fundamentals. And again, we must understand that each view has evangelical representatives. Too many contemporary evangelicals believe

---

[11] Actually this is not true in the ultimate sense because the Bible is a preterist book and its sells millions of copies every year.

we have only two views of Revelation: their own view and the liberal view.

Origins of Preterism

Some dispensationalists like to point out that a Roman Catholic priest, Luis De Alcazar (1554–1613), presents the first formal, full-scale preterist approach to Revelation. By emphasizing his Roman Catholic convictions, they seek to write off the view without further reflection. This, of course, is a classic example of the "genetic fallacy," discounting a position because of its early use by an unpopular advocate.

Furthermore, this practice overlooks two countervailing facts: (1) We may discover preterist elements among the early Church fathers in a number of passages, including Matthew 24 (e.g., Eusebius, *Eccl. Hist.* 3:7) and Revelation (e.g., Andreas of Cappadocia's commentary on Revelation). Alcazar simply presents a more consistent, full-scale preterist approach to Revelation. (2) The futurist system itself is also highly developed by another Jesuit priest from the same era. Dispensationalists Thomas D. Ice writes: "Jesuit Francisco Ribera (1537–1591) was one of the first to revive an undeveloped form of futurism around 1580."[12] Thus, the same "problem" of Roman Catholic involvement is true with a formal, full-scale *futurist* approach to Revelation.

System Differences

As with any system developed by fallen men and held in fallen minds, we must recognize that no hermeneutic approach can be pure. Consider the "futurism" of dispensationalism, for instance. No dispensationalist is a "pure" futurist. He believes *some* prophecies of Scripture have already occurred, and therefore must be interpreted preteristically. For instance, Isaiah 7:14 prophesies the virgin birth of Christ. This is a past event in our day, which we cannot interpret futuristically. We could mention any number of other passages dealing with the coming of the Messiah in the first century. Modern orthodox Jews may be futuristic in their handling of Messianic passages, such as the Suffering Servant passage in Isaiah 53, but not

---

[12] Ice in Thomas Ice and Timothy Demy, *When the Trumpet Sounds* (Eugene, Ore.: Harvest, 1995), 16. He confesses this just two pages after citing Merrill C. Tenney's statement that "the first systematic presentation of the preterist viewpoint originated in the early seventeenth century with Alcazar, a Jesuit friar" (14). Premillennialist Chung also recognizes this derivation of futurism: Craig L. Blomberg and Sung Wook Chung, eds., *A Case for Historic Premillennialism: An Alternative to "Left Behind" Eschatology* (Grand Rapids: BakerAcademic, 2009), 9.

even the dispensational *futurist* would agree at this point. Indeed, they are manifestly preteristic on the relevant passages.

In fact, preterism has a sound basis in New Testament theology, textual exegesis, and historical analysis, as we may see in both the Olivet Discourse and Revelation.[13] Consequently, we should not discount a preterist approach to Revelation, for instance, as rendering Revelation irrelevant today, as some do. Shall we declare that the many Old Testament prophecies concerning the coming of Christ are "irrelevant" because they involve historical matters already occurring in our past? Are we to set aside historical references to Christ in the Gospels and the apostles in Acts, simply because they are dealing with "ancient history"? Surely not.

We must also remember that almost all of the New Testament epistles are what we call "occasional epistles." That is, they are dealing with specific occasions regarding the historical experiences of the first century Christians. For instance, 1 Corinthians deals with several particular sins in a local church existing almost 2000 years ago. Is it therefore irrelevant to us today because we are not fighting over whether we will follow Paul or Apollos or Cephas (1Co 1:12; 3:4, 22)? The Epistle to the Hebrews warns first-century Jewish converts to Christianity that it is both dangerous and pointless to return to temple-based Judaism because the temple system is "about to disappear" (Heb 8:13). The temple system disappeared long ago. Indeed, the writer sends this glorious epistle to "Hebrews." Is it irrelevant to those of us who are *Gentiles* living centuries *after the temple's destruction*?

We should understand several very important "relevancies" of fulfilled prophecies such as in Revelation:

First, they demonstrate the general truth that God's prophetic word will come to pass, for in several places we already see a past fulfillment. Thus, when we read such passages, they affirm the truthfulness of God's Word, thereby encouraging us in our confidence regarding Scripture.

Second, though Revelation prophesies events that occur almost 2000 years ago, we can learn principles of God's operations in history from those events. We see God protecting his people, warring against his enemies, leaving a witness behind for the ongoing Church, and demonstrating the catastrophic results of rebellion against him by those who are his people. We may discern ethical

---

[13] See for instance: Kenneth L. Gentry, Jr., *Perilous Times: A Study in Eschatological Evil* (Texarkana, Ark.: CMF, 1999). Gary DeMar, *Last Days Madness: Obsession of the Modern Church* (Atlanta: American Vision, 1994).

and spiritual lessons through those first century trials of faith. And more.

Third, since Revelation largely speaks of events occurring in and around A.D. 70, we have an inspired interpretation about what becomes of the temple and Israel, both of which had been central to redemptive history for centuries. We see that God overthrows the temple and judges Israel in order to send his new covenant Church in new directions, not tying it to a particular race, a specific land, a single temple, and a ritualistic worship. Preterists believe with Paul that fulfilled, historic Scriptures are "written for our admonition" (1Co 10:11).

Part 2

SPECIAL ISSUES IN REVELATION

4

THE SEALED SCROLL
AS A DIVORCE CERTIFICATE

And I saw in the right hand of Him who sat on the throne a book written inside and on the back, sealed up with seven seals. (Rev 5:1)

Introduction

In my first three chapters I deal with general issues necessary for *approaching* Revelation's drama. Now I will move beyond the basics to analyzing specific issues that arise *within* Revelation. The reader should recall a point I make in the Preface: These studies require a basic understanding of redemptive-historical preterism, which I deal with elsewhere. This and the following chapters are for the "initiated," as it were.

In this chapter I will be focusing on the important scroll in Revelation 5. Revelation is performative drama that employs *forensic* rhetoric. The succession of scenes will increasingly inform the audience of the legal action undertaken within. The identity of this scroll will exercise a large interpretive influence over the later chapters of Revelation.

Overview of Revelation's Plot-line

By way of introducing this court-drama I will trace in broad strokes Revelation's interesting legal plot-line, then I will backup and provide the particular evidence that leads me to this understanding.

(1) John opens by announcing in no uncertain terms the absolute authority of his message. It comes ultimately from God through Christ to the angel and finally to John (Rev 1:1). With such a chain of authority, John in legal fashion amply "bore witness" (Rev 1:2) to the message. Witnesses and testimony play an important role throughout the book. The Greek word for "witness" (*martus*) has as a primary meaning the idea of a *legal* witness, as in a court case (cf. Dt 17:6; 19:15; Mt 18:16; 26:65; Ac 6:13; 7:58; 2Co 13:1; 1Ti 5:19; Heb 10:28).[1]

(2) John declares that Revelation's events are historically pressing issues *imminent* in his own day. They must "shortly take place"

---

[1] BAGD, 619.

(Rev 1:1) for "the time is near" (Rev 1:3). Later he will conclude his drama by reaffirming the nearness of the prophetic events (Rev 22:6, 10). Whatever may be the drama that requires such authority and legal witness, it must directly relate to the first century Church — for it will play out in her experience.

(3) As John prepares to state his theme, he focuses on Christ as "the faithful witness" (Rev 1:5; cp. also 3:14). Clearly the original audience is to recognize the legal character of what is to follow.

(4) He then establishes his legal theme which focuses on Christ's judgment-coming against the Jews who had crucified Christ: "Behold, He is coming with the clouds, and every eye will see Him, even those who pierced Him; and all the tribes of the earth (lit.: "land") will mourn over Him. Even so. Amen" (Rev 1:7). (For evidence that his theme portrays Christ's judgment of first century Israel, see Ch. 8 in my *Before Jerusalem Fell*.) In fact, two of the Seven Letters specifically warn the recipients about the antagonism of the racial Jews. In his estimation the Jews are not worthy of the name "Jew" (cp. Ro 2:28–29) for they are of the "synagogue of Satan" (Rev 2:9; 3:9; cp. Jesus' similar denunciation, Jn 8:44).[2]

In keeping with Revelation's imminency-expectation and Israel-judgment theme, Christ even promises that those Jews so troubling them will soon be brought low — evidently in A.D. 70: "Behold, I will cause those of the synagogue of Satan, who say that they are Jews, and are not, but lie — behold, I will make them to come and bow down at your feet, and to know that I have loved you" (Rev 3:9; cp. Mt 24:2, 16; 1Th 2:15–16).

(5) Christ appears in Revelation's inaugural vision (Rev 1:13–20) to formally and authoritatively commission John to write the prophecy, further enhancing the authority of John's witness: "Write therefore the things which you have seen, and the things which are, and the things which shall take place after these things" (Rev 1:19). In fact, the Lord lays his hand upon him to lift him up for his task (Rev 1:17). Jesus explains that he himself "was dead" but is now "alive forevermore" (Rev 1:18), despite the fact that the Jews "pierced him" to death (Rev 1:7).

(6) The actual judgment process begins with John being summoned before God where he sees the Lord seated on his judicial throne: "After these things I looked, and behold, a door standing open in heaven, and the first voice which I had heard, like the sound of a trumpet speaking with me, said, 'Come up here, and I will show you what must take place after these things.' Immediately I was in

---

[2] For a response to those who charge that such a view of Revelation is anti-Semitic, see my Appendix.

the Spirit; and behold, a throne was standing in heaven, and One sitting on the throne" (Rev 4:1–2). God is surrounded by his heavenly court, the twenty-four elders sitting on their thrones (Rev 4:4). John frequently mentions God's throne and the heavenly control of earthly events in Revelation (see esp.: Rev 1:4; 4–5; 6:16; 7:10; 12:5; 19:4; 20:11).

(7) As John looks about this heavenly court he notices a sealed document in God's right hand (Rev 5:1). This document involves the central matter for which he has been summoned to court, for the entire heavenly court focuses attention on it (Rev 5:2–4) and it initiates the first judgments to follow (Rev 6:1–8:1). After some consternation regarding who can open it (Rev 5:2–4) he soon discovers that the "Lamb" who had been "slain" (as per the theme, Rev 1:7) is the only one worthy of opening the court document (Rev 5:2, 5). The victim is the witness. The scroll's being sealed and its handling in God's court suggests it is some sort of legal document.

(8) In keeping with Revelation's judgment theme against Israel (Rev 1:7) John presents the Lamb in very Judaic imagery: "Behold, the Lion that is from the tribe of Judah, the Root of David, has overcome so as to open the book and its seven seals" (Rev 5:5). This slain but living Lamb becomes the dominant figure of Revelation, appearing twenty-seven times in chapters 5–7, 12–15, 17, 19, 21–22. In the initial drama he appears between God's throne and the elders (Rev 5:6) and is praised along with God (Rev 5:13). Later he appears "in the center of" and "on" the throne (Rev 7:17; 22:1, 3).

(9) As the slain but living Lamb begins unsealing this legal scroll, judgments pour out upon "the land"[3] of Israel (Rev 6–19[4] with interludes). At the opening of the fifth seal John sees the souls of deceased saints crying out for God's "judging and avenging" their blood on those who "dwell in the land [literally]" (Rev 6:10). They are promised that they must wait only "a little while longer" (Rev 6:11). This scene reminds us of Jesus' parable in Luke 18:1–8 where he promises God will speedily exercise justice for his elect who cry out day and night to him (Lk 18:7–8).[5] We should also compare the scene to Christ's denunciation of Israel's leaders in Matthew 23. He promises their soon judgment (Mt 23:36) for shedding innocent blood (Mt 23:34–35). These victims of the Jews were persecuted because of their alignment with Christ (Rev 17:6; 19:2; cp. 7:14; 12:11):

---

[3] See discussion of *tēs gēs* ("the land") at Rev 1:7 in Gentry, *The Book of Revelation Made Easy*.

[4] See especially: Rev 6:4, 10, 15; 8:5, 13; 9:3; 14:3, 16, 18–19; 16:1; 19:2.

[5] See my exposition in Kenneth L. Gentry, Jr., *He Shall Have Dominion: A Postmillennial Eschatology* (3d. ed.: Draper, Vir.: ApologeticsMedia, 2009), 490–93.

they have their names written in his Book of Life (Rev 3:5; 13:8; 17:8).[6]

(10) In Revelation 10 we see the scroll fully opened and in a strong angel's hand (Rev 10:2). This is Christ appearing as the "Angel of the Covenant" who is expected in Malachi 3:1 for the purpose of bringing judgment upon Israel.[7] He appears here in angelic form, because he is a "messenger" [aggelos] swearing an oath as a legal witness (Rev 10:1, 5, 6). This vision appears just before Revelation's clearest statement regarding the earthly temple in Jerusalem: Revelation 11:1-2 (see next point).

(11) Then the scene turns to the trampling of the earthly temple (God's house) by the nations (Rev 11:1-2):

> And there was given me a measuring rod like a staff; and someone said, "Rise and measure the temple of God, and the altar, and those who worship in it. And leave out the court which is outside the temple, and do not measure it, for it has been given to the nations; and they will tread under foot the holy city for forty-two months."

This statement is clearly based on Jesus' prophecy in Luke 21:24 wherein he denounces the temple (cf. Lk 21:5-6). This trampling is legally affirmed once again, this time by "my two witnesses" (Rev 11:1-3). In God's Law two is the essential number for court testimony and is particularly important in capital cases (cp. Nu 35; Dt 17:6; 19:15; Jn 18:17; Heb 10:28).

(12) As the drama moves ever forward to its climax, John brings to the forefront two female personages. One is the Babylonian harlot (Rev 14:8; 16:19; 17:1; 18:2, 10, 21; 19:2), who is described in great detail for emphasis (Rev 17:1-7). This harlot symbolizes historical Jerusalem, the capital of old covenant Israel (see Ch. 11 below). The other female is the Lamb's bride (Rev 19:7-9; 21:2 – 22:5), who is the "new Jerusalem," the very goal of Revelation.[8] She is also described in detail for emphasis (Rev 21:10 – 22:5). As Witherington notes:

---

[6] The Gospels speak of the persecution of Christ's followers in the same terms as they do their treatment of him, drawing an intentional parallel between the Lord and his disciples (Mt 10:17-18; Mk 10:33; Lk 21:12; Jn 15:20). See: Claudia Setzer, *Jewish Response to Early Christians: History and Polemics, 30-150 C.E.* (Minneapolis: Fortress, 1994), 38..

[7] Pieter A. Verhoef, *The Books of Haggai and Malachi* (NICOT) (Grand Rapids: Eerdmans, 1987), 289-90.

[8] "The Apocalypse moves toward the great climax of destruction and renewal in the description and comparison (*ekphrasis* and *synkrisis*) of Babylon and the heavenly Jerusalem." Robert M. Royalty, *The Streets of Heaven: The Ideology of Wealth in the Apocalypse of John* (Macon, Geo.: Mercer University Press, 1998), 177.

"The entire book has been pressing forward toward a conclusion, which is revealed in these two sections [Rev 17 and 22] involving the destruction of Babylon and its replacement by the New Jerusalem."[9] The witness of the two prophets

> is to prophesy against the earthly Jerusalem and the earthly Temple, and to announce the heavenly Jerusalem and the heavenly temple. The latter half of the book exactly corresponds to this programme. The earthly Jerusalem, under the figure of Babylon, is doomed and destroyed; the heavenly Jerusalem takes its place.[10]

"The whole literary framework of the book becomes clear and simple once the Harlot Babylon is identified with Jerusalem."[11]

(13) These two women play out the judgment theme in terms of both its negative and positive implications: the harlot is publically stoned to death for her harlotry (Rev 16:19–17:1) so that the new bride of the Lamb may descend from heaven to take her place on the earth (Rev 21:2, 10). This portrays the judgment and removal of Israel in A.D. 70 so that Christianity might remain as the final redemptive-historical reality (cp. Mt 8:10–12; 19:28; Heb 12:18–28).

(14) The Babylonian harlot's judgment gives way to a celebratory "marriage supper" (Rev 19:7, 9). This leads to Christ's judgment-appearing in A.D. 70 as the Avenger-witness who is "Faithful and True" for "in righteousness He judges and wages war" (Rev 19:11).

(15) Then Revelation focuses on the taking of a new "bride" (Rev 19:7; 21:2, 9), which is the "new Jerusalem" (Rev 21:2, 10). "The very close resemblance of the wording of [Rev 21:9] to 17:1, where the judgment of the great harlot is announced, renders obvious the parallel intended" between the bride and the harlot.[12] This "new Jerusalem" obviously replaces the old Jerusalem, following not only John's story-line but also the pattern of Paul and Hebrews (Gal 4:25–26; Heb 12:18, 22).[13]

In a nutshell this is how Revelation's forensic drama unfolds as it plays out its stated judgment theme (Rev 1:7). I will flesh out this movement in great detail in my commentary, but for now let me

---

[9] Ben Witherington, *Revelation* (NCBC) (Cambridge: Cambridge University Press, 2003), 20.

[10] Philip Carrington, *The Meaning of Revelation* (Eugene, Ore.: Wipf & Stock, 2007 [rep. 1931]), 195.

[11] Carrington, *Revelation*, 345.

[12] Raymond C. Ortlund, *Whoredom: God's Unfaithful Wife in Biblical Theology* (Grand Rapids: Eerdmans, 1996), 167.

[13] See Ch. 15 below.

consider the redemptive-historical imagery that informs this approach.

Covenantal Marriage

We must recognize at the outset that Revelation is an extremely Hebraic book that draws heavily from the Old Testament. And we should understand that John's theme verse warns of Christ's judgment-coming against the Jews.[14] In order to understand John's court drama better, we must consider the all-important Old Testament backdrop, which all agree is so important for interpreting Revelation. John's book is the capstone of biblical revelation; it is "the crowning finish of the entire Scripture, both Old and New Testament."[15] Not only does it draw freely from the Old Testament,[16] but it presents in bold relief the enormous redemptive-historical implications of the incarnational coming and work of Christ in the New Testament era. His advent transforms the biblical faith from its temporary, national, typological seed in Israel into its permanent, international, full fruit in the Church as "the Israel of God" (Rev 6:16).[17]

The particular imagery John employs to this end is remarkable. We must recall that "throughout the Bible, God's relationship to his people is pictured as a marriage."[18] In the Old Testament particularly, "the relationship between God and Israel was . . . very frequently viewed as analogous to that of husband and wife."[19] Consequently, marriage appears as the dominant metaphor portraying Israel's relation to God. As the Old Testament clearly declares: "Your husband is your Maker, / Whose name is the Lord of hosts" (Isa 54:5a; cp. Isa 50:1; 62:4; Jer 2:2; 3:14, 20; 31:32; Hos 1:2; 2:2, 7, 16; 5:4; 9:1, 10). Even the land is deemed "married" to God (Isa 62:4). Thus, when Israel falls into idol worship she is in essence seeking to marry foreign gods: "Judah has dealt treacherously, and an abomination has been committed in Israel and in Jerusalem; for Judah has

---

[14] See exposition in Gentry, *The Book of Revelation Made Easy* (Powder Springs, Geo.: American Vision, 2008).

[15] André Feuilett, *Johannine Studies*, trans. by Thomas E. Crane (Staten Island, N.Y.: Alba, 1964) 14.

[16] See my understanding of Lk 21:22 in *He Shall Have Dominion*, 542–44. Jesus sees all the Old Testament warnings of Jerusalem's judgment coming to pass in A.D. 70.

[17] David E. Holwerda, *Jesus and Israel: One Covenant or Two?* (Grand Rapids: Eerdmans, 1995). Roderick Campbell, *Israel and the New Covenant* (Tyler, Tex.: Geneva Divinity School, 1954 [rep. n.d.]).

[18] DBI, 538.

[19] ABD, 1:1195. See also: TDNT 4:1101–03.

profaned the sanctuary of the Lord which He loves, and has married the daughter of a foreign god" (Mal 2:11; cp. Eze 23).

Ezekiel "develops the metaphor to its greatest extent," presenting the clearest imagery of God's actually marrying Israel (Eze 16).[20] Ezekiel 16:8 reflects on God's original taking her for his wife in the wilderness after leaving Egypt: "'Then I passed by you and saw you, and behold, you were at the time for love; so I spread My skirt over you and covered your nakedness. I also swore to you and entered into a covenant with you so that you became Mine,' declares the Lord God."

Jeremiah comes in a close second to Ezekiel in this regard. He also speaks directly of Israel's original betrothal to God: "Go and proclaim in the ears of Jerusalem, saying, 'Thus says the Lord, "I remember concerning you the devotion of your youth, the love of your betrothals, your following after Me in the wilderness, through a land not sown"'" (Jer 2:2; cp. Hos 2:15–16 which also recalls that happy occasion).

Rabbinic Judaism picks up on this imagery and speaks of the Mount Sinai covenant as being Israel's "Day of Espousal," with the Shekinah cloud's descent upon the tabernacle portraying the marital consummation.[21] "Rabbis extolled the conclusion of the covenant at Sinai as the marriage of Yahweh with Israel."[22] Her marital "I do" appears in her vocal commitment: "All the words which the Lord has spoken we will do!" (Ex 24:3). Interestingly, Exodus 24 also includes a throne vision when the elders "saw the God of Israel; and under His feet there appeared to be a pavement of sapphire, as clear as the sky itself" (Ex 24:10).[23] God's covenantal marriage is legally affirmed. Ezekiel 16:8 shows "that entering into berith [covenant] with Israel is called a marrying her"; Hosea "identified the berith-idea and his favorite idea of marriage between Jehovah and Israel."[24]

Thus, the temple (and its precursor, the tabernacle) is God's "house" wherein he dwells with his wife: "Let them construct a sanctuary for Me, that I may dwell among them" (Ex 25:8). Many references to the temple (or tabernacle) speak of its being God's spe-

---

[20] DBI, 538.

[21] J. Massyngberde Ford, *Revelation* (Garden City, N.Y.: Anchor, 1975), 165.

[22] TDNT, 4:1101–03.

[23] Several Old Testament passages, including Ex 24, "feature visions of the divine throne, or throne-chariot, and its occupant." Peter R. Carrell, *Jesus and the Angels: Angelology and the Christology of the Apocalypse of John* (Cambridge: Cambridge University Press, 1997), 11.

[24] Geerhardus Vos, *Biblical Theology: Old and New Testaments* (Grand Rapids: Eerdmans, 1948), 278, 279

cial dwelling place with his people (Ex 29:45; Lev 26:9-13; 1Ki 8:10-13; Ps 132:13-15; Mt 23:21; Jub 1:17; 25:21[25]). This is emphasized in Ezekiel's prophecy of the future temple, where he reminds Israel of her past failure to live in covenant with God: "when you brought in foreigners, uncircumcised in heart and uncircumcised in flesh, to be in My sanctuary to profane it, even My house, when you offered My food, the fat and the blood; for they made My covenant void — this in addition to all your abominations" (Eze 44:7; cp. 37:26-28). God's house is located in the city of Jerusalem where he has chosen for his name to "dwell" (Dt 12:5, 11; 26:2). As Josephus laments after Jerusalem's destruction in A.D. 70: "Where is this city that was believed to have God himself inhabiting therein?" (J.W. 7:8:7).

As we continue reflecting on the marital imagery, "in the Pentateuch we hear of Yahweh's jealousy, an emotion that is only proper to an exclusive relationship like marriage (Ex 19:3-6; 20:2-6; 34:14)."[26] Jealousy is appropriate and even expected in marital relationships (Nu 5:14, 29, 30; Pro 6:32-34; Song 8:6). The word "jealous" (*qanah*) is the same as used in the law of jealousy designed for the husband to discover if his wife has committed adultery (Nu 5:11-31). As in a marital union "the jealousy of Yahweh insists that his people observe his exclusive claims upon them (Dt. 6:13-15)."[27] The many references to God's jealousy are significant in that "the word means conjugal zeal specifically, jealously in the married relation."[28] See: Exodus 20:5; 34:14; Numbers 25:11; Deuteronomy 4:24; 5:9; 6:15; 29:20; 32:16, 21; Joshua 24:19; 1 Kings 14:22; Psalms 78:58; 79:5;

---

[25] Devout Jews called the temple "God's house," e.g., *Ant.* 3:8:5; 4:8:22; 7:14:1; 8:2:6; 8:3:7; 8:4:3; *J.W.* 4:3:10; 4:4:4; 6:2:1; 6:5:3. In Scripture the temple (and its tabernacle precursor) is often called "the house of the Lord" (Ex 23:19; 34:26; Dt 23:18; Jos 6:24; 1Sa 1:7, 24; 3:15; 2Sa 12:20; 1Ki 3:1; 6:1, 37; 7:12, 40, 45, 48, 51; 8:10-11, 63-64; 9:1, 10, 15; 10:5, 12; 12:27; 14:26, 28; 15:15, 18; 2Ki 11:3-4, 7, 10, 13, 15, 18-19; 12:4, 9-14, 16, 18; 14:14; 15:35; 16:8, 14, 18; 18:15; 19:1, 14; 20:5, 8; 21:4-5; 22:3-5, 8-9; 23:2, 6-7, 11-12, 24; 24:13; 25:9, 13, 16; 1Ch 6:31-32; 9:23; 22:1, 11, 14; 23:4, 24, 28, 32; 24:19; 25:6; 26:12, 22, 27; 28:12-13, 20; 29:8; 2Ch 4:16; 5:1, 13; 7:2, 7, 11; 8:1, 16; 9:4, 11; 12:9, 11; 16:2; 20:5, 28; 23:5-6, 12, 14, 18-20; 24:4, 7-8, 12, 14, 18, 21; 26:19, 21; 27:3, 28:21, 24; 29:3, 5, 15-18, 20, 25, 31, 25; 30:1, 15; 31:10-11, 16; 33:4-5, 15; 24:8, 10, 14-15, 30; 25:2; 36:7, 14, 18; Ezr 1:3, 5, 7, 2:68; 3:11; 7:27; 8:29; Neh 10:35; Ps 23:6; 27:4; 92:13; 118:26; 122:1, 9; 134:1; 135:2; Isa 2:2; 37:1, 14; 38:20, 22; 66:20; Jer 17:26; 20:1-2, 7; 26:9-10; 27:18, 21; 28:1, 5; 29:26; 33:11; 35:2; 36:5, 10; 38:14; 41:5; 52:13; 52:17, 20; Lam 2:7; Eze 44:4-5; Hos 8:1; 9:4; Joel 1:9, 14; 3:18; Mic 4:1; Hag 1:2, 14; Zec 7:3; 8:9; 11:13; 14:21.

[26] *DBI*, 539.

[27] Ortlund, *Whoredom*, 29.

[28] Vos, *Biblical Theology*, 152.

Ezekiel 16:38, 42; 23:25; 36:5–6; 29:25; Nahum 1:2; Zephaniah 1:18; Zechariah 1:14; 8:2.

Very early in her national history, Israel's potential for worshiping false gods is portrayed as prostitution against her husband whose name is "Jealous" (Ex 34:14). Hence, Israel's obligation to "cling/cleave" to the Lord (Dt 10:20; 11:22; 13:4) is the same word (*dabaq*) which is used in Genesis 2:24 of a man cleaving to his wife.[29]

In Scripture God ordains human marriage from the beginning so that two "shall become one flesh" (Ge 2:24). Thus, later in Scripture we learn that human marriage is established by covenanting before God, which effects a binding legal union (Mt 19:6). We see this covenantal reality behind two important Old Testament texts: In Proverbs 2:17 the adulteress who leaves her husband legally "forgets the covenant of her God." In Malachi 2:14 God is "witness" against Israel because men are dealing treacherously with their wives, and a wife is deemed a "wife by covenant."

Marital Unfaithfulness

In Jeremiah's new covenant promise, God complains of Israel's unfaithfulness noting that they broke his covenant, though "I had mastered [*ba'l*] them as a husband" (Jer 31:32). This verb derives from a root meaning "to become master." Therefore, it means to marry "with an emphasis on the rights and authority the husband exercised,"[30] cp. Genesis 20:3; Numbers 5:19–20, 29; Deuteronomy 21:13; 22:22. Whereas the word for "husband" (*'hś*) "is apparently an endearing expression", *ba'l* "emphasizes the legal position of the husband as lord and 'owner' of his wife."[31] The legal relation and subsequent obligation is clearly in view.

Scripture often expresses Israel's turning to other gods as marital infidelity in breach of God's legal covenant with her. In Deuteronomy God tells Moses that after he dies Israel will "play the harlot with the strange gods of the land" which will "break My covenant" (Dt 31:16). In fact, the most common use of *znh* ("act as a harlot") in the Old Testament refers to "covenantal unfaithfulness on Israel's part."[32] Moses even warns against individual Israelites "playing the harlot" by worshiping false gods (Lev 20:5–6). Aune mentions "the analogy of the covenant between Yahweh and Israel and marriage

---

[29] Ortlund, *Whoredom*, 146.

[30] Gerald L. Keown, *Jeremiah 26–52* (WBC) (Dallas, Tex.: Word, 1995), 132

[31] Hans Walter Wolff, *Hosea: A Commentary on the Book of the Prophet Hosea*, trans. by Gary Stansell, ed. by Paul D. Hanson (Philadelphia: Fortress, 1974), 49.

[32] Willem VanGemeren, ed., *New International Dictionary of Old Testament Theology & Exegesis* (Grand Rapids: Zondervan, 1997), 1:1123.

contracts (Lev 17:7; 20:5–6; Num 14:33; 15:39; Deut 31:16; Judg 2:17; 8:27; 1 Chr 5:25; 2 Chr 21:11; Ps 73:27), a metaphor found with particular frequency in the prophets Hosea (1:2; 2:4 [MT: 6]; 4:15; 9:1), Jeremiah (2:20; 3:2, 9, 13; 5:7, 11; 13:27), and Ezekiel (6:9; 16; 23; 43:7, 9)."[33]

The prophets speak of Israel's unfaithfulness through idolatry as hurtful to her husband: "Then those of you who escape will remember Me among the nations to which they will be carried captive, how I have been hurt by their adulterous hearts which turned away from Me, and by their eyes, which played the harlot after their idols" (Eze 6:9a).

Hosea develops the theme of harlotry throughout his entire book, even marrying a harlot to illustrate Israel's sin (Hos 1:2; 3:1–3). For instance, Hosea 2:2 reads:

Contend with your mother, contend, / For she is not my wife, and I am not her husband; / And let her put away her harlotry from her face, / And her adultery from between her breasts.

Jeremiah 3:6 speaks similarly: "Then the Lord said to me in the days of Josiah the king, 'Have you seen what faithless Israel did? She went up on every high hill and under every green tree, and she was a harlot there.'"

Ortlund well notes of this harlotry theme that "what begins as Pentateuchal whispers rises later to prophetic cries and is eventually echoed in apostolic teaching."[34] Eventually this harlotry image is used by the prophets Hosea, Jeremiah, and Ezekiel who "exploit it to the fullest."[35] Jeremiah and Ezekiel particularly develop it "into elaborate images."[36] The harlot metaphor is applied to Israel time and again in the Old Testament.[37]

We must realize that although the charge of harlotry tends to focus on its most egregious manifestation in actual idolatry, it is not limited to idol worship. In the biblical view of marriage, the wife's faithfulness involves a wholesale relationship of loving obedience (Nu 5:29; Jer 31:32; Eph 5:22–23; 1Pe 3:1, 6), not just her avoiding adultery. Consequently, there are places where charges of harlotry

---

[33] David E. Aune, *Revelation 17–22* (WBC) (Dallas, Tex.: Word, 1998), 930.

[34] Ortlund, *Whoredom*, 8.

[35] VanGemeren, *New International Dictionary*, 1:1123.

[36] Ortlund, *Whoredom*, 77.

[37] Ex 34:15–16; Lev 17:7; Nu 15:39; 25:1; Dt 31:16; Jdg 2:17; 8:27, 33; 1Ch 5:25; 2Ch 21:11, 13; Ps 106:39; Isa 1:21; Jer 2:20; 3:1–9; 5:7; Eze 6:9; 16:15–17, 20, 22, 25–36, 41; 23:5–8, 11, 14, 15–19, 27–30, 35, 44; 43:7, 9; Hos 1:2, 2:2, 4–5; 3:3; 4:10–15, 18; 5:3–4; 6:10; 9:1; Joel 3:3; Am 7:17; Mic 1:7; Nah 3:4.

against Israel speak of situations not involving actual, formal idolatry.

When lawlessness (not idolatry) prevails in Jerusalem, the "faithful city" becomes a "harlot" (Isa 1:21–23). The same is true when a person consults a medium, seeking counsel (revelation) apart from God (Lev 20:6). This seems to be Gideon's sin in making the ephod (for seeking revelatory counsel) which Scripture deems harlotry (Jdg 8:27). Israel sins as a harlot (Hos 6:10) in not trusting in God but in seeking alliances with Egypt and Assyria in Hosea 7:10–11.[38]

In Hosea 7:11 the prophet "calls the dove 'easily seduced' (*pitāh*); it is 'inexperienced' and 'unintelligent' (*'en leb*). The dove represents Israel, who is easily mislead politically by the powerful nations."[39] Rossing agrees: "Israel's 'prostitution' may include economic indictment of Israel's foreign liaisons in additions to changes [*sic*] of idolatry. . . . Alice A. Keefe suggests that Israel's foreign lovers in Hosea 'are not fertility gods but Israel's foreign allies and trading partners.'"[40]

As God's wife, Israel must be faithful to her covenant with God. She must follow after "all My commandments" rather than following her own desires, in order to avoid harlotry (Nu 15:38–40). Wolff well captures the significance of this for us:

> The net force of the declaration is that all the sinful preferences of the autonomous self, running contrary to the law of God, are a kind of whoredom, as if Yahweh's wisdom and ways were not trustworthy.[41]

Israel is legally bound to God just as a wife is bound to her husband through mutual covenant.

Covenantal Divorce
In the Old Testament economy God's prophets function as his lawyers.[42] They prosecute Israel's breaches of God's covenantal law

---

[38] Ortlund, *Whoredom*, 47–48.

[39] Hans Walter Wolff, *Hosea: A Commentary on the Book of the Prophet Hosea*, trans. by Gary Stansell, ed. by Paul D. Hanson (Philadelphia: Fortress, 1974), 41.

[40] Barbara Rossing, *The Choice Between Two Cities: Whore, Bride, and Empire in the Apocalypse* (Harrisburg, Penn.: Trinity Press International, 1999), 69n.

[41] Ortlund, *Whoredom*, 37. In the New Testament "friendship with the world" is a form of adultery for the believer (Jas 4:4).

[42] Willem Gemeren, *Interpreting the Prophetic Word* (Grand Rapids: Zondervan, 1990), 290ff; O. Palmer Robertson, *The Christ of the Prophets* (Phillipsburg, N.J.: P & R, 2004), 121–126, 143–199). See also: G. E. Wright, "'The Lawsuit of God': A Form-Critical Study of Deuteronomy 32," in Bernard W. Anderson and Walter J. Harrel-

by bringing his legal case (*riyb*) against them. Just as God was married to Israel at his throne (Ex 24:10), so her divorce issues from his throne.

In Isaiah 1:2 the heavens and earth are called as witnesses against Israel, as per the Mosaic example (Dt 4:26; 30:19; 31:26, 28). In Isaiah 3:14 the Lord "enters into *judgment* with the elders and princes" (cp. Isa 41:21; 43:26; 45:21). In Micah 6:2 we read: "Listen, you mountains, to the *indictment* of the Lord, / And you enduring foundations of the earth, / Because the Lord has a *case* against His people; / Even with Israel He will dispute." The passage in which Micah 6:2 appears is "an elaborate representation of a legal case 'Yahweh v. Israel,' in which God brings a grievance against his people" in this "covenant lawsuit."[43] In Jeremiah 30:13–14 the Lord speaks through Jeremiah stating "there is no one to plead your cause" for "all your lovers have forsaken you."

The prophet Hosea is a classic example of God's "lawyer" bringing a lawsuit against his unfaithful wife. He writes that the Lord "has a *case* against the inhabitants of the land" (Hos 4:1) and "has a *dispute* with Judah" (Hos 12:2). Hosea 2 is especially compelling. His "use of the key word *rib* ("to contend, accuse," 2:4[2]; 4:4; 'lawsuit,' 4:1; 12:3 [2]) clearly indicates that his proclamation of the divine word is modeled after the legal procedure in the city gate."[44]

In addition, "Hosea likens the relationship of Yahweh to Israel to a marriage, a metaphor which he combines in chapter 2 with the image of a trial. Yahweh is the husband who accuses his wife, Israel, of infidelity. The 'trial' thus suggests the form of a divorce proceeding."[45] God pursues formal divorce, even though she has left and married another: "she is not my wife, and I am not her husband" (Hos 2:2b); she says "I will go back to my *first* husband" God (Hos 2:7c).

Clearly then, "the prophets had spoken as God's covenant prosecutors bringing God's charge and stating God's verdict."[46]

---

son, eds., *Israel's Prophetic Heritage: Essays in Honor of James Muilenberg* (New York: Harper, 1962), 26–67. James Limburg, "The root *Rib* and the Prophetic Lawsuit Speeches," *JBL* 88 (1969): 291–304.

[43] Leslie C. Allen, *The Books of Joel, Obadiah, Jonah, and Micah* (Grand Rapids: Eerdmans, 1976), 363.

[44] Hans Walter Wolff, *Hosea: A Commentary on the Book of the Prophet Hosea.*, trans. by Gary Stansell, ed. by Paul D. Hanson (Philadelphia: Fortress, 1974), xxiii.

[45] Kirsten Nielsen, *Yahweh as Prosecutor and Judge: An Investigation of the Prophetic Lawsuit (Rîb-Pattern)*, trans. by Frederick Cryer (Sheffield: JSOT, Sup. Ser. 9), 34.

[46] VanGemeren, *Interpreting the Prophetic Word*, 296.

In that marriage is a legal covenant, it can only be set aside on sufficient grounds and by means of court proceedings issuing forth in a divorce certificate (Dt 24:1-4). Because of the marital relationship existing between God and Israel, God's Old Testament lawyers (the prophets) can speak of his issuing a "bill of divorce" against her when she sins against him, thereby justifying her temple's destruction and her Babylonian captivity:

> Thus says the Lord, / "Where is the certificate of divorce, / By which I have sent your mother away? / Or to whom of My creditors did I sell you? / Behold, you were sold for your iniquities, / And for your transgressions your mother was sent away." (Isa 50:1)

> And I saw that for all the adulteries of faithless Israel, I had sent her away and given her a writ of divorce, yet her treacherous sister Judah did not fear; but she went and was a harlot also. (Jer 3:8)

In that God's covenant "established a legally defined relationship" the "marriage exists under a marriage-law. Israel is charged not merely with having been deficient in love and affection, but with having violated distinct promises. She is legally guilty."[47]

Jeremiah 2-3 is a very interesting passage in this regard. Chapter 2 speaks of Israel's sin, while chapter 3 calls her to repentance from it. "The whole [second] chapter has strong reminiscences of a legal form which was well known in the secular world, the so-called *rib* pattern. . . . Israel is, as it were, in the law court being arraigned by Yahweh in a lawsuit (*rib*)."[48] After reminding Israel of "the love of your betrothals" (Jer 2:2), God calls her to listen (Jer 2:4-5), "contends" with her (Jer 2:9), and calls heaven as witness (Jer 2:12). He is effectively asking her in a court of law to explain what led her astray from him.

In that God is bringing a lawsuit against her, he appeals to the Mosaic law as the standard of justice. In Jeremiah 3 "the opening verse contains a much condensed paraphrase of the legislation pertaining to marriage, divorce, and remarriage in Deut 24:1-4"[49]:

> God says, "if a husband divorces his wife, / And she goes from him, / And belongs to another man, / Will he still return to her? / Will not that land be completely polluted? / But you are a harlot with many lovers; / Yet you turn to me," declares the Lord.

---

[47] Vos, *Biblical Theology*, 282.

[48] J. A. Thompson, *The Book of Jeremiah* (NICOT) (Grand Rapids: Eerdmans, 1980), 159, 60.

[49] Peter C. Craigie, Page H. Kelley, and Joel F. Drinkard, Jr., *Jeremiah 1-25* (WBC) (Dallas, Tex.: Word, 1991), 51.

We must note that he not only specifically mentions "divorce" and alludes to the Mosaic divorce legislation, but that he also repeatedly calls her a "harlot" (Jer 3:1–3, 6, 8–9) while once again reminding her of her youthful betrothal to God (Jer 3:4; cp. Hos 2:15).

In Isaiah we learn of the importance of a bill of divorce. In Isaiah 50:1 God calls upon Israel to produce her bill of divorce. Why? As Alexander puts it: "That we may see the cause of her repudiation."[50] This is necessary in that the people are complaining that God lacks a just cause for turning from her: "Zion said, 'The Lord has forsaken me, / And the Lord has forgotten me'" (Isa 49:14). But he argues in court that he did repeatedly call to her, yet she did not answer (Isa 50:2; cp. Jer 7:13). Jeremiah's prophecy notes the same type of problem: Israel does not ask for God (Jer 2:6), nor did her priests (2:8). This disinterest in the Lord, this refusal to come back to him reminds us of Israel in the New Testament (Jn 1:11; Mt 10:6, 15–20; 15:7–9; 22:1–7; 23:37).

Jerusalem is the City of God wherein God dwells in his temple (2Ki 23:27; Ps 68:29). So when Jerusalem is destroyed in the Old Testament Babylonian Captivity, and her inhabitants are cast out, they are effectively cast out of the house, away from the God's presence:

> For because of the anger of the LORD this happened in Jerusalem and Judah, that He finally cast them out from His presence. (2Ki 24:20; Jer 52:3)

> "And now, because you have done all these things," declares the Lord, "and I spoke to you, rising up early and speaking, but you did not hear, and I called you but you did not answer, therefore, I will do to the house which is called by My name, in which you trust, and to the place which I gave you and your fathers, as I did to Shiloh. And I will cast you out of My sight, as I have cast out all your brothers, all the offspring of Ephraim." (Jer 7:13–15)

In 1 Kings 6:11–13 God promises to live with Israel in this house if she would remain faithful (cp. Dt 12:10–11 and his earlier promise to live in his tent with her, Ex 25:8; 29:44–45). Thus, when she becomes unfaithful God issues his covenantal wife a divorce decree before he "sends her out from his house" (Dt 24:1), destroying her temple and sending her off into captivity (cp. Jer 15:1–2): "I have forsaken My house, / I have abandoned My inheritance; / I have given the beloved of My soul / Into the hand of her enemies" (Jer 12:7). In Jeremiah 11:15 he complains against Israel's attempts to

---

[50] J. A. Alexander, *Commentary on the Prophecies of Isaiah* (Grand Rapids: Zondervan, rep. 1977 [1875]), 2:248. John N. Oswalt, *The Book of Isaiah, Chapter 1–39* (NICOT) (Grand Rapids: Eerdmans, 1986), 318.

come to the temple while rebelling against him with strange gods: "what right has My beloved in My house?"

God is not simply abandoning Israel without warrant. He is suing her in "court" with just cause, proper witnesses, and legal evidence. He even calls her by pagan names to demonstrate the enormity of her unfaithfulness to him. In several places he calls Israel "Sodom" (Isa 3:8–9; Jer 23:14; Lam 4:6; Eze 16:46, 48–49, 55–56; Am 4:11), just as does John in Revelation 11:8 (cf. Mt 10:15; 11:23–24).

In the Ezekiel 16 passage the prophet is dealing with Israel as a harlot. Even the wicked Philistines are embarrassed at Israel's evil conduct (Eze 16:27). The destruction of God's temple speaks of his abandoning Israel for disobedience (1Ki 9:6–9; Jer 22:5; Lam 2:7; Mic 3:12; Bar 2:26; *T. Levi* 15:1; *1 Enoch* 89:56; *Pesiq. R.* 138a; 146a), for "the temple [is] a symbol of the rise and fall of God's people according to their moral, ethical and spiritual condition."[51] The land's desolation also speaks of Israel's troubled marriage (Isa 62:4). In the first century the Qumran community denounces Jerusalem as a hated wife (4QLam 179).

By the grace of God, later in the Old Testament period Israel eventually returns to her land from deportation (Ezr 2; Neh 7:6ff; 11:1ff) and rebuilds God's house (Ezr 5:14–15), though on a smaller scale than Solomon's original. Centuries later Herod greatly expands and magnificently adorns it (Jn 2:20) making it "the biggest structure of its kind in the ancient Near East,"[52] "the largest, grandest, and shortest-lived of the Jerusalem temples."[53] This refurbished temple is God's "house"[54] which Christ and the apostles visited.

Christ's Coming and Its Consequences

Interestingly, Christ alludes to the Old Testament marriage imagery and relates it to his own coming and ministry. In the several places where he touches on this theme, he "moves wholly within the circle of ideas of His contemporaries when he expresses the meaning and glory of the Messianic period in the images of the wedding and wedding feast."[55]

Early in his ministry Jesus uses wedding imagery to explain why John the Baptist's disciples fast though his do not: "While the bride-

---

[51] *DBI*, 851.

[52] *DBI*, 849.

[53] ABD, 6:365. This article distinguishes Herod's Temple as effectively a third temple (see pages 351, 363).

[54] Mt 12:4∥; 21:13∥; 23:38; Lk 11:51; Jn 2:16–17; 14:2; Ac 7:47, 49.

[55] TDNT 1:654. Jesus also alludes to the coming Messianic wedding "possibly even in Jn. 2:7ff" in his first miracle at the wedding in Cana (*TDNT* 1:654 n43).

groom is with them, the attendants of the bridegroom do not fast, do they? So long as they have the bridegroom with them, they cannot fast" (Mk 2:19‖). "It is clear . . . that in this connection the bridegroom is an allegorical indicator of the Messiah,"[56] with the wedding imagery being built upon the Old Testament relationship of God to Israel.[57]

With this announcement, Mounce notes of Matthew's parallel account and its Old Testament backdrop that "the messianic wedding feast is under way."[58] Indeed, the marriage analogy was "so widely used by the Jews with reference to the kingdom of God that bridegroom = Messiah would have been immediately understood."[59] Here "the Lord identifies himself with the Bridegroom of O.T. prophecy."[60]

His next statement "strikes a jarring note"[61]: "But the days will come when the bridegroom is taken away from them, and then they will fast in that day" (Mk 2:20). "The idea of the bridegroom being removed from the wedding scene comes as a jarring surprise," especially in light of all the rejoicing.[62] Here and in Matthew's parallel, the bridegroom's being "taken away" (apairein) echoes Isaiah 53:8 and implies violence. This serves as an early pointer to Christ's rejection and death at the hands of the Jews, as many commentators observe.[63]

---

[56] Herman Ridderbos, The Coming of the Kingdom (Phillipsburg, N.J.: P & R, 1962), 160.

[57] James R. Edwards, Gospel according to Mark (PNTC) (Grand Rapids: Eerdmans, 2002), 90–92; William Hendriksen, Exposition of the Gospel according to Mark (Grand Rapids: Baker, 1975), 100–102; William L. Lane, Gospel according to Mark (NICNT) (Grand Rapids: Eerdmans, 1974), 110. Joseph Addison Alexander, The Gospel according to Mark (Grand Rapids: Baker, n.d. [rep. 1858]),

[58] Robert H. Mounce, Matthew (NIBC) (Peabody, Mass.: Hendrikson, 1991), 85.

[59] D. E. Nineham, Saint Mark (WPC) (Philadelphia: Westminster, 1963), 102. On p. 103 he mentions the marriage relation between God and Israel.

[60] Henry Barclay Swete, Commentary on Mark (Grand Rapids: Kregel, 1913), 44. Cp. A. T. Robertson, Word Pictures in the New Testament (Nashville: Broadman, 1930), 272. George Milligan, The Book of Revelation (New York: Armstrong, 1903), 321–22.

[61] Ben Witherington, The Gospel of Mark: A Socio-Rhetorical Commentary (Grand Rapids: Eerdmans, 2001), 124.

[62] Robert A. Guelich, Mark 1–8:26 (WBC) (Dallas, Tex.: Word, 1989), 112.

[63] James R. Edwards, Gospel according to Mark (PNTC) (Grand Rapids: Eerdmans, 2002), 91; David Wenham, The Parables of Jesus (Downers Grove, Ill: InterVarsity, 1989), 29; Ridderbos, The Coming of the Kingdom, 160; Heinrich August Meyer, Critical and Exegetical Handbook to the Gospel of Matthew, tran. by Peter Chris-

The following two parables in Mark 2:21–22 also exhibit a like incongruity: using new material as a patch on a new garment and pouring new wine into old wineskins are both unwise actions. The new garment may represent a wedding garment and the new wine may portray the celebration of a new marriage, as we may surmise from ancient culture in general and the biblical record in particular — even in this very context (see: Mk 2:19–20‖; cp. Mt 22:2–12; Jn 2:1–10; cf. Isa 62:5). These parables indicate that the old Judaistic forms would not allow expansion and must be wholly replaced and they also leave the clear impression that Christianity is the system that will replace them.

Early also is the ministry of John the Baptist. John understands his own role as fulfilling Scripture (Jn 1:23) in calling Israel to repentance (Mt 3:1–2) in preparation for the Messiah (Jn 1:23–27). As the last of the Old Testament prophets (Mt 11:13) and being well acquainted with Old Testament imagery, he also recognizes and announces the significance of Christ's coming in terms of covenantal wedding symbolism. This is noteworthy in that John's preaching represents some of the earliest revelation in the New Testament (after the birth and infancy of Christ):

> You yourselves bear me witness, that I said, "I am not the Christ," but, "I have been sent before Him." He who has the bride is the bridegroom; but the friend of the bridegroom, who stands and hears him, rejoices greatly because of the bridegroom's voice. And so this joy of mine has been made full. (Jn 3:28–29)

Morris, citing Murray, notes of this passage that "God Himself was in Christ betrothing His bride to Himself afresh."[64] John understands that "his office is to bring groom and bride together."[65] In this his final witness to Christ, he clearly bases his imagery on the Old Testament symbolism of God's marriage relation to Israel.[66] In fact, his rejoicing with the bridegroom echoes Isaiah 62:5 where "as the

---

tie (Winona Lake, Ind.: Alpha, rep. 1883), 199. R. T. France, *Mark* (PBC) (Oxford: Bible Reading Fellowship, 1996), 34.

[64] Leon Morris, *The Gospel according to John* (NICNT) (Grand Rapids: Eerdmans, 1971), 241.

[65] A. T. Robertson, *Words Pictures in the New Testament* (Nashville: Broadman, 1930), 5:56.

[66] See: D. A. Carson, *The Gospel according to John* (Grand Rapids: Eerdmans, 1991), 211. Leon Morris, *The Gospel according to John* (NICNT) (Grand Rapids: Eerdmans, 1971), 241. F. F. Bruce, *The Gospel of John* (Grand Rapids: Eerdmans, 1983), 95.

bridegroom rejoices over the bride, so your God will rejoice over you."[67][68]

Even Christ's first miracle appears to serve as a metaphor (a *semeiōn*) of his presenting himself to Israel in terms of marriage imagery (wine is associated with the messianic banquet, Isa 25:6; Joel 3:18; Am 9:13). In John's Gospel his "beginning of signs" (Jn 2:11) to Israel turns water into wine at a wedding feast (Jn 2:1–10). As Barclay observes (with many others), we must read John on two levels, a surface level that is obvious, but also on a deeper level which presents a bigger theological picture.[69] Ridderbos concurs.[70] Morris notes that this "signifies that there is a transforming power associated with Jesus. He changes the water of Judaism into the wine of Christianity."[71]

Morris, Michaels, and others see this miracle paralleling the synoptic use of wedding feast and bridegroom images drawn from the Old Testament, and therefore exhibiting Christ as the bridegroom who has come.[72] Indeed, there is "little doubt" that this miracle is a sign of the coming of God's kingdom pictured in the Old Testament wedding feast imagery.[73] And just as the other wedding imagery alluded to his coming death, this miracle does also (Jn 2:4; cp. Jn 7:30; 8:20; Mt 26:18) and is followed by more detail of his eventual violent death (Jn 2:19–21).

And once again we witness the replacement motif substituting the better wife (Christianity) with the old unfaithful wife (Israel); we see this in mere water being transformed into wine. And not only so, but it is surprising even to those who do not know of the miracle, because the "good wine" is brought to the wedding *after* the first wine (Christianity comes after Judaism) (see above discussion of Mk 2 and Jn 2). In addition, Jesus produces a large quantity of wine (120+ gallons) in vessels filled to the brim (*heōs anō*, Jn 2:7). As Feuillet points out, "Cana is a sign, a symbol of the new Covenant" and the miracle is part of a leitmotif in Jn 2–4 where we see the old

---

[67] Bruce, *John*, 95.

[68] Rodney A. Whitacre, *John* (IVP NTC) (Downers Grove, Ill.: InterVarsity, 1999), 77.

[69] William Barclay, *The Gospel of John* (DBSS) (Philadelphia: Westminster, 1956), 1:80.

[70] Herman Ridderbos, *The Gospel of John: A Theological Commentary*, trans. by John Vriend (Grand Rapids: Eerdmans, 1997), 100–01.

[71] Morris, *John*, 176.

[72] Morris, *John*, 176–77; J. Ramsey Michaels, *John* (NIBC) (Peabody, Mass: 1989), 47.

[73] George R. Beasley-Murray, *John* (WBC) (Dallas, Tex.: Word, 1999), 36.

temple compared to the perfect temple (Jn 2:13–22), the old birth into Israel compared to the new birth of the Spirit (Jn 3:1–21), and Jacob's well paling in comparison to Christ's living water (Jn 4:1–42).[74]

Interestingly, Ridderbos, citing Olsson, sees John 2–4 against the "Sinai screen" of Exodus 19.[75] Olsson draws strong parallels between the Jewish interpretation of Exodus 19 and this section of John's Gospel (Jn 1:19–2:11).[76] And since Exodus 19 presents the covenantal formation of Israel as a nation and bespeaks her marriage to God, this is quite significant. "The Jewish tradition concerning the events at Sinai often mentions *the marriage of the Lord and Israel.*"[77]

So then, during his three and one-half year ministry, the Lord comes to his own but they do not receive him (Jn 1:11). The Apostle John is particularly concerned to demonstrate this recurring problem (Jn 12:37–41),[78] so that he characteristically calls them "the Jews"[79] in order "to denote the Jewish nation as hostile to Jesus."[80] And no wonder! They are of their father the devil (Jn 8:44). Early in John's Gospel we witness the Baptist's wilderness message (Jn 1:23) which

---

[74] André Feuilett, *Johannine Studies*, trans. Thomas E. Crane (Staten Island, N.Y.: Alba, 1964), 33.

[75] Ridderbos, *John*, 109.

[76] Olsson focuses on John's phrases "the third day," "invited," "whatever he says to you, do it," "manifested his glory," "they believed in him," and other portions of Jn 1:19 – 2:22. For example, the third day time frames match (2:1; cp. Ex 19:10, 11, 15–16 LXX). The obedience motif picks up on Israel's hearing and obeying God (Jn 1:37; 2:5, 7–8, 11; cp. Ex 19:5, 8). The purifying vessels and the purging of the temple by Jesus reflect Israel's consecration (Jn 1:29; 2:6, 14–17; cp. Ex 19:10, 14, 19). Jesus as the "lamb of God" echoes the sacrificial blood (Jn 1:29, 36; cp. ex 24:5–8). The parallel between Jesus and Moses being invited (Jn 2:2; cp. Ex 19:20, 25). The presence of Jesus' mother (she is emphasized though unnecessary to explaining the miracle, 2:1, 3, 5) represents the Israelites at Sinai. Jesus's manifested "glory" reminds us of God's glorious enveloping of Mt. Sinai (Jn 2:11; cp. Ex 19:16–20). He even notes that "Cana" means "possession," which reminds us that God took possession of Israel in marriage at Sinai (Ex 19:5). Birger Olsson, *Structure and Meaning in the Fourth Gospel: A Text-Linguistic Analysis of John 2:1–11 and 4:1–42* (Lund, Sweden: Gleerup, 1974), 102–14.

[77] Olsson, *Structure and Meaning*, 107.

[78] Morris, *John*, 97–97; William Hendriksen, *Exposition of the Gospel according to John* (Grand Rapids: Baker, 1953), 80; Carson, *John*, 124–25; Heinrich August Meyer, *Critical and Exegetical Handbook to the Gospel of John*, tran. by Peter Christie (Winona Lake, Ind.: Alpha, rep. 1883), 57. This reminds us of Israel's Old Testament problem, Is 65:2–3; Jer 7:25–26.

[79] Jn 1:19; 2:13, 18, 20; 3:1; 4:9, 22; 5:1, 10, 15; 6:4, 41, 52; 7:1, 11, 35; 8:22, 31, 48, 52, 57; 9:18; 10:19, 24, 31; etc.

[80] Morris, *John*, 131.

reminds us of God's marrying Israel in the wilderness (Ex 19:1-2[81]);
see an allusion to the coming destruction of the temple (Jn 2:19);
learn of the dullness of Israel's leaders (Jn 3:10); and discover that
worship will be de-centralized away from the temple (Jn 4:21-23). In
John's Gospel "Jesus is largely rejected in Jerusalem and Judaea"
whereas "it is in Galilee and Samaria that he is received and that
many believe in him."[82] In Jerusalem "'the judgment of this world'
and of its ruler takes place."[83]

Christ's tender calling to Israel falls upon deaf ears, so that he
deems first century Israel — like her Old Testament fathers — "an
adulterous generation" (Mt 12:38-39; 16:4; Mk 8:38; cp. Jos., *J.W.*
5:9:4). It is "skeptical Jews who ask for signs as 'this adulterous generation.'"[84] Thus, in John a "common theme in 2:1-4:42" is Jesus'
teaching on the "replacement of the old with the new," the replacement of Israel's story with that which Christ brings about: Israel's
water is replaced with Christianity's wine (Jn 2:1-11), the temple is
replaced by Christ himself (Jn 2:14-19), the old birth into Israel with
the new birth (Jn 3:1-21), the old well water with the new living
water (Jn 4:7-15), and finally the replacement of Zion as the place of
worship with universal worship in Christ (Jn 4:16-26).[85] Interestingly, in the *pericope de adultera* we discover that though they are
presenting a woman allegedly caught in adultery, not one of them
is without guilt so that he can properly witness against the woman
(Jn 8:7-11).

As I show in Chapter 1 above Matthew drives home the Jewish
rejection of Christ throughout his gospel. In fact, Telford cites Barclay in noting that "there is no gospel which so unsparingly con-
demns the Jews, and especially the Pharisees."[86] I will repeat some

---

[81] The "wilderness of Sinai" is frequently mentioned in the context of Israel's formation. In Numbers it is mentioned ten times. Jeremiah's important marriage passage mentions God's betrothal there (Jer 2:2), as does Hosea (Hos 2:3; 13:4-6). Cp. Eze 20:10-16.

[82] Charles H. H. Scobie, "The Origins and Development of Samaritan Christianity," *New Testament Studies* 19 (1972-73): 404.

[83] Scobie, "Origins," 404.

[84] Rick Van De Water, "Reconsidering the Beast from the Sea (Rev 13.1)," *New Testament Studies* 46 (April, 2000): 256.

[85] Rodney A. Whitacre, *John* (IVP NTC) (Downers Grove, Ill.: InterVarsity, 1999),77. See also: Carson, *John*, 166.

[86] William R. Telford, *The Barren Temple and the Withered Tree: A Redaction-critical Analysis of the Cursing of the Fig-Tee Pericope in Mark's Gospel and Its Relation to the Cleansing of the Temple Tradition* (Sheffield: JSNT Supp. 1, 1980), 93.

of Matthew's later material that I rehearsed in Chapter 1 and make a few additional observations relevant to the present argument.

During the last few days before his crucifixion, Jesus increasingly denounces Israel and prophesies her coming destruction for rejecting his overtures. After zealously attacking the corruption in the temple, he charges that it has become a "robber's den" and cites Scripture calling it "My house" (Mt 21:13). Shortly thereafter he curses the barren fig tree and calls for an unyielding faith from his disciples (Mt 21:18–22). This is clearly a symbol of Israel's curse for "the passage coheres with Jesus' teaching about impending judgment on the temple, his teachings about radical faith, and his commissioning disciples to carry on his work."[87] Thus, "the ravaged or withered fig-tree is a vivid emblem of God's active *punishment* of his people in Jer. 5.17; 8.13; Hos. 2.12; 9.10, 16 and Am. 4.9 (cf. also Ps. 105.33; Is. 28.4; 34.4; Na. 3:12)."[88]

The lesson from the withered fig tree intensifies in Jesus' response to his disciples' surprise: "And Jesus answered and said to them, 'Truly I say to you, if you have faith, and do not doubt, you shall not only do what was done to the fig tree, but even if you say to this mountain, "Be taken up and cast into the sea," it shall happen'" (Mt 21:21). Here Jesus urges his disciples to believe that the temple Mount will be destroyed for it "in like manner has failed to fulfil its raison d'être."[89]

Shortly thereafter he presents the Parable of the Landowner which shows God's loving care for Israel and her continuing disregard for him (Mt 21:33–44), while warning that "the kingdom of God will be taken away from you and given to a people producing the fruit of it" (Mt 21:43).

Then his next parable picks up on the image of marriage which introduced his ministry (Mt 22:1–7). The Parable of the Marriage Feast presents a king (God) preparing "a wedding feast for his son" (Mt 22:2). The call goes out to invite all to the feast, only to be rejected (Mt 22:3–6) causing the king to be so "enraged" that he sends his armies to destroy "those murderers and set their city on fire" (Mt 22:7). The A.D. 70 destruction of the temple "is here clearly predicted."[90] This parable once again shows the faithless "lack of re-

---

[87] Craig S. Keener, *A Commentary on the Gospel of Matthew* (Grand Rapids: Eerdmans, 1999), 503.

[88] Telford, *Barren Temple*, 145.

[89] Telford, *Barren Temple*, 59; cp. 95, 163.

[90] William Hendriksen, *Exposition of the Gospel according to Matthew* (Grand Rapids: Baker, 1973), 795.

sponse among the Jews to Jesus and his message."[91] Regarding this recurring wedding motif in Christ's teaching: "the image can hardly be accidental."[92]

In Matthew 22:14 he holds out hope for a remnant in Israel, for "many are called, but few are chosen." That is, many (all) of Israel received the call, but only a few (the remnant) were chosen and accept it. In Revelation 7:4 John pictures these few as the 144,000 "out of all the tribes of the sons of Israel" (*ek pases phulēs huion Israel*). They appear again in Revelation 14 with the Lamb on heavenly Mount Zion. In Revelation 14:4 they are designated as "chaste (lit., "virgins" *parthenoi*), which sets them apart from "adulterous" Israel (Mt 12:38–39; 16:4; Mk 8:38). They are an important part of those appearing in Revelation as the "purchased" ones (Rev 5:9) — they have been purchased with the *bride price* (Ge 29:18; 34:12; Ru 4:10; cp. m. Ket 4:4, 7–8) leading to their marital union with the Lamb in Revelation 21–22.

In Matthew 23 Jesus denounces Israel's religious leaders, then weeps over Jerusalem for spurning his loving overtures: "O Jerusalem, Jerusalem, who kills the prophets and stones those who are sent to her! How often I wanted to gather your children together, the way a hen gathers her chicks under her wings, and you were unwilling" (Mt 23:37).[93] He then not only declares the temple "desolate," but no longer calls it "my house" (cp. Mt 21:13; cp. Lk 2:49; Jn 2:16[94]) but "your house"[95] (Mt 23:38[96]) as he prepares to dramatically depart from it (Mt 24:1). "In doing so he took the presence of God with him, confiscating it from the Temple."[97] Indeed, "Jesus' final

---

[91] Donald A. Hagner, *Matthew 14–28* (WBC) (Dallas: Word, 1995), 626–27.

[92] *TDNT*, 1:655.

[93] Luke adds the parable of the fig tree planted in the vineyard wherein the vineyard keeper gave the tree three years (the length of Jesus' ministry) to bear fruit. He allows just one more season (another six months), then cuts it down. Lk 13:6–10.

[94] God calls the temple "my house": 1Ch 17:14; 28:6; Isa 56:5, 7; Jer 11:15; 12:7; 23:11; Eze 23:39; 44:7; Hos 9:15; Hag 1:9; Zec 1:16; 3:7; 9:8; Mal 3:10.

[95] Stephen does the same sort of distancing in his sermon to the Jews. When he speaks of Old Testament Israel as faithful, he calls them "our fathers" (Ac 7:11, 12, 15, 19, 38, 39, 45), but in vv 51–52 he speaks of their rebellion, calling them "your fathers."

[96] Feuillet, *Johannine Studies*, 235; Peter W. L. Walker, *Jesus and the Holy City: New Testament Perspectives on Jerusalem* (Grand Rapids: Eerdmans, 1996), 62; James C. DeYoung, *Jerusalem in the New Testament: The Significance of the City in the History of Redemption and in Eschatology* (Kampen: J. H. Kok, 1960), 89.

[97] Walker, *Jesus and the Holy City*, 31.

departure from the temple should be understood as a sign that the sentence of God's judgment in the words 'your house is abandoned to you' is *immediately* being brought to realization."[98]

After his declaring the temple is desolate, he pronounces its coming total destruction (Mt 24:2). In the Old Testament God's judgment on Israel's sin included his forsaking of his house (1Ki 9:6–9; Jer 12:7; 22:5; Eze 8:6; cp. Ps. Sol. 7;1). In fact, Ezekiel sees the Spirit departing the temple to stand over the Mount of Olives (Eze 11:22–25), which Jesus re-enacts by leaving the temple desolate and walking to the Mount of Olives (Mt 23:38; 24:1–3; cp. 24:15). The New Testament hereinafter expects the closing down of the temple system (Heb 8:13; 12:25–27[99]).

Surprisingly, Josephus records various remarkable signs that the temple is now without God's presence. He records one of these as follows:

> as the priests were going by night into the inner [court of the temple], as their custom was, to perform their sacred ministrations, they said that, in the first place, they felt a quaking, and heard a great noise, and after that they heard a sound as of a great multitude, saying, "Let us remove hence." (*J. W.* 6:5:3).

This is even recorded by the Roman historian Tacitus who was born during the reign of Nero:

> There had been seen hosts joining battle in the skies, the fiery gleam of arms, the temple illuminated by a sudden radiance from the clouds. The doors of the inner shrine were suddenly thrown open, and a voice of more than mortal tone was heard to cry that the Gods were departing. At the same instant there was a mighty stir as of departure. (*Hist.* 5:13)

Though Matthew emphasizes Jesus' confirming his ministry to the Jews (Mt 10:6; 15:24), it is to no avail for they eventually demand his crucifixion — even though Pilate declares his innocence (Mt 27:17–24). In the end they cry out: "His blood shall be on us and on our children!" (Mt 27:25) — which language is picked up from the first temple's destruction in the Old Testament (Eze 33:4–5). Matthew appropriately closes his Gospel with the Great Commission to

---

[98] DeYoung, *Jerusalem*, 88. Emph. added.

[99] The "created things" soon to be shaken (i.e., destroyed) in Heb 12:27 are the tangible elements of the temple system. See: Heb 9:6, 8, 11, 24. In Heb 12:27 the author of Hebrews "speaks more emphatically than ever about the end of the earthly cultus, though that end still lies in the future." Paul Ellingworth, *The Epistle to the Hebrews* (NIGNTC) (Grand Rapids: Eerdmans, 1993), 687.

"all nations" (Mt 28:19), just as John closes Revelation with the new Jerusalem coming down from heaven with God's provision for the "nations" (Rev 21:24; cp. 21:3).

In the first century the temple's final destruction accomplishes God's conclusive divorce of Israel. In his New Testament divorce action God so dis-establishes her that redemptive history is no longer the story of a Jewish-focused, Israel-exalting, geo-political work as in the Old Testament (Mt 8:11; 21:43; cp. Am 3:2a; Ps 147:19–20). God's work now reaches out to "all nations" (Mt 28:19; Ac 1:8; 13:46–48; Col 1:6) whom will marry in Christ (Eph 5:25b–27, 32; 2Co 11:2).

The Apostle John's early statement that "He came to his own but his own received him not" (Jn 1:11) is recalled in one of his closing scenes:

> As a result of this Pilate made efforts to release Him, but the Jews cried out, saying, "If you release this Man, you are no friend of Caesar; everyone who makes himself out to be a king opposes Caesar." When Pilate therefore heard these words, he brought Jesus out, and sat down on the judgment seat at a place called The Pavement, but in Hebrew, Gabbatha. Now it was the day of preparation for the Passover; it was about the sixth hour. And he said to the Jews, "Behold, your King!" They therefore cried out, "Away with Him, away with Him, crucify Him!" Pilate said to them, "Shall I crucify your King?" The chief priests answered, "We have no king but Caesar." So he then delivered Him to them to be crucified. (Jn 19:12–16)

Revelation 5 and Divorce Grounds

Covenantal marriage requires formal, legal grounds for divorce. In Deuteronomy 24:1 we read that the husband must find something morally "unclean" (*ervah*) in her. Jesus affirms the moral grounds for issuing a covenantal divorce in Matthew 5:31–32 and 19:7–9: "fornication" (*porneia*). In Isaiah 50:1 God's divorce decree against Israel mentions her "iniquities" (*peshaim*). In Jeremiah 3 her divorce decree appears in the context of a statement regarding her being covenantally "faithless" (*meshubah*) and "treacherous" (*bagad*) (Jer 3:6, 8). Whatever these terms mean, they show the necessity of moral grounds for divorce. In biblical law no one could secure a divorce for "any cause at all" — contrary to the Pharisees' challenge to Jesus (Mt 19:3; see also: Jos., *Ant.* 4:8:23; *m. Gitt.* 9:10).

In Isaiah 1:21 Isaiah declares that the "faithful city has become a harlot" because she was "full of justice" and "righteousness" but "now murderers." The "faithful [Heb., *amen*] city" is now acting like a "harlot," the most unfaithful of women. As Young explains: Jerusalem's "infidelity is one of the heart and can express itself in various ways. . . . One of these may have been idolatry, but since the following words seem to be explanatory, we may say that the presence of murderers and the general corruption of the state which has been described were also manifestations of this unfaithfulness. The word 'harlot' is emphatic; 'how has become a harlot . . . . the faithful city!'"[100] Isaiah had already deemed Old Testament Jerusalem like Sodom (Isa 1:10), a city well-known in Scripture for gross wickedness (Ge 13:13; 19:4–5; Jer 23:14; Eze 16:49; 2Pe 2:6–7; Jude 7) with no mention of idolatry.

Revelation 5 presents Christ before the throne in such a way as to highlight the just grounds for God's divorcing Israel. In Revelation 1:7 the whole theme of Revelation is rooted in Israel's judgment for crucifying Christ (cp. Mt 21:33–40; 27:25; 1Th 2:14–16). In the court scene in Revelation 5 Christ is repeatedly (emphatically) referred to as the "Lamb that was slain" (Rev 5:12; cp. 6, 9). He is not just a Lamb who was once dead but is now alive (as per Rev 1:5, 18; 2:8, *nekrōn, nekros*); rather he is the Lamb who had been "slain" (*esphagō*), that is, ruthlessly murdered (Rev 5:6, 9, 12; cp. 13:8). Even Pilate wants to release Christ (Mt 27:18, 19, 23a, 24), but the Jews persist (Mt 27:20, 23b, 25) even bringing in false witnesses against him (Mt 26:60).[101] John emphasizes that the Jews seek his death through much of his ministry (Jn 5:18; 7:1, 11; 10:31–33; 11:8, 47–53; 18:14; 19:7).

In Revelation this innocent Lamb is the only one in the Universe who is "worthy" to open the seals (Rev 5:2) and he was worthy *because* he had been ruthlessly slaughtered (Rev 5:9), even though innocent. His worthiness is emphasized three times (Rev 5:2, 9, 12), as well as necessitated by his heavenly praise as equal to God in blessing, honor, glory and dominion (Rev 5:13). Hence, the legal decree is justified in court.

Conclusion

Revelation comes late in the period of canonical revelation, 1500 years after the Mosaic revelation. It appears at the great redemptive-historical juncture reached in the first century with the coming of Christ. As God turns to the Gentiles he will soon finally remove his old covenant temple. The A.D. 70 catastrophe is a major event in re-

---

[100] E. J. Young, *The Book of Isaiah* (Grand Rapids: Eerdmans, 1965), 1:80.

[101] R. Travers Herford, *Christianity in Talmud and Midrash* (New York: KTAV, 1975 [rep. London: Williams and Norgate, 1903]), 81, notes that "as early as the time when the Tosephta was compiled, there was a tradition that the condemnation of Jesus had been obtained by the fraudulent means described above" (though those means differ from the Gospel record).

demptive history that an intensely Jewish-flavored book such as Revelation would not overlook. This opens the very strong possibility that the scroll in Revelation 5 represents God's legal judgment against Israel, especially given the large role that Israel's judgment plays elsewhere in the New Testament record (note for instance Luke's four major Jerusalem oracles, 13:32–35; 19:41–44; 21:20–24; 23:38–31).[102] The judgments of Revelation "are best understood in the light of the 'sevenfold chastisement' that is evolved within Jewish legal theology as a scheme of punishment for disobedience to God" (cf. Lev 6:18, 21, 24, 28).[103] This is affirmed by a mass of related contextual evidence in Revelation as well, which I develop in my forthcoming commentary.

In addition, the evidence even suggests that this judgment scroll is a divorce decree against God's unfaithful wife, Israel. According to Christ's own teaching, no man may divorce his wife to take another apart from proper moral justification and his securing a divorce certificate (Mt 5:31–32; 19:9). God certainly does this in the Old Testament in response to Israel's engaging in harlotry (Isa 50:1; Jer 3:8). The moral justification which Christ demands for such a radical breach of covenant is *porneia* (fornication), which happens to be related to the word used for Revelation's "harlot": *pornes*. In fact, the harlot is guilty of *porneia* (Rev 14:8; 17:1–2; 18:2–3).

Revelation shows God issuing a divorce decree against his harlot-wife in a dramatic heavenly court-room setting before taking a new bride, the "new Jerusalem," the Church of Jesus Christ. The local movement in this section of Revelation is from God's throne (Rev 4), the presentation of the divorce decree and Christ's opening it (Rev 5), the judgments flowing from it (Rev 6), to a pause to consider the faithful remnant of Jews (the 144,000 from the twelve tribes), and the resulting universal growth of the Christian Church (Rev 7). This movement parallels in important respects the revisiting of the scroll (Rev 10), the destruction of the temple in the holy city (Rev 11:1–2) in the presence of witnesses (Rev 11:3–8), with a reiteration of its universal consequences (Rev 11:15) and its viewing of the heavenly temple (Rev 11:16–18) which is now opens (Rev 11:19). The divorce of Israel leads to enormous redemptive-historical changes.

Clearly "in Israel some kind of written document appears to have been necessary" to effect divorce,[104] and this requires formal

---

[102] See especially: Walker, *Jesus and the Holy City* (1996).

[103] John M. Court, *Myth and History in the Book of Revelation* (Atlanta: John Knox, 1979), 80.

[104] James D. Martin, "The Forensic Background to Jeremiah III 1," *Vetus Testamentum* 19 (1969): 89. Cp. *m. Gitt.* 2:7. See the care taken in writing the divorce cer-

court proceedings and proper witnesses (as the Mishnah, *Gittin* shows[105]). Consequently, I believe Ford's approach is correct when she writes: "the bride and adulteress motifs in Revelation . . point to such a scroll. It might easily be a bill of divorce; the Lamb divorces unfaithful Jerusalem and marries the new Jerusalem."[106] This identification of the scroll and the consequent dramatic movement of Revelation will become more evident as we continue through chapter 5 and through the remainder of the book.

---

tificate, *m. Gitt.* 2:3–4; 3:2; 6:2.

[105] E.g., *m. Gitt.* 1:3; 3:6–7; 4:3; 6:2, 7; 8:9; 9:3–4, 8. Though unusual to us, the means of issuing a bill of divorce were governed by certain rules, *Gitt.* 8:1–3. In earlier days a man could set up a court of three men in order to secure his divorce, *Gitt.* 4:2.

[106] J. Massyngberde Ford, *Revelation* (Garden City, N.Y.: Anchor, 1975), 93.

5

THE JEWISH PERSECUTION OF CHRISTIANITY

And I saw the woman drunk with the blood of the saints, and with the blood of the witnesses of Jesus. And when I saw her, I wondered greatly. (Rev 17:6)

Introduction

Redemptive-historical preterism understands Revelation as focusing *primarily* on Jerusalem's fall and the temple's destruction as Christ judges Israel in A.D. 70. However, the enormity of that judgment reverberates beyond Jerusalem, even shaking the wider Roman Empire. In addition, to this Jewish focus, commentators agree that Revelation is an extremely Judaic book, with allusions to hundreds of Old Testament passages, scores of old covenant images, a Hebraicized form of Greek grammar, the inclusion of several Hebrew words, and more. We should expect this when we properly understand Revelation's theme verse — Revelation 1:7 — as dealing with Christ's judgment-coming against Israel.

But Revelation is not one dimensional. It is also a book that expresses a deep, visible, and unrelenting concern for Christian martyrs in the first century — both those who will actually be put to death (e.g., Rev 6:9–10; 14:13), as well as those who will endure terrible persecutions short of death (Rev 2:9–10; 3:10). Given Revelation's theme regarding Israel's judgment and the entire book's Hebraic character, we should not be surprised that we find within it significant references to *Jewish* persecution of the budding Christian faith. This realization is significant not only for interpreting Revelation itself, but for understanding Christianity's earliest experience and Israel's dramatic rebellion against God.

John emphasizes in his introduction that a major sub-theme in Revelation is Christ's vindication of his people who are suffering for their testimony of faith in him. There he not only mentions his own persecutional suffering (obviously at the hands of the Romans who banish him to the Roman penal colony on Patmos), but expresses his concern for the saints elsewhere: "I, John, your brother and *fellow partaker* in the *tribulation* and kingdom and *perseverance* which are in Jesus, was on the island called Patmos, because of the word of God and the testimony of Jesus" (Rev 1:9). He frequently mentions Christian suffering — sometimes at the hands of the Romans, sometimes at the hands of the Jews. Indeed, as we shall see, the evidence suggests that Christians will eventually be persecuted by the Romans *because of the Jews*.

Revelation appears to present an unholy alliance against Christianity, a Roman-Jewish alignment. In Revelation 2:9–10, a portion of the letter to the church at Smyrna, we read about opposition from the synagogue, which results in Christian suffering that will eventually involve imprisonment. Imprisonment requires Roman action, since Jewish synagogues could not imprison their opponents in Smyrna. Yet Christ links these pagan and Jewish cultures against his followers in the letter to Smyrna: "I know your *tribulation* and your poverty (but you are rich), and the blasphemy by those who *say they are Jews* and are not, but are a *synagogue of Satan*. Do not fear what you are about to *suffer*. Behold, the devil is about to *cast some of you into prison*, that you may be tested, and you will have *tribulation* ten days. *Be faithful until death*, and I will give you the crown of life."

Mayo comments on Revelation 2:9 (and its similar statement in 3:9) that the "most widely held and most compelling interpretation is that these two churches were in some way in conflict with the Jewish communities of Smryna and Philadelphia."[1] He further observes that "the close contextual proximity of the 'synagogue of Satan' in 2.9 and the activity of the 'devil' in 10b argues powerfully that the so-called Jews were instigating civil persecution." And in John's view "any involvement of the Jews with the Romans against the Christians merited mention and serious condemnation."[2] Charles agrees, noting that "the persecution with which the Church is here threatened shows that the Jews were acting in concert with the heathen authorities."[3]

John symbolizes this Jewish-Roman linkage in several places in Revelation. For instance, in Revelation 13:11ff we see the second beast from "the land" (literally) serving the first beast from the sea (Rev 13:1), whom I show elsewhere is Rome.[4] As I demonstrate in Chapter 9 below, the land beast (also known as the "false prophet," Rev 19:20), represents the Jewish High Priestly aristocracy, who has sold out to Rome. Josephus shows that the High Priests are appointed by Roman authorities in the first century (*Ant* 14:8:5; 15:2:7; 15:3:1; 17:13:1; 20:8:11; 20:9:4; 20:10:4, 5).

---

[1] Philip L. Mayo, *"Those Who Call Themselves Jews": The Church and Judaism in the Apocalypse of John* (Eugene, Ore.: Wipf and Stock, 2006), 51.

[2] Mayo, *"Those Who Call Themselves Jews,"* 66.

[3] R. H. Charles, *The Revelation of St. John* (ICC), (Edinburgh: T & T Clark, 1920), 1:58. See also: J. P. M. Sweet, *Revelation* (Philadelphia: Westminster, 1979), 28–30.

[4] See: Kenneth L. Gentry, Jr., *The Beast of Revelation* (Powder Springs, Geo.: American Vision, 2002).

Speaking of the sixty year line of six priests issuing from Annanus b. Sethi (*Ant* 18:26), Goodman observes that "in every case their right to lead the Jewish nation rested . . . entirely on the whim of the Romans, or in later cases Herodian princes, who appointed them."[5] This corruption of the High Priesthood is a large issue with the Jewish community in Qumran that separates from Israel. As a consequence the Qumran community deems Jerusalem as defiled and worthy of divine curse (CDC 1:3; 4:18; 5:6; 6:16; 12:1–2), as did much of the Jewish apocalyptic literature beginning as early as 200 B.C. (1 Eno 83–89; Apoc Weeks; T. Levi 17:10; Jub. 23:21).

This Judeo-Roman alignment appears symbolically in Revelation 17:3 where the Jerusalem harlot (see: Ch. 11 below) sits on the Roman beast. In Revelation, sitting on something symbolizes a position of influence or control, such as God's sitting on his throne to rule (Rev 4:2), or the four horsemen sitting on their horses to create havoc (Rev 6:2–8), or Christ's sitting on his white horse to judge (Rev 19:11). Thus, the imagery in Revelation 17:3 portrays the Jewish authorities influencing Rome against Christianity (cf. Rev 17:6).

Christ warns against this alliance in Mark 10:17–18: "But beware of men; for they will deliver you up to the courts, and scourge you in *their synagogues*; and you shall even be brought before *governors and kings* for My sake, as a testimony to them and to the Gentiles." We see it operating against Christ during his trial, which shifts back-and-forth between Roman and Jewish courts:

> Early in the morning the *chief priests* with the elders and scribes, and the whole Council, immediately held a consultation; and binding Jesus, they led Him away, and delivered Him up to *Pilate*" (Mk 15:1).

> As a result of *this Pilate made efforts to release Him*, but *the Jews cried out*, saying, "If you release this Man, *you are no friend of Caesar*; everyone who makes himself out to be a king opposes Caesar. . . ." They therefore cried out, "Away with Him, away with Him, crucify Him!" Pilate said to them, "Shall I crucify your King?" *The chief priests answered, "We have no king but Caesar"* (Jn 19:12, 15).

Peter's Pentecostal sermon to those in Jerusalem alludes to this problem: "this Man, delivered up by the predetermined plan and foreknowledge of God, *you* [Jews] nailed to a cross *by the hands of godless men* [Romans] and put Him to death" (Ac 2:23). We see this again in Acts 4:27: "For truly in this city there were *gathered together* against Thy holy servant Jesus, whom Thou didst anoint, both Her-

---

[5] Martin Goodman, *The Ruling Class of Judaea: The Origins of the Jewish Revolt Against Rome A.D. 66–70* (Cambridge: Cambridge University Press, 1987), 44.

od and Pontius Pilate, *along with* the Gentiles *and* the peoples of Israel."

In Revelation the persecution of Christians appears in many passages, such as: Revelation 2:9–10; 3:9–10; 6:9–11; 11:7–8, 11–13, 18; 12:10; 13:10; 14:11–13; 16:5–6; 17:6; 18:20, 24; 19:2; 20:4, 6. Because of the enormous social and cultural forces set against them, John exhorts the beleaguered first century saints to have patience, to withstand, to persevere, to overcome: Revelation 1:9; 2:7, 11, 17, 26; 3:5, 12, 21; 7:3; 12:15–16; 21:7. He especially encourages Jewish Christians who are under tremendous pressure from their racial brethren for having aligned themselves with Christ's Church. This is a serious problem the New Testament expresses elsewhere (Mt 10:17–18; 23:34; 1Th 2:14–17; Heb 10:32; 11:26; 12:4; 13:13). John designs his vision-set to embolden them to recognize that their Christ-denying Jewish persecutors (the church's first and main enemy, see below) will be overwhelmed by the wrath of God who avenges his true people (cp. Lk 18:7–8; Ro 12:19; Heb 10:30; 1Pe 4:14–17).[6]

This Jewish opposition is all the more significant when we realize that the Jewish-Christian element was a small remnant of a vast Jewish community of the first century (Ro 11:5). In fact, in the first century, Jews represent between nine and fifteen per cent of the Roman Empire's population. In this regard Paul Barnett notes that "successive Roman rulers for more than a century had prudently recognised both the size of the Jewish community within the empire (approximately 15% overall) and the peculiar character of Jewish religious nationalism."[7]

Thus, we must understand the Jewish persecution setting of Revelation — even while recognizing that Nero will eventually initiate Rome's first imperial persecution of Christianity. The problem arising from an antagonistic Judaism for young Christianity is felt even in the communities in Asia Minor to which John writes (see Ch.8 for additional information on the significance of Judaism for Asian Christians). See further material on this matter under point 4 below.

I will now succinctly present under several headings the anti-Christian activities of the first-century Jews.

---

[6] Howard Kee Clark, *Understanding the New Testament* (Englewood, N. J.: Prentice-Hall, 1983), 292.

[7] Paul Barnett, *Behind the Scenes of the New Testament* (Downer's Grove, Ill.: Inter-varsity, 1990), 158.

Jesus Prophesies Jewish Persecution

Early in his ministry the Lord warns his disciples that he is sending them to the house of Israel (Mt 10:6, 17, 23) where they will be terribly treated: "But beware of men; for they will deliver you up to the courts, and scourge you in their synagogues; and you shall even be brought before governors and kings for My sake, as a testimony to them and to the Gentiles" (Mt 10:17-18).

> It is noteworthy that the idea of *prosecuting* is included in the concept of *persecution*. Jesus connected the idea of being persecuted with being brought before rulers and being arraigned for one's witness. . . . This background of a legal process against Christians has a bearing on the calls for vengeance in Revelation.[8]

The very real prospect of economic deprivation leads Jesus to warn: "no one of you can be My disciple who does not give up all his own possessions" (Lk 14:33), which alludes to the economic consequences of following him in that day. Jewish Christians risk being hounded out of town, driven from city to city, and being subjected to arrest, all of which create extreme difficulties for providing a living (Mt 10:23; Ac 8:1; 11:19; 13:50; 14:2, 19; 17:5-8, 13; 18:12; 25:2; 1Th 2:14-15a). Mark 13:12 records Christ warning that among the Jews "brother will deliver brother to death, and a father his child; and children will rise up against parents and have them put to death."

In his parables and discourses Jesus often focuses on Israel's rebellion and looming destruction — with almost *no* reference to Rome's future persecution: "in the gospels, Jesus shows no particular hostility towards the Roman occupation. The placing of the responsibility for his death on the [Jewish] religious leaders, rather than on the Romans who executed has been treated extensively."[9]

---

[8] Joel Nobel Musvosvi, "The Concept of Vengeance in the Book of Revelation in its Old Testament and Near Eastern Context" (Ph.D. Dissertation: Andrews University, March 1986), 151.

[9] Rick Van De Water, "Reconsidering the Beast from the Sea (Rev 13.1)," *New Testament Studies* 46 (April, 2000):246. For the Israel-judgment emphasis in Christ's ministry (and in the Gospel record as such), see: N. T. Wright, *Jesus and the Victory of God* (Minneapolis: Fortress, 1996) and Peter W. L. Walker, *Jesus and the Holy City: New Testament Perspectives on Jerusalem* (Grand Rapids: Eerdmans, 1996). The same is true regarding Paul's epistles. Despite faddish academia charging Paul with explicit challenges to Roman authority (as per N. T. Wright, Karl Donfried, J. R. Harrison, Abraham Smith, and Helmut Koester), Seeyon Kim presents several strands of evidence against such: (1) Paul never expressly critiques Roman hegemony; (2) he specifically affirms Rome's authority both directly (Ro 13:1-7) and by

The Lord even teaches that the Jews who persecute Christians believe they are serving God — just as much as worshiping him in the temple: "They will make you outcasts from the synagogue, but an hour is coming for everyone who kills you to think that he is offering service to God" (Jn 16:2). Thus, he relates Jerusalem's demise (Mt 23:35–24:2) to Israel's persecution of the saints (which is, in effect, persecuting Christ (Mt 5:10–13; 25:34–40; Ac 9:4):

> Therefore, behold, I am sending you prophets and wise men and scribes; some of them you will kill and crucify, and some of them you will scourge in your synagogues, and persecute from city to city that upon you may fall the guilt of all the righteous blood shed on earth, from the blood of righteous Abel to the blood of Zechariah, the son of Berechiah, whom you murdered between the temple and the altar. (Mt 23:34–35)

Hare calls this an "unambiguous reference to Jewish persecutors."[10]

Beagley argues that "John's Apocalypse is greatly concerned with the Church's conflict with unbelieving and persecuting anti-Christian Judaism as an immediate problem."[11] This sort of treatment should not surprise us in that:

Ancient Jews Show a Violent Tendency

Hare notes that "the Jews of first-century Palestine and the diaspora were in fact often fanatical and violent, if even a portion of what Josephus reports is accurate."[12] Some of the Josephan evidence appears in his *Jewish War*:[13] Josephus himself receives threats of death by the Pharisees who are associated with the Sanhedrin (*Life* 39–40).

We see this violent response in the Jewish Qumran dissenters. Their *War Scroll* calls on the community to be ready to slay the wicked (1QM 6:17), as does the *Temple Scroll* (64:1–2). Johnson comments

---

his appeal to Nero (Ac 25:11; 28:19); (3) he never mentions the emperor cult; (4) his mission work leaves him no time for labor for political change; (5) he promotes an ethic of non-retaliation; and (6) he expects to be acquitted when he appears before a Roman court. Kim, *Christ and Caesar: The Gospel and the Roman Empire in the Writings of Paul and Luke* (Grand Rapids: Eerdmans, 2008).

[10] Douglas R. A. Hare, *The Theme of Jewish Persecution of Christians in the Gospel according to St. Matthew* (Cambridge: University Press, 1967), 80.

[11] Alan James Beagley, *The "Sitz im Leben" of the Apocalypse with Particular Reference to the Role of the Church's Enemies* (New York: Walter de Gruyter, 1987), 112.

[12] Hare, *Theme of Jewish Persecution*, 19–79.

[13] *J.W.*, 1:4:3; 1:7:5; 1:29:11; 2:1:3; 2:3:1; 2:4:3; 2:9:2; 2:12:13; 2:12:2; 2:13:6; 2:17:2; 2:17:4; 2:18:3; 4:3:3; 4:3:12; 4:5:1; 4:6:3; 4:9:4; 7:8:7; 7:10:1; 7:11:1.

that "an interesting but difficult line of inquiry would be to trace the polemic between the Pharisaic schools Beth Hillel and Beth Shammai. The Talmud retains intriguing glimpses into the fierceness of those disputes."[14] He notes that *y. Sabb.* 1:4 speaks of the murder of the disciples of Beth Hillel by those of Beth Shammai. Josef Blinzler shows that the Jews were prone to lynchings, as with Stephen.[15] See Acts 5:26; 9:29; 21:30ff; 22:22–24; 23:12; 25:2ff. Again we must remember Paul's own zeal in persecuting Christians (Ac 8:3; 9:2; 22:4; 26:11).

Pearson notes that as Judaism reorganizes after A.D. 70: "Christians are being cursed in the synagogues and excommunicated therefore; their prophets and teachers are being persecuted, and denounced as 'children of hell.' These developments are not limited only to Palestine, but are apparently also felt in the Diaspora."[16]

The Jews Cause Christ's Death

Despite his disciples' disbelief, Christ warns them that the Jewish leaders will kill him: "Behold, we are going up to Jerusalem; and the Son of Man will be delivered to the chief priests and scribes, and *they will condemn Him to death*, and will deliver Him to the Gentiles to mock and scourge and crucify Him, and on the third day He will be raised up" (Mt 20:18–19; cp. Mt 16:21; 17:22–23; Mk 9:31; Lk 17:25; 18:32).

The biblical record shows that they accomplish their evil task in delivering him to Pilate to suffer capital punishment: "And early in the morning the chief priests with the elders and scribes, and the whole Council, immediately held a consultation; and binding Jesus, they led Him away, and delivered Him up to Pilate" (Mk 15:1). The Jewish culpability in the matter is frequently repeated,[17] for they *demand* his crucifixion (Mt 23:37ff.; Jn 19:12–16). According to R. Travers Herford, while commenting on the Talmud reference at San-

---

[14] Luke T. Johnson, "The New Testament's Anti-Jewish Slander and the Conventions of Ancient Polemic," *Journal of Biblical Literature* 108 (1989):439.

[15] Josef Blinzler, *The Trial of Jesus: The Jewish and Roman Proceedings Against Jesus Christ Described and Assessed from the Oldest Accounts,* trans from 2d ed. by Isabel and Florence McHugh (Westminster, Maryland: Newman, 1959), 163.

[16] Birger A. Pearson, "1 Thessalonians 2:13–16: A Deutero-Pauline Interpolation," *HTR* 64 (1971): 93.

[17] Mt 26:59; Mk 14:64; Lk 23:20–23; 24:20; Jn 18:29–31; Ac 2:22–23, 36; 3:13–15a; 4:10; 5:28, 30; 7:52; 10:39; 13:27–29; 26:10; 1Th. 2:14–15.

hedrin 9:7, even "the Talmudic story of the execution of Jesus does not implicate the civil government at all."[18]

The Jews Persecute Christians

Carson observes that "there should be little doubt that the first virulent opposition Christians faced came from the Jews, precisely because the Church sprang out of Judaism and all of its earliest members were Jews. It is not surprising that Paul five times received the thirty-nine lashes (2Co 11:24) — a distinctive punishment meted out by synagogue authorities."[19] Indeed, the Book of Acts is virtually a running report of Jewish resistance to fledgling Christianity.[20]

In Acts Luke traces the growing vehemence of Jewish opposition strengthening from mockery (Ac 2:12-13), to threats (Ac 4:1-3, 21), to flogging (Ac 5:40), and finally to death (Ac 7:58-59). The persecution motif leads up to Stephen's important message (Ac 2:22-23, 36; 3:13-15a; 4:10; 5:28, 30), concludes it (Ac 7:52), and follows it (Ac 10:39; 13:28-29). Luke emphasizes Stephen's message, for it appears as the longest recorded statement in Acts (Ac 7:2-53), is given by a man highly praised (Ac 6:5, 8, 10, 15; 7:55-56, 60; 8:2), and sets the stage for the fuller Jewish persecution of Christianity (Ac 6:10-15; 7:58-8:1).

At Stephen's execution a full-scale Jewish persecution breaks out against Christians (Ac 8:1), leading Saul (Paul) and others to seek their death (Ac 12:2; 13:28; 26:10). We read after Stephen's martyrdom that "a great persecution arose against the church in Jerusalem" (Ac 8:1; cp. 11:19). At that point Saul breathes out "threats and murder against the disciples of the Lord" and "went to the high priest, and asked for letters for him to the synagogues at Damascus, so that if he found any belonging to the Way, both men and women, he might bring them bound to Jerusalem" (Ac 9:1-2, 14, 21). In fact, the chief priests give him the "authority" (*exousian*, Ac 9:14) and a "commission" (*epitropēs*, Ac 26:12) to bring them to Jerusalem.

As a zealous Jew before his conversion, Paul persecutes Christians (Ac 7:58; 8:1-3; 9:1-9, 21; 22:4-5; Gal 1:13; Php 3:6; 1Co 15:8; 1Ti

---

[18] R. Travers Herford, *Christianity in Talmud and Midrash* (New York: KTAV, 1975), 89-90.

[19] D. A. Carson, *The Gospel according to John* (Grand Rapids: Eerdmans, 1991), 531.

[20] See in: Acts 4:3; 5:17-18; 6:12-13; 7:58; 8:1, 3; 9:1-2, 13, 23, 29; 12:1-4; 13:45-50;14:2-5, 19; 17:5; 18:6, 12, 17; 20:3, 19; 21:11, 27-28; 22:3-5; 23:12-15, 20-21; 24:27; 26:10, 21; 28:18-29. See elsewhere: Ro 15:31; 2Co 11:24; Heb 10:33-34. See also: Eusebius *Eccl. Hist.* 3:5. Paul Barnett, *Jesus & the Rise of Early Christianity: A History of New Testament Times* (Downers Grove, Ill.: InterVarsity, 1999), 158.

1:12–13), even noting in his later testimony the blind fury involved in this disruptive and terrifying activity: "as I punished them often in all the synagogues, I tried to force them to blaspheme; and being furiously enraged at them, I kept pursuing them even to foreign cities" (Ac 26:11). Many Jewish Christians also have their property seized (Heb 10:32–34). Paul's ministry (which dominates the last half of Acts) shows that because of their hard hearts God is turning from the Jews to the Gentiles (Ac 13:46–47; 18:6; 22:21). Because of the danger, Christ has to "deliver" Paul from the Jews so that he might engage this ministry (Ac 26:17) which will be effectual (Ac 28:8). He asks the Roman Christians to pray "that I may be delivered from those who are disobedient in Judea" (Ro 15:31). Later he himself suffers persecution by the Jews (2Co 11:23–29; Gal 5:11; 6:12).

Hare observes that upon "reviewing the evidence of Acts, we find that Jews are reported as instigating action against Christians by (1) poisoning the mind of the populace, (2) stirring up the rabble to attack the Christians, (3) bringing Christians before Gentile tribunals on charges of having broken Gentile law, and (4) inciting Gentiles to hale Christians into court on such charges."[21] We see this conduct in Acts 13:45, 50; 14:2, 5, 19; 17:5–8, 13.

Thus, the record of Jewish opposition, which results in Israel's consequent judgment in A.D. 70, shows that it arises earlier than the Roman persecution. Israel historically begins directly persecuting the Church in A.D. 33 (Ac 8:1–3; A.D. 33) three decades before both the Neronic persecution (A.D. 64ff) and the Jewish War (A.D. 67–70). In fact, it is largely due to Jewish activity that Rome eventually becomes aware of Christianity as a distinct movement and begins persecuting it. "NT persecution as a whole began with the Jews' attacks upon the Church, but before long they sought the assistance of Gentiles, esp. the Rom. authorities."[22] Lund observes that in Revelation 2:9 the Jews in Smyrna are "acting as informers for the Roman authorities."[23] This opens Nero's *Circus Maximus* to the bloody repression of the faith (cf. Jn 19:12, 15; Ac 12:1–3; 14:2; 17:5–7; 25:24–26).

Van de Water notes that we may discern "the common reflection of Jewish opposition in the NT writings."[24] The Epistle to the Hebrews provides us a clear insight into growing defections back into

---

[21] Hare, *The Theme of Jewish Persecution*, 75.

[22] *ZPEB*, 4:705.

[23] Nils Wilhelm Lund, *Studies in the Book of Revelation* (n.p.: Covenant, 1955), 80.

[24] Van de Water, "Reconsidering the Beast from the Sea (Rev 13.1)," 248.

Judaism because of Jewish pressures.[25] Eusebius records the widely held belief that Christians flee Pella so that "the judgment of God might at last overtake them for all their crimes against the Christ and his Apostles" (*Eccl. Hist.* 3:5:3).

In the New Testament record the Jews are constantly "casting out" Christians either from their synagogues or their cities. And oftentimes for purposes of physical persecution. Stephen is "cast out" [*ekballō*] from Jerusalem before the Jews stone him (Ac 7:58). The Jews "drove out" (*exebalon*) Paul and Barnabas from the city on their first missionary journey (Ac 13:50). The disciples of Christ are constantly fleeing from the Jews (Ac 14:1–6, 19–20; 17:5–9, 13–14; 18:6, 12–17). John's Gospel records the fear of the Jews among Christ's followers even *during* his ministry (Jn 7:13; 19:38; 20:19; cp. 3:1).

Excommunication is such a serious matter in ancient Judaism that it can — and often *does* — involve persecution. Martin notes that ultimately "the demise of Jewish membership in the Christian Church was hastened by punishment and persecution of Christian Jews within the synagogue, eventually followed by expulsion from the synagogue."[26] (See: *m. Mid.* 2:2; *m. Mo'ed Qat.* 3:1–2; *m. Sanh.* 1:2; 3:6; 4:1; *m. Mak.* 3:4, 7; *m. Hul.* 12:4.)

This ecclesiastical exclusion not only involves social ostracizing from family and friends (Mt 10:21, 34–39), but outside the borders of Israel it legally endangers the individual in that "expulsion from the synagogue deprived Christians of the shelter of Judaism and left

---

[25] "These people were converted Jews who had nevertheless retained their allegiance to Judaism and were in danger of falling between two stools, or even of leaving the Christian church and returning to their former Jewish faith. To appreciate the strong pull of Judaism on Christians who were formerly Jews, it must be remembered that Christianity could offer no parallel to the ritual trappings to which they had been accustomed. . . . The attraction of apostasy in the sense of returning to an outward allegiance to Judaism would have been strong for those who found it hard to face the determined opposition of their Jewish compatriots (*cf.* 10:32)." Donald B. Guthrie, *Hebrews* (TNTC) (Grand Rapids: Eerdmans, 1985), 32; C. F. D. Moule, *The Birth of the New Testament* (3d ed.: New York: Harper & Row, 1982), 59–60; D. A. Carson, Douglas J. Moo, and Leon Morris, *An Introduction to the New Testament* (Grand Rapids: Zondervan, 1992), 400–04; I. Howard Marshall, Stephen Travis, and Ian Paul, eds., *Exploring the New Testament: A Guide to the Letters & Revelation* (Downers Grove, Ill: InterVarsity, 2002), 231–32.

[26] Ralph P. Martin, and Peter H. Davids, eds., *Dictionary of the Later New Testament & Its Development* (Downers Grove, Ill.: InterVarsity, 1997), 165.

them vulnerable to the Romans."[27] Jesus warns his disciples that in their ministry to Israel the Jews will drag them before the *sunedria* (legal courts) and scourge them in the synagogues (Mt 10:16–18). But he promises this persecution will be cut short by his judgment-coming against Israel: "But whenever they persecute you in this city, flee to the next; for truly I say to you, you shall not finish going through the cities of Israel, until the Son of Man comes" (Mt 10:23; cp. Rev 1:7; 3:9, 11).

Eusebius writes: "Now after the ascension of our Saviour in addition to their crime against him the Jews at once contrived numberless plots against his disciples" and "the other Apostles were driven from the land of Judaea by thousands of deadly plots" (*Eccl. Hist.* 3:4:5). Tertullian calls the "synagogues of the Jews, fountains of persecution" (*Scorp.* 10; see also *A.D. Nationes* 1:14). Apolinarius (quoted by Eusebius, *Eccl. Hist.* 5:16:12) writes: "Or was any one of the women ever scourged in the synagogues of the Jews or stoned?" He uses this to show that the Montanists are not true prophets because they do not suffer under the hands of the Jews like orthodox Christians.

We see this embodied in the later Jewish writings, which probably reflect actions beginning even from before the temple's destruction.

> The *Minim* [apostate Jews, those in "sects"] including Jewish Christians, were indeed excluded from the synagogue, but by other means than the *cherem* [formal excommunication] or *niddui* [a formal ban for a set period of time]: all personal and business contact with them were formally cursed in the *Shemoneh Esreh*.[28]

In the Jewish Tosefta we read of the Jew's treatment of *Minim*: "One does not sell to them or receive from them or take from them or give to them. One does not teach their sons a trade'" (*t. Hullin* 2:20) and "the Minim and the apostates and the betrayers are cast in [a pit] and not helped out" (*t. B. Mezia* 2:33).

Justin records Trypho the Jew as stating: "Sir, it were good for us if we obeyed our teachers, who laid down a law that we should have no intercourse [communication] with any of you" (*Dial.* 38 §138). This comports with Justin's reference regarding the first century activities by the Jews: "at that time [after Christ's crucifixion] you selected and sent out from Jerusalem chosen men through all the land [*eis pasan tēn gēn*] to tell that the godless heresy of the Christians

---

[27] Claudia Setzer, *Jewish Response to Early Christians: History and Polemics, 30–150 C.E.* (Minneapolis: Fortress, 1994), 87.

[28] Hare, *Jewish Persecution of Christians*, 49.

had sprung up, and to publish those things which all they who knew us not speak against us" (*Dial.* 17). He also complains to Trypho:

> For the expression, "He that is afflicted [and driven out]," i.e., from the world, [implies] that, so far as you and all other men have it in your power, each Christian has been driven out not only from his own property, but even from the whole world; for you permit no Christian to live. But you say that the same fate has befallen your own nation. Now, if you have been cast out after defeat in battle, you have suffered such treatment justly indeed, as all the Scriptures bear witness; but we, though we have done no such [evil acts] after we knew the truth of God, are testified to by God, that, together with the most righteous, and only spotless and sinless Christ, we are taken away out of the earth. (*Dial.* 36)

The Jews Involve Gentiles in Persecution

Not only do the Jews directly engage in Christian persecution, but they constantly agitate against the Christians so as to involve the Romans in their persecution (Ac 4:27; 16:20; 17:5-8; 18:12; 21:11; 22:22-23; 24:1-9; 25:1-2, 24; 28:17). Indeed, scholars generally admit that the Jews were responsible for Roman repression of Christianity.

Throughout Acts Rome is largely indifferent to Christianity — and even a source of refuge for Paul (Ac 25:11-12; 26:32; 28:30). Indeed, in Acts "one gets not the slightest hint . . . that Christianity faced any difficulty from the Roman authorities."[29] But we see trouble brewing for Christians due to Jewish riots against the faith. Rome would have to enter the fray. In Acts 18:2 we read that Claudius "had commanded all the Jews to leave Rome." This apparently is due to Jewish violence against Christian preaching about Christ,[30] for Suetonius writes that "as the Jews were indulging in constant riots at the instigation of Chrestus ["Christ"], he banished them from Rome" (*Claud.* 25:4). This speaks of "dissension and disorder in the Jewish community at Rome resulting from the introduction of

---

[29] Jack T. Sanders, *The Jews in Luke-Acts* (Philadelphia: Fortress, 1987), 313.

[30] For a helpful discussion see: Harry J. Leon, *The Jews of Ancient Rome* (rev. ed.: Peabody, Mass.: Hendrikson, 1995), 25-27. Suetonius: *The Twelve Caesars*, trans. Robert Graves; rev. by Michael Grant (New York: Penguin, 1979), 202. See: Albert A. Bell, Jr., *A Guide to the New Testament World* (Scottsdale, Penn.: Herald, 1994), 82. Mary E. Smallwood, *The Jews Under Roman Rule: From Pompey to Diocletian* (Boston: Brill, 2001), 211-15.

Christianity into one or more of the synagogues of the city."[31] Because of Paul's constant trouble with the Jews in Acts requiring his appeal to Caesar, negative attention was being drawn to Christianity. "The frequent riots instigated by Jewish opponents against Christians in many cities seem to have predisposed Roman authorities against Christianity. Legislation against it was only a small step away."[32] Thus considered, Revelation serves "as a kind of sequel to the Acts of the Apostles."[33]

That being so, as I noted previously we learn that a number of historians surmise that even the Neronic persecution may have been partly due to "the promptings of orthodox Jews."[34] Regarding Nero's search for scapegoats on which to blame the Roman fires of July, A.D. 64 (Tacitus, *Ann.* 15:41), Gibbon sees the Jews behind Nero's choice of Christians. He notes that the Jews "possessed very powerful advocates in the palace, and even in the heart of the tyrant: his wife and mistress, the beautiful Poppaea, and a favourite player of the race of Abraham." These two suggested to Nero "the new and pernicious sect of Galileans," the Christians.[35]

On this matter, Adolf Harnack writes: "Unless the evidence is misleading, they instigated the Neronic outburst against the Christians; and as a rule whenever bloody persecutions are afoot in later days, the Jews are either in the background or the foreground."[36] Workman concurs: "The Jews, working probably through Poppaea, the famous mistress and wife of Nero, whose superstitious nature led her to dally with Judaism, or through Aliturus, a favourite Jewish mime, took the opportunity of the great fire and the need for a

---

[31] F. F. Bruce, *The Book of the Acts* (NICNT) (Grand Rapids: Eerdmans, 1980), 368. Cp. Leon 25–26.

[32] Joel Nobel Musvosvi, "The Concept of Vengeance in the Book of Revelation in its Old Testament and Near Eastern Context, Ph.D. Dissertation: Andrews University (March 1986), 158 n 16.

[33] M. Hopkins, "The Historical Perspective of Apocalypse 1–11" *Catholic Biblical Quarterly* 27 (1965):45.

[34] W. H. C. Frend, *The Rise of Christianity* (Philadelphia: Fortress, 1984), 109.

[35] Edward Gibbon, *The Decline and Fall of the Roman Empire*, 1:16. See also: ABD, 4:1080; BEB, 1:396; Miriam T. Griffin, *Nero: The End of a Dynasty* (New Haven: Yale University Press, 1985), 133; Albert A. Bell, Jr., *A Guide to the New Testament World* (Scottsdale, Penn.: Herald, 1994), 82–83.

[36] Adolf Harnack, *The Expansion of Christianity in the First Three Centuries*, trans. by James Moffatt (New York: Putnams, 1904), 1:66.

scapegoat to save themselves and at the same time to wreak ven-geance on the Christians."[37] Frend and Canfield agree.[38]

In *1 Clement* 6:5 the first century churchman Clement claims that the Neronic persecution was prompted "through envy [*dia zelos pathontēs*]," which many scholars believe refers to the Jews (e.g., Workman, Canfield; Renan, Harnack, Uhlhorn, and Barnett).[39] The gospels record their peculiarly virulent envy in Christ's trial: "he was aware that the chief priests had delivered Him up because of envy" (Mk 15:10). In supplementing the evidence from Clement, we should note that

> the apologist Melito of Sardis, writing a half-century later, says that Nero and Domitian were persuaded to persecute the Christians by certain malicious slanderers. . . . Klette's explanation that the calu-miantors were the Jews is a point well taken. He argues that the slanderers in the first place must have been well acquainted with the distinction between Jews and Christians, and in the second place they must have hated the Christians with an unrelenting hatred. One does not have to go far to discover who these malicious advisers are likely to have been. . . . The malicious slanderers then would seem to have been none other than the Jewish advisers of Nero.[40]

Keresztes offers a particularly compelling argument regarding this meaning in Clement.[41] Much of the following is based on his re-search. (1) Acts shows the Jews violently attacking Christians (Ac 8:1; 13:45; 14:2, 19; 17:5, 3; 21:27; 25:2-3), even putting some to death (Ac 7:1-2, 59; 9:1-2; 12:1-3). They have deadly designs on Paul (Ac 28:17-29). They complain that Christians are nullifying Moses and

---

[37] Herbert B. Workman, *Persecution in the Early Church: A Chapter in the History of Renunciation* (Cincinnati: Jennings and Graham, 1906), 57.

[38] W. H. C. Frend, *Martyrdom and Persecution in the Early Church: A Study of a Conflict from the Maccabees to Donatus* (Garden City: Anchor, 1967), 126; Leon H. Canfield, *The Early Persecutions of the Christians* (New York: Columbia University Press, 1913), 49.

[39] Workman, *Persecution in the Early Church*, 365; Canfield, *The Early Perse-cutions*, 50ff; Joseph-Ernest Renan, *Renan's Antichrist*, trans. William G. Hutchison (London: Walter Scott [rep.: Whitefish, Mont.: Kessinger, n.d.]), 80–81; Adolf Har-nack, *The Expansion of Christianity in the First Three Centuries*, trans. by James Moffatt (New York: Putnams, 1904), 1:65ff; Gerhard T. Uhlhorn, *The Conflict of Christianity with Heathenism*, trans. by Egbert C. Smyth and C. J. H. Ropes (3d ed.: New York: Scribner's, 1912) 246; Barnett, *Behind the Scenes of the New Testament*, 303.

[40] Canfield, *Early Persecutions of the Christians*, 52.

[41] Paul Keresztes, *Imperial Rome and the Christians*, vol. 1: *From Herod the Great to about A.D. 200* (Lanham, Mary.: University Press of America, 1981), 404–13.

proselytizing (Ac 21:21, 28; cp 13:16–50; 14:1, 6, 18; 17:4, 10–14). They charge before Roman authorities that Christians are upsetting the world (Ac 17:6) and are "spoken against everywhere" (Ac 28:22). But Rome barely notices Christians: "the imperial Roman government showed no hostility towards Christianity."[42] Luke presents Roman legal authorities in a favorable light allowing Paul to appeal to Caesar for protection from the Jews (Ac 25:11; 28:19).

(2) Suetonius (*Claud.* 25:4; cp. Dio 60:66:6; Orosius 7:6:15–16) shows that the Jews were expelled from Rome under Claudius around A.D. 50 for causing riots in confrontations with Christians (cp. Ac 18:2; 24:5). The Jews were disliked by the Romans (Josephus, *Ap* 2:66–92) and frequently stirred up trouble in Rome causing them to be expelled from Rome on other occasions (Suetonius, *Tib.* 36; Tacitus *Ann.* 2:85; Josephus, *Ant* 8:3:5). They would rightly fear that blame for the Roman fire might fall upon them and would therefore be moved to deflect attention to the Christians.

(3) In 1 Clement, "the context of the Roman tragedy [i.e., Neronic persecution] rather suggests that it was the result of fratricidal jealousy similar to the examples just mentioned from the history of the Chosen People,"[43] for Clement had just traced such a history among the Jews (*1 Clem.* 3–4). As Frend puts it:

> Clement has just been describing the dire effect of envy and jealousy in the Israelite community down through the ages, and it was to drive home his conclusion that he "ceases from the examples of old time" to speak of his own day. It looks from the context as though "envy and jealousy" were symptoms of internal conflict among a Jewish community, especially as Clement time and again draws his readers" attention to fratricidal struggles in Jewish history, such as Cain and Abel, Jacob and Esau, Joseph and his brethren. In this case, the warring brothers could be the Old Israel and the New (cf. Acts 13:45). . . . One may perhaps draw the same conclusion from the use of the term in St. Mark"s Gospel (15:10) where the Jewish high priests are described as delivering up Our Lord "through envy" (*dia epthonon*).[44]

Thus, "the natural inference is that the Jews, because of their jealousy of the Christians, had stirred up the [Neronic] persecution directed against the Christians."[45]

---

[42] Keresztes, *Imperial Rome and the Christians*, 67.
[43] Keresztes, *Imperial Rome and the Christians*, 411.
[44] Frend, *Martyrdom and Persecution*, 125.
[45] Canfield, *Early Persecution of the Christians*, 48.

(4) Clement specifically mentions the martyrdom of Peter and Paul in this context. And we know the Jews persecute them (Ac 4:1-2; 5:17-19, 28; 12:3-5; 17:5, 3; 21:27; 25:2-3).

(5) We know that Paul's missionary practice was to go first to the Jewish synagogues and preach (Ac 9:20; 13:5, 14-15; 14:1; 17:1, 10; 18:4, 26).

(6) We also know that Paul appeals to Caesar (Ac 25:11-12; 26:32; 28:19), arrives at Rome around A.D. 62 just two years before the persecution (Ac 27:1; 28:14), and preaches freely to the Jews in Rome (Ac 28:16-17, 23, 30-31). Thus, he is not afraid of Rome, but is informed by Roman Jews that they had heard that "this sect" (of Christians) "is spoken against everywhere" (Ac 28:22). But now Caesar would have recently heard the Jews vigorously complain against Paul and therefore Christianity. Nero would doubtless be reminded of that by his cunning wife Poppaea at this time of great political concern.

Keresztes concludes his analysis of Clement: "There can be little doubt that, seeing the activities and the great success of Paul and other leaders of the Church in Rome, such as Peter, the Synagogue, moved by jealousy and envy, enlightened, as explained above, Nero and the Imperial government about a sect waiting for the coming of the Kingdom of God."[46] Eusebius concurs with Clement, citing Melito's reference to "malicious people" (*Eccl. Hist.* 4:26:9) which suggests the Neronic persecution was "engineered by the Jews."[47] Frend notes regarding his survey of the evidence:

> The persecution represented a triumph for the orthodox Jews, who were able, through influence at Court, to shift the odium of the outbreak onto the hated schismatics, the Christian synagogue. This they hoped to destroy at a single tremendous blow. In the persons of Pappaea Sabina and the actor Tigellinus they had the ear of the Emperor, and they succeeded in so far as a great number of Christians were killed, including the leaders, Peter and Paul.[48]

Historian Schaff comments that "it is not unlikely that in this (as in all previous persecutions, and often afterwards) the fanatical Jews, enraged by the rapid progress of Christianity, and anxious to avert suspicion from themselves, stirred up the people against the

---

[46] Keresztes, *Imperial Rome and the Christians*, 411.

[47] Mary E. Smallwood, *The Jews Under Roman Rule: From Pompey to Diocletian* (Boston: Brill, 2001), 218.

[48] Frend, *Martyrdom and Persecution*, 126.

hated Galileans."[49] Hence, the extreme danger of the slander ("blasphemy") of the Jews (Rev 2:9; 3:9) and Christ's prior warning about their bringing Christians before kings (Mt 10:17–18). They hound the Christians throughout the Apostolic period (Acts; Rom 15:31; 1 Thess 2:14–16). Origen reports that:

> when Christianity began to be first preached, [the Jews] scattered abroad false reports of the gospel, such as that "Christians offered up an infant in sacrifice, and partook of its flesh"; and again, "that the professor of Christianity, wishing to do the 'works of darkness', used to extinguish the lights, and each one to have sexual intercourse with any woman whom he chanced to meet." (*Cels.* 6:27; cp. Tacitus, *Ann.* 15:44)

Most would agree that "in S. John's day the Jews had considerable influence at Rome."[50] In terms of sheer numbers, this should not be surprising: Jews probably made up over ten percent of the population of the empire.[51] In fact, "the eastern provinces probably [had] as high as 20% of the population as Jewish."[52] Josephus notes that "there is no region of the world without its Jewish colony" (*J.W.* 2:16:4). In fact, Jews were in "every important city of Asia Minor."[53] In Rome itself existed "a total community of a very large size."[54]

But the Jews also had well-placed advocates. Again Josephus reveals the probable Jewish access to Caesar when he notes:

> I became acquainted with Aliturius, an actor of plays, and much beloved by Nero, but a Jew by birth; and through his interest became known to Poppaea, Caesar's wife, and took care, as soon as possible, to entreat her to procure that the priests might be set at liberty. And when, besides this favor, I had obtained many presents from Poppaea, I returned home again. (*Life*, Pref. 3)

---

[49] Philip Schaff, *History of the Christian Church* (Grand Rapids: Eerdmans, rep. n.d. [1910]), 1:383.

[50] James J. L. Ratton, *The Apocalypse of St. John: A Commentary on the Greek Text* (London: R & T Washbourne, 1915), 48.

[51] Mireille Hadas-Lebel, *Flavius Josephus: Eyewitness to Rome's First-Century Conquest of Judea*, trans. by Richard Miller (New York: Macmillan, 1993), 53–54.

[52] Neil Faulkner, *Apocalypse: The Great Jewish Revolt Against Rome AD 66–73* (Gloucestershire, Eng.: Tempus, 2002), 38; cp. Roland H. Worth, Jr. *Seven Cities of the Apocalypse and Roman Culture* (New York: Paulist, 1999), 72.

[53] Worth, *Seven Cities of the Apocalypse and Roman Culture*, 72.

[54] Smallwood, *The Jews Under Roman Rule*, 131.

According to Josephus elsewhere, Nero's acting in favor of a certain Jewish petition "showed favour to his wife Poppaea, who was a worshipper of God [*theasebēs*] and who pleaded on behalf of the Jews" (*Ant* 20:8:11).[55] Interestingly, the Roman historian Tacitus has nothing good to say about Poppaea whereas the Jewish historian Josephus praises her. And besides all of this, Nero believes he is destined to rule a kingdom in Jerusalem were he to fall from favor in Rome (Suetonius, *Nero* 40).

We have already seen that in *1 Clement* 5:5 and 6:1 Clement blames the martyrdom of both Peter and Paul on "jealousy and envy." These are words Luke uses in Acts to describe motives to Jewish opposition (Ac 5:17; 13:45; 17:5; cp. Mt 27:18‖). Paul sees this as fulfilling the Deuteronomy 32:21 prophecy: "I will make you jealous by that which is not a nation, by a nation without understanding will I anger you" (Ro 10:19; 11:11, 14). Van De Water notes that "this implied Jewish influence behind the demise of the two apostles coincides with a vivid account recorded in the *Acts of Peter and Paul*."[56]

In the first four paragraphs of *1 Clement* we read that Roman Jews successfully denounce Paul before Nero. They argue that he should not allow Paul to come to Rome in pursuit of his judicial appeal. This leads to warnings to Paul that "'we have heard from the rabbis of the Jews that are in this Rome . . . that they have asked Caesar to send into all his governments in order that wherever you may be found, you may be put to death,' whereupon Paul, then Peter, was martyred." Van De Water also cites Barnard noting that opposition to Christianity in *Barnabas* "has been described as 'the assaults of a militant Judaism.'"[57] Clearly the early Church is "persecuted by the Jews, behind which they never ceased to see the work of Satan."[58]

We find graphic evidence of Jewish interest in Christian persecution in later works such as *The Martyrdom of Polycarp* and Justin's

---

[55] She may have actually converted to Judaism. F. W. Farrar, *The Early Days of Christianity* (London: Cassell, 1884), 36–37) points out that she at least adopted their ways: she wanted to be buried at death rather than cremated (Tacitus, *Ann.* 16:16), wore a veil in public (*Ann.* 13:45), favored Aliturus and Josephus (Josephus *Life* 4; *Ant.* 2:8:11), and was deemed by Josephus a *theosebes*.

[56] Rick Van De Water, "Reconsidering the Beast from the Sea (Rev 13.1)," *New Testament Studies* 46 (April, 2000): 249.

[57] Van De Water, "Reconsidering the Beast," 249.

[58] S. Giet, *L'Apocalypse et l'histoire* (Paris: Presses universitaires de France, 1957), 105. As translated and cited in Van De Water, 254. In 1Th 2:18 Paul speaks of Satan's resisting him, which appears to refer to Jewish antagonism (cp. 1Th 2:14–16).

Apology. In the former we read: "the multitude of heathen and Jews living in Smyrna cried out with uncontrollable wrath" (*Mart. Pol.* 12:2). In Justin's work we discover that "they slay and punish us wherever they are able" so that Barchocba decrees that "Christians alone should be led to cruel punishments, unless they would deny Jesus Christ, and utter blasphemy" (*Apol. 1:* 31). In their analysis of Revelation 2:9 Bratcher and Hatton see the blasphemy as *slander* consisting in "false accusations made by their enemies for the purpose of getting them into trouble with the Roman authorities."[59]

Very often the Jews haul Christians before Roman legal authorities. In Thessalonica the Jews attack Paul and Silas and drag them before city rulers (Ac 17:5-6). They are charged with acting "contrary to the decrees of Caesar, saying that there is another king, Jesus" (Ac 17:7). This reflects Jesus' trial where the religious authorities cry out "we have no king but Caesar" (Jn 19:15). Later, Jews bring him before the proconsul of Achaia (Ac 18:12). Agabus warns that "the Jews at Jerusalem will bind" Paul and "deliver him into the hands of the Gentiles" (Ac 21:11; cp. Ac 24:2-10; 25:2; 26:2, 7).

Farrer notes the seriousness of Jewish slander when he comments on Revelation 2:9: "They slander his people and this is serious. By repudiating the Christians they deny them the legal protection extended to the synagogue, and expose them to Roman persecution as an unlawful society or 'religion.'"[60] He continues: "Indeed they are a synagogue of Satan for 'Satan' means 'adversary' or 'legal accuser'" which means that Christians can be thrown in prison (Rev 2:10). Thus, as the dragon does before God (Rev 12:10), so the Jews act before the Romans.

---

[59] Robert G. Bratcher and Howard A. Hatton. *A Handbook on The Revelation to John* (New York: United Bible Societies, 19934), 6-47; cp. Nils Wilhelm Lund, *Studies in the Book of Revelation* (n.p.: Covenant, 1955), 80.

[60] Austin Farrer, *The Revelation of St. John the Divine* (Oxford: Clarendon, 1964), 72.

6

THE "CAST OUT" TEMPLE

And there was given me a measuring rod like a staff; and someone said, "Rise and measure the temple of God, and the altar, and those who worship in it." And leave out the court which is outside the temple, and do not measure it, for it has been given to the nations; and they will tread under foot the holy city for forty-two months. (Rev 11:1–2)

Introduction

In that Revelation's theme is Christ's judgment on Israel, we would expect to find specific references to the temple. In fact, we find a remarkable reference to the temple and its coming destruction in Revelation 11:1–2. I deal with the general implications of this passage in *Before Jerusalem Fell*. But in my present context I want to look a little more deeply at it in light of the divorce motif in Revelation (see Ch. 4 above). The phrase I will focus on is: "leave out the court which is outside the temple."

John's Command Given

We should note that John is not simply commanded: "do not measure it," which would be sufficient to direct him in his task. Rather, the verb translated rather blandly (and uniquely for the New Testament) as "leave out" is actually the dramatic and forceful *ekbale*, which means "cast out." Not only so, but John seems to emphasize it, for the Greek literally reads: "And the court outside of the temple cast out, outside." The verb *ekbale* sufficiently directs that the court be "cast out," but John emphasizes that it must be "cast out outside": *ekbale exothen*.

The primary meaning of *ekballō* means "cast out" "with the included notion of more or less violence."[1] We can see that the idea can involve destruction when we note the parallelism in Deuteronomy 33:27 (LXX): "He drove out the enemy from before you / and said, "Destroy!" The immediate significance of this strong phraseology in Revelation is that the historical result of this casting out was so destructive that "the great temple of Herod was devastated, never to be rebuilt. . . . So violent was the Roman assault on the city

---

[1] Joseph Henry Thayer, *A Greek-English Lexicon of the New Testament*, (New York: American Book, 1889), 192.

that its physical appearance was permanently changed."[2] The Romans' scorched-earth policy even alters the landscape for miles around, for "wherever they passed, they left a desert of devastation and death."[3]

However, there is more here than meets the eye. Not only does John prophesy the temple's coming destruction in A.D. 70, but he does so in a fascinating manner quite in keeping with the overall drift of the book. You will need to keep in mind two important matters:

(1) As I argue in *The Book of Revelation Made Easy* (Ch. 2), Revelation 1:7 provides the theme of Revelation, which is Christ's judgment-coming against those who pierced him. They are the Jews who demand his crucifixion (Mt 20:18–19; 27:11–25; Mk 10:33; 15:1; Lk 18:32; 23:1–2; Jn 18:28–31; 19:12, 15; Ac 3:13; 4:26–27) and whom the apostles blame for it (Ac 2:22–23; 3:13–15a; 5:28, 30; 7:52; 10:39; 1Th 2:14–15).

(2) As I argue in Chapter 4 above the Seven Sealed Scroll in Revelation 5 is God's divorce decree against Israel (his Old Testament wife, Isa 50:1; 54:5–6; 62:4–5; Jer. 3:14, 20; 31:32; Eze 16:7–14, 31–32; Hos 1:2; 2:2, 7, 16, 19; 5:4; 9:1, 10) so that he can (in Christ) take a new bride, the "*new* Jerusalem" (Rev 21:2). We see the scroll fully opened in Revelation 10, where it presents the inclusion of the Gentiles in God's kingdom. This fits the meaning of the "mystery" in Revelation 10:7, as Paul explains in Romans 16:25–26; Colossians 1:26–27; 2:2; 4:3; 1 Corinthians 2:1; Ephesians 1:9–10; 3:3; 6:9.

John's Command Explained

The foundational meaning of *ekballō* is: "force to leave, drive out, expel."[4] Scripture uses this term in three conceptually related ways that are of particular interest for our understanding of Revelation 11:2, each of which is found in the first definition of the term in BAGD. This is especially significant in that scholars recognize "the Johannine love of multiple meaning."[5]

The three closely related uses of the term all signify forceful removal of something from its home area: exorcism, excommunication, and divorce. Interestingly, Christ alludes to each of these ideas in his original commissioning of his disciples as he prepares to

---

[2] Paul Barnett, *Behind the Scenes of the New Testament* (Downer's Grove, Ill.: Inter-varsity, 1990), 226, 228.

[3] Neil Faulkner, *Apocalypse: Great Jewish Revolt Against Rome A.D. 66–73* (Gloucestershire, Eng.: Tempus, 2002), 106.

[4] BAGD, 299.

[5] BAGD, 299.

send them to the "house of Israel" (Mt 10:6): *exorcism*, involving Satan (Mt 10:8, cp. v 25); *excommunication*, involving persecution (Mt 10:17–19, 23, 28, 34) and *divorce*, involving home disruption (Mt 10:21, 35–36).

First, *ekballo* is very commonly used for casting out demons (e.g., Mt 12:26, 28; Mk 1:34;16:9; Jos., *Ant* 6:11:1) from where they "have settled in men as in a house" (cf. Mt 12:43–44). This is particularly remarkable given that Revelation's "first woe" (the fifth trumpet) brings demons upon the Land (Rev 9:1–11). Later John declares her to be "the dwelling place of demons" (Rev 18:2). Thus, this "cast out" language becomes most relevant to the flow of the drama.

The use of *ekballō* for demon exorcism is important for at least two reasons: (1) John repeatedly notes in his Gospel that the Jewish leaders charge Jesus with being in league with the devil and demons (Jn 7:20; 8:48–52; 10:20). This issue even results in a major exchange with the Jews regarding the signs of the kingdom. They claim he was in league with Beelzebul (Mt 12:22–29; cp. 10:25), which leads to his warning them that the demons he cleared out of the land will come back seven times worse (Mt 12:43–45).

(2) John (alone among the Gospel writers) records Jesus' charge that the Jews are of their "father the devil" who was "a liar from the beginning" (Jn 8:44). Jesus effectively repeats this in John's Revelation when he twice calls the Jewish synagogue a "synagogue of Satan" and charges the Jews with lying about their claim (Rev 2:9; 3:9). The outpouring of demons on the land in Revelation 9 is just as Jesus warns in Matthew 12:45b (cf vv 43–45a). The verb *ekballō* in Revelation 11:2 echoes Christ's concern in a startling way: Whereas he cast out demons, their temple ("your house," Mt 23:38) will itself be cast out like a demon.

Second, *ekballō* is used for excommunication from one's faith community (e.g., 3 Jn 10). This is significant in that the Jews are constantly "casting out" Christians either from their synagogues or their cities. A key issue in Revelation is the persecution of believers by the Jews.

The clearest, most detailed, historical example of synagogue excommunication appears in John's Gospel. There the parents of the blind man whom Jesus heals (Jn 9:1–7) fear being "put out of the synagogue" (*aposunagōgos*, not *ekballō*, v. 22). After the Jews confront the man himself, "they put him out" (*exabalon auton exō*, Jn 9:34–35). John mentions this danger also in John 12:42–43 and 16:2 (though employing the other, uniquely New Testament term, *aposunagōgos*). In John 16:2 they believe they are doing God a spiritual service (*latreian*). *Latreia* is used of tabernacle/ temple service, making it appropriate for our concerns in showing the temple's judgment (Ro 9:4; Heb 9:1, 6).

Thus, the irony: whereas, the Jews are casting out Jewish converts to Christ, God is going to cast out their temple.

Third, *ekballō* speaks of divorcing one's wife by sending her out of the house. "As a [technical term] of the Septuagint for expulsion of a wife, *ekballō* appears in the citation of Gen 21:10 in Gal 4:30" where Paul refers to the expulsion of Hagar from Abraham's house.[6] In that the judicial backdrop of Revelation is God's divorce decree against Jerusalem/Israel, this fits perfectly with John's theme. The excommunication concept (discussed in our previous point) fits nicely also with God's sending Israel out of his house as a divorced wife.

And though the common Septuagint and New Testament term for divorce is *apostasion* (from *apolyo*, to set free), we find the Septuagint using forms of *ekballō* when speaking of a divorced woman as one "cast out" (Lev 21:7, 14; 22:13–14; Nu 30:9; Eze 44:22). Each of these cases (except for Nu 30:9) appears in levitical discussions. The two Leviticus 21 statements forbid a priest from marrying divorcees because he is "holy to his God." Interestingly, when Ezekiel uses the term (*ekbeblēmenēn*, Eze 44:22) of divorced women whom priests are forbidden to marry, he does so while speaking of the temple and in defining the difference between "the holy and the profane" (Eze 44:23). These levitical uses remind us of Revelation where John is speaking of the temple and worship while distinguishing between that which God accepts (the inner temple, the *naos*, Rev 11:1) and that which he rejects (the outer temple, the physical structure itself, Rev 11:2; cp. Rev 21:27).

All three connotations of *ekbale* as found in Revelation 11:2 are related to each other and relevant to John's theme. All three involve removal from a protective home place: Demons in Israel are cast out of the "house" they have taken up in a man (Mt 21:44). Synagogue excommunicants are cast out of their social community which revolves around God's house (Jn 9:34–35). Divorced wives are cast out of their husband's homes (Gal 4:30).

Conclusion

Thus, we see in Revelation a merging of biblical themes in the prophecy of the temple's destruction. And these merged sub-themes fit perfectly with John's over-arching theme of judgment upon Israel for crucifying Christ. And remarkably they help flesh out the redemptive-historical theme of God's divorcing his old covenant wife in order to take his new covenant wife.

---

[6] EDNT, 1:406.

7

THE JEWISH TEMPLE AS AN IDOL

But he who kills an ox is like one who slays a man;
He who sacrifices a lamb is like the one who breaks a dog's neck;
He who offers a grain offering is like one who offers swine's blood;
He who burns incense is like the one who blesses an idol. (Isa 66:3a)

Introduction

In Chapter 5 above, I point out the Jewish pressure on Rome to persecute Christians. I also note that the Jewish High Priestly aristocracy controls the corrupted temple, which itself is sold-out to the Romans. Here I will note John's further symbolic portrayal of this historical backdrop in his forensic drama.

For almost a century before the destruction of the temple, Israel exists as a part of the Roman regime, enjoying special leagues of "friendship and mutual alliance" beginning with Julius Caesar (Jos., *Ant* 14:10:1).[1] The Jews' love for Caesar was so great that after his murder, they weep for many nights at the site of his cremation (Suetonius, *Jul.* 84:5). Josephus praises Julius and records many of the treaties which he and later Roman authorities establish (*Ant.* 14:10:2–25). He then declares: "there are many such decrees of the senate and imperators of the Romans and those different from these before us" (*Ant* 14:10:26).

We must recognize that Israel engages in this practice *despite* her Old Testament prophets condemning such unholy alliances as harlotry (e.g., Isa 30:1; 36:12–18; Eze 23:5–7, 11–21; Hos 7:11; 8:9). According to John, the land beast (the Jewish High Priestly aristocracy, see Ch. 9 below) exercises his authority "in his [the Roman emperor's] presence" (Rev 13:1a), that is, in submission to Rome. In Revelation 17 we see John's portraying her alliance with Rome by the image of a harlot sitting on the beast.

Christ repeatedly forewarns his disciples about the nefarious designs the religious rulers have in mind: "from that time Jesus Christ began to show His disciples that He must go to Jerusalem, and suffer many things from the elders and chief priests and scribes, and be killed, and be raised up on the third day" (Mt 16:21‖).

---

[1] Harry J. Leon, *The Jews of Ancient Rome* (Rev. ed.: Peabody, Mass.: Hendrikson, 1995), 8–11.

"Behold, we are going up to Jerusalem; and the Son of Man will be delivered to the chief priests and scribes, and they will condemn Him to death" (Mt 20:18‖).

In John's Gospel we discover the point in time at which Israel finally and legally becomes apostate: when she chooses Caesar over Christ during his judicial trial. The Jewish religious authorities ("chief priests and the officers," Jn 19:6; cp. Jn 18:13, 19, 22, 24) go to great lengths to employ Rome's authority so that they might kill him: they "kept trying to obtain false testimony against Jesus" even bringing "many false witnesses" (Mt 27:59–60). They were "accusing Him vehemently" (Lk 23:1–10, 13–20).

The Roman procurator Pilate sees that Jesus is actually innocent, so he "made efforts to release Him, but the Jews cried out, saying, 'If you release this Man, you are no friend of Caesar; everyone who makes himself out to be a king opposes Caesar'" (Jn 19:12; cp. Ac 17:7). This "friend [philos] of Caesar" statement reminds us of the famous leagues of "friendship" (philian) with Caesar (Ant. 14:10:1). Philo mentions that the Jews are "friends to Caesar" (Embassy 36). So then, the "city of the great King" denounces her rightful King. And that denunciation seals her doom (see Jesus' warnings about his approaching betrayal and death, Mt 21:33–45; 22:2–14).

It is finally in her assertion of Roman judicial authority that Israel stumbles in her transgression (Ro 11:11–12) leading to her rejection (Ro 11:15). In that context she cries out for her own judgment: "And all the people answered and said, 'His blood be on us and on our children!'" (Mt 27:25; cp. Ac 5:28). Operatives of the first beast drive the nails in Christ's hands at the second beast's insistence (Jn 19:12, 15; Ac 2:23; 3:13–14) — and the dragon is behind it all (Jn 13:2, 27; cp. Col 2:15; Rev 12:4b; cf. Jn 8:44). We should recall once again that Israel's putting Christ to death is the central theme of John's drama (Rev 1:7). Thus, the slaughtered Lamb becomes its leading figure (Rev 5:6–13; 13:8). With her glorious heritage and privileges (Ro 3:1–2; 9:1–6; Eph 2:12) Israel should know better (Lk 23:34; Ac 17:30; Eph 4:17–18).

Temple Abuse; Temple Transience

Over and over again the Old Testament prophets disparage the temple cult — when Israel sins (e.g., Isa 1:10–17; 29:13; 43:23–24; Jer 6:20; 7:1–6, 21–22; 11:15; Eze 20:25; Hos 6:5–6; Am 4:4–5; 5:21–25; 9:1; Mic 6:1–8; Mal 1:10). Jeremiah presents God as denying he ever directed Israel to sacrifice: "For I did not speak to your fathers, or command them in the day that I brought them out of the land of Egypt, concerning burnt offerings and sacrifices. But this is what I commanded them, saying, 'Obey My voice, and I will be your God, and you will be My people; and you will walk in all the way which I command you, that it may be well with you'" (Jer 7:22–23).

In the Gospel record Jesus' overt teaching and his subtle conduct prepare us for the temple's removal as both liturgically no longer necessary and spiritually corrupted. John's Gospel is especially interesting in this regard: In John 1:14 he presents Christ as God's true "tabernacle" (*eskenōsen en emin*). This theme of Jesus replacing Israel's religious features recurs repeatedly in his ministry: In John 1:51 he, rather than the temple or High Priest, is the nexus between heaven and earth because "the angels of God [are] ascending and descending on the Son of Man." In John 2:19–21 he declares his body to be the true temple. In John 4:21–23 he tells the Samaritan woman the physical temple will soon be unnecessary.

When he attends the festival of Tabernacles (cf. Jn 7:2ff), he presents himself as the living water (Jn 7:37–39). This festival reminds Israel of Moses' producing water from the rock (Ex 17:1–7; Nu 20:8–13). It also reflects the temple promise (Zec 14:8; Eze 47:1–11). In John 8:12 he calls himself "the light of the world," which reflects the festival ceremony (*Sukkah* 5:1).

In the "I am" debate in John 8:13–59 Jesus appropriates to himself the whole essence of the temple as being the dwelling-place of the divine Name. In John 10:22–39, while the Jews are celebrating the Feast of Lights which recalls the re-consecration of the temple under the Maccabees, he presents himself as the one who is "sanctified and sent." Immediately after declaring himself "I am" (Jn 8:58) he departs from the temple (Jn 8:59), which in John's Gospel serves as his sign that God has departed her temple. This appears to be why John does not mention the temple confrontation episode at the close of his ministry: because in John's structure he has Jesus depart the temple at John 8:59, taking God's presence with him.

In John 10 Christ comes to the Feast of Dedication in Jerusalem, which celebrates the Maccabean victory in reclaiming the temple and re-consecrating the altar and temple. Jesus does not enter the temple at this time, but comes only to Solomon's portico (Jn 10:23; cp. 11:56). Here he declares himself to be the one "whom the Father consecrated and sent into the world" (Jn 10:36). In John 12:41, while referring to Isaiah 6:5, Christ becomes the Shekinah glory of the temple. Walker argues that the upper room episode (Jn 13–17) reflects a "temple-experience" beginning with foot-washing as an initiation ritual (Jn 13:3ff) and ending with the "high-priestly prayer" (Jn 17). Thus, it appears "John's over-riding message is that the Temple has been *replaced* by Jesus." On and on we could go. In fact, in all the Gospels "there was no denial of its previous theological status, but that status was now appropriated by Jesus."[2]

Not only so, but on several occasions before Christ's coming, the temple undergoes various "cleansings" because of profanations by Ahaz (2Ch 29:12ff), Mannaseh (2Ch 34:3ff), Tobiah (Neh 13:4–19), and Antiochus (1Mac 4:36ff; 2Mac 10:1ff). The temple of Christ's day is corrupt, once again, for Christ denounces it when he opens his ministry (Jn 2:13–17) and as he closes it (Mt 21:12–13). It is corrupt even though it is under the direct, daily, fully-functioning administration of the High Priesthood. As Horsley well notes: "Once in Jerusalem, [Jesus] moves directly into the symbolic and material center of the society, the power base of the ruling aristocracy" to challenge it.

In fact, Horsley argues, "Jesus attacks the activities in which the exploitation of God's people by their priestly rulers was most visible."[3] He calls the temple they are controlling a "robbers' den" (Mt 21:13) only to later have the "chief priests and the elders" demand the release of the robber Barabbas over him (Mt 27:40; Jn 18:40). Furthermore, they ask him on what authority he drives out the moneychangers and teaches in the temple, since they had not commissioned him to clean up the corruption (Mt 21:23). As Galambush observes: "It is no coincidence that Matthew's extravagant assertions of Jesus' authority are placed in the context of confrontations with the Pharisees."[4]

DeYoung argues that Christ's actions are not an effort at reform but a testimony against the present cultus.[5] This is evident in that in the first episode he alludes to its destruction (Jn 2:19) and in the immediate context of the second he curses the fig tree as symbol of Israel's corruption (cf. Hos 9:10, 16; Mic 7:1). Hahn agrees: "The procedure of Jesus in the temple precincts can only be understood as a symbolic action proclaiming judgment and punishment on the Jewish sanctuary if it is connected with the cursing of the fig tree, as it is in the present redactional context."[6]

---

[2] Peter W. L. Walker, *Jesus and the Holy City: New Testament Perspectives on Jerusalem* (Grand Rapids: Eerdmans, 1996), 170.

[3] Richard A. Horsley, *Galilee: History, Politics, People* (Valley Forge, Penn.: Trinity, 1995), 300.

[4] Julie Galambush, *The Reluctant Parting: How the New Testament's Jewish Writers Created a Christian Book* (San Francisco: HarperSanFrancisco, 2005), 101.

[5] James C. DeYoung, *Jerusalem in the New Testament: The Significance of the City in the History of Redemption and in Eschatology* (Kampen: J. H. Kok, 1960), 63.

[6] Ferdinand Hahn, *The Titles of Jesus in Christology: Their History in Early Christianity*, trans. Harold Knight and George Ogg (New York: World, 1969), 155.

The temple authorities, including especially the High Priests, were irrevocably corrupt long before the Jewish War. Josephus writes that "the principal high-priestly families, with their hired gangs of thugs, not only were feuding among themselves, but had become predatory, seizing by force from the threshing floors the tithes intended for the ordinary priests" (*Ant.*20:8:8). The Babylonian Talmud laments: "Woe is me because of the house of Boethus; woe is me because of their staves! . . . Woe is me because of the house of Ishmael the son of Phabi; woe is me because of their fists! For they are High Priests . . . and their servants beat the people with staves" (*Pesah.* 57a). "Starting by about 58 or 59, the high priests began surrounding themselves with gangs of ruffians, who would abuse the common priests and general populace."[7] In fact, "the high priests and royalists actually contributed to the breakdown of social order through their own aggressive, even violent, predatory actions."[8]

Completely frustrated at the High Priests' continuing collaboration with the Romans, "a group of sages/teachers called Sicarii or 'Daggermen' turned to assassinating key high-priestly figures (*B.J.* 2.254-57). . . . The population of Jerusalem was as dependent on the Temple-high-priesthood system as the high-priestly aristocracy was on their Roman sponsors."[9] In fact, "when the Roman troops under Cestius finally came to retake control of Jerusalem . . . the priestly aristocracy attempted to open the gates to them . . . (November 66; *B.J.* 2.517-55)."[10]

Jesus preaches against the temple's degenerate condition when he mentions the death of the son of Berechiah who was "murdered between the temple and the altar" (Mt 23:35). When we last hear him publicly referring to the temple he calls it "*your* house" rather than *God's* house (Mt 23:38). Then he declares it "desolate" and ceremoniously departs from it (Mt 23:38-24:1). And it "is extremely significant that the declaration of abandonment (v 38) is preceded by the seven woes upon the religious hierarchy of Jerusalem (vv 13-36)."[11] The Qumran community existed largely because of their disdain for the corruption of the temple.

---

[7] Richard A. Horsley, "High Priests and the Politics of Roman Palestine: A Contextual Analysis of the Evidence in Josephus" *Journal for the Study of Judaism in the Persian, Hellenistic, and Roman Period*, 17 (1986): 45.

[8] Horsley, "High Priests," 24.

[9] Richard A. Horsley, *Galilee: History, Politics, People* (Valley Forge, Penn.: Trinity, 1995), 73-74.

[10] Horsley, *Galilee*, 74.

[11] DeYoung, *Jerusalem in the New Testament*, 91.

As the very heartbeat of their religion, the temple is a key element in the singular pride of the Jew, for rabbis exclaim: "He who has not seen the temple of Herod has never in his life seen a beautiful structure" (*B. Bat.* 4a; cf. Mt 24:2; Lk 21:5; Philo, *Spec.* 1, 72, 73; Jos., *Ant.* 15:11:3). Even the Lord's disciples are enamored by the temple's majesty (Mt 24:1‖). The revolutionaries in Israel during the Jewish War are confident God's temple will survive the assault of Rome, while they use seducers and false prophets (*J.W.* 6:5:2). Prior to A.D. 70 the temple's significance is such that it is the very "foundation and focus of national worship," one of "the three great pillars of popular Jewish piety," "the cardinal postulates" of the Jewish faith, which included also the Land and the Law.[12] And given the structure of ancient life in merging religious and political outlooks, "the function of the Temple was more extensive and central in Jewish society than the typical modern theological reduction to the religious dimension allows."[13]

Jewish Temple as Pagan Idol

In the final analysis the temple system becomes for Israel an idol substituting for a right relationship with God. Formalism replaces vitalism in worship, externalism pushes out spirituality. The Lord rebukes the Pharisees and scribes for their empty traditionalism which "invalidated the word of God" (Mt 15:1-6), making them "hypocrites" (15:7), and showing that "this people honors Me with their lips, / But their heart is far away from me, / But in vain do they worship Me, / Teaching as doctrines the precepts of men" (15:8-9). He chastises Peter for not understanding the hypocrisy involved in Pharisaic hand washing rituals (Mt 15:15-20), for "not what enters into the mouth defiles the man, but what proceeds out of the mouth, this defiles the man" (Mt 15:11).

The Lord warns his followers: "The scribes and the Pharisees have seated themselves in the chair of Moses; therefore all that they tell you, do and observe, but do not do according to their deeds; for they say things, and do not do them" (Mt 23:2-3). The temple's dead ritualism is brought into the very context of the temple when Christ curses the fig tree for showy leaves but no fruit (Mk 11:12-14‖) after surveying the temple (Mk 11:11) and just before driving out the moneychangers (Mk 11:15).

---

[12] Richard N. Longenecker, "Acts," in Frank E. Gaebelein, ed., *The Expositor's Bible Commentary* (Grand Rapids: Zondervan/Regency, 1976-91), 9:336, 337.

[13] Richard A. Horsley *Jesus and the Spiral of Violence: Popular Jewish Resistance in Roman Palestine* (Minneapolis: Fortress, 1987), 286.

We see in the Old Testament the same problem of devotion to the temple rather than concern for God. Regarding the first temple's destruction, Israel believes false prophecies (Jer 5:31; 20:6; 27;15; 29:9, 21; Eze 13:7, 9; 22:28; cp. Rev 16:13). God warns Old Testament Israel: "Do not trust in deceptive words, saying, 'This is the temple of the Lord, the temple of the Lord, the temple of the Lord'" (Jer 7:4). He threatens: "therefore, I will do to the house which is called by My name, in which you trust, and to the place which I gave you and your fathers, as I did to Shiloh" (Jer 7:14). Elsewhere they arrogantly declare: "Is not the Lord in our midst? / Calamity will not come upon us" (Mic 3:11). The Lord warns: "What right has My beloved in My house / When she has done many vile deeds? / Can the sacrificial flesh take away from you your disaster, / So that you can rejoice?" (Jer 11:15).

God powerfully asserts this temple-as-idol problem against rebellious Israel in Isaiah 66, which "contains one of the strongest denunciations of cult in the Bible."[14] The prophet compares the sacrificial actions in the temple system to various sins — *including idolatry*:

> But he who kills an ox is like one who slays a man; / He who sacrifices a lamb is like the one who breaks a dog's neck; / He who offers a grain offering is like one who offers swine's blood; / *He who burns incense is like the one who blesses an idol.* / As they have chosen their own ways, / And their soul delights in their abominations. (Isa 66:3)

According to several competent exegetes, Isaiah's prophecy has an ultimate fulfillment in the Herodian temple after Jesus' death. For instance, Young argues that they "continued offering the sacrifices even after the one true Sacrifice had been offered."[15] Alexander states that this passage teaches "the general doctrine that sacrifice is hateful in the sight of God if offered in a wicked spirit, but with a special reference to the old sacrifices after the great Sacrifice for sin was come, and had been offered once for all."[16]

Gaston argues for "a definite anti-cultic polemic in the tradition behind the gospel according to Mark."[17] Thus, in Mark 14:58 the Lord himself alludes to the temple as an idol for Israel. There we

---

[14] John N. Oswalt, *The Book of Isaiah* (40–66) (NICOT) (Grand Rapids: Eerdmans, 1998), 2:667.

[15] E. J. Young, *The Book of Isaiah* (Grand Rapids: Eerdmans, 1965), 3:520.

[16] J. A. Alexander, *Commentary on the Prophecies of Isaiah* (Grand Rapids: Zondervan, rep. 1977 [1875]), 2:460.

[17] Lloyd Gaston, *No Stone On Another: Studies in the Significance of the Fall of Jerusalem in the Synoptic Gospels* (Leiden: Brill, 1970), 75–76.

read witnesses against him declaring: "We heard Him say, 'I will destroy this temple *made with hands* [*cheirpoiēton*] and in three days I will build another made without hands.'" We see *cheirpoiton* frequently used of idols in the LXX in the place of *eidōlon* or *tupos*. In the Septuagint the term "almost always"[18] refers to pagan idols (see: Lev 26:1; Dt 4:28; 2Ki 19:18; 2Ch 32:19; 27:15; Ps 115:4; 135:15; Isa 2:8; 10:11; 16:12; 19:1; 21:9; 31:7; 46:6; Hab 2:18).

Simon notes that "*chiropoiēton* is the technical term, so to say, by which the Septuagint and the Greek-speaking Jews describe the idols."[19] We also find it in Philo (*Vit. Mos.* 1:303; 2:51, 88, 165, 168) and the Sibylline Oracles (*Sib. Or.* 3:650ff; 4:8–12). Consequently, Evans notes that "made with hands" is a "hint at [the temple's] idolatrous status"[20]; Lightfoot agrees.[21] Therefore, Walker calls this phrase "potentially incendiary."[22]

This idolatry-equation is almost certainly Stephen's intent as we can discover from his defense. He is standing before the religious authorities of Israel (elders, scribes, Sanhedrin, and the high-priest; Ac 6:12, 15; 7:1). There his accusers charge that he is preaching as Christ did on the subject: "we have heard him say that this Nazarene, Jesus, will destroy this place" (Ac 6:14; cp. Mk 14:58). Instead, of disputing the charge, he provides a redemptive-historical argument *defending* his teaching — even to the point of bringing in the additional fact from Christ's trial that their temple was "made with hands" (Ac 7:48). In this he utters a "radical condemnation" regarding the temple.[23]

Remarkably, just before Stephen speaks of the temple as "made with hands," he mentions Israel's fathers making the golden calf and "rejoicing in the works of their hands [*en tois ergois tōn cheirōn*]" (Ac 7:41b) while they were "unwilling to be obedient" (Ac 7:39). He then reminds them that God declares their sacrifices in the wilderness were "not to me" but for Moloch and "the star of the god Rompha" (Ac 7:42–43; here he is referencing Amos 5:25–26). Scobie observes that "the superstitious attachment of the Jews to their temple is

[18] TDNT, 9:436.

[19] Marcel Simon, "Saint Stephen and the Jerusalem Temple" *The Journal of Ecclesiastical History*, 2 (1951): 133.

[20] Craig A. Evans, *Mark 8:27 – 16:20* (WBC) (Nashville: Nelson, 2001), 446.

[21] J. B. Lightfoot, *Saint Paul's Epistles to the Colossians and to Philemon* (Grand Rapids: Zondervan, n.d. [rep. 1879]), 183; William J. Larkin, Jr., Acts (IVP NTC) (Downers Grove, Ill.: InterVarsity, 1995), 118.

[22] Walker, *Jesus and the Holy City*, 10.

[23] Simon, "Saint Stephen," 134.

made to appear as a continuation of their idolatry in the desert."[24] Stephen's "condemnation of the Temple includes condemnation of the sacrificial cult" in that sacrifices are not mentioned by Stephen "in connection with the Temple, but in relation to the [golden] calf."[25]

By several means Stephen diminishes the temple and suggests that it is now an idol for Israel: (1) He speaks highly of the "tabernacle" over against the temple, calling it "the tabernacle of testimony" (Ac 7:44a), whereas the temple is spoken of more negatively (Ac 7:48–50). (2) He notes that the tabernacle is erected by God's word to Moses (Ac 7:44b). (3) The tabernacle leads Joshua in dispossessing the nations as he secures the promised land (Ac 7:45). (4) The tabernacle is in use until the time of David, who "found favor in God's sight" (Ac 7:46).

(5) Then over against beloved David he states: "*But* it was *Solomon* who built a house for Him" (Ac 7:47). He probably has in mind Solomon as the one whose "wives turned his heart away after other gods; and his heart was not wholly devoted to the Lord his God, as the heart of David his father had been" (1Ki 11:4; cp. vv 4–9). Solomon's actions lead to his ruin: "So the Lord said to Solomon, 'Because you have done this, and you have not kept My covenant and My statutes, which I have commanded you, I will surely tear the kingdom from you, and will give it to your servant'" (1Ki 11:11). Thus, the one who builds the temple brings idolatry into Israel where it continually arises as a recurring plague.

Most significantly, Stephen supports his argument against the temple by specifically citing Isaiah 66:1–2 (Ac 7:49–50) — the two verses leading up to God's denouncing Israel's temple worship as idolatrous (Isa 66:3; see discussion above). He then concludes by equating the temple's current authorities with their idolatrous forbears, calling them "stiff-necked and uncircumcised in heart and ears" for "always resisting the Holy Spirit . . . *just as your fathers did*" (Ac 7:51; v 39). The idolatrous overtones are clear and unmistakable: he "suggests that the Temple was a form of idolatry"[26] — in the way they revere it.

---

[24] Charles H. H. Scobie, "The Origins and Development of Samaritan Christianity," *New Testament Studies* 19 (1972–73): 394–95.

[25] Simon, "Saint Stephen," 134.

[26] Clifton J. Allen, ed., *The Broadman Bible Commentary* (Nashville: Broadman, 1970–73), 10:53; William Neil agrees (*The Acts of the Apostles* [Grand Rapids: Eerdmans, 1973]), 117.

Marshall concludes that Stephen "rests on the negative point, that temple-worship imposes a false limit on the nature of God."[27] That is, it suggests limits such as associated with idols housed in shrines. According to Witherington, the point of these verses

> is not that God's presence can't be found in the temple . . . , but that God's presence can't be *confined* there, nor can God be controlled or manipulated by the building of a temple and by the rituals of the temple culture or the power moves of the temple hierarchy. What is being opposed is a God-in-the-box theology that has magical overtones, suggesting that *if God can be located and confined, God can be magically manipulated and used to human ends. Such an approach is idolatry* — the attempt to fashion or control God with human hands according to human devices.[28]

Later in the same book Paul preaches to the Athenians about their many idols, one even "To an unknown God" (Ac 17:16, 23): "God who made the world and all things in it, since He is Lord of heaven and earth, does not dwell in temples made with hands [*cheiropoiētois*]" (Ac 17:24). This also picks up on Jesus' statement and, like Stephen's defense, alludes to Isaiah 66:1-3. Later Paul is accused of turning people from idolatry "saying that gods made with hands [*dia cheirōn ginomenoi* (a different expression)] are no gods at all" (Ac 19:26). Revelation 9:20 also mentions the idols which were "the works of their hands [*ergōn tōn cheirōn*]."

Conclusion

We must remember that Jesus calls first century Israel under its unbelieving authorities an "adulterous generation" (Mt 12:39‖; 16:4‖). That charge harkens back to Old Testament Israel's unfaithfulness through idolatry. Thus, the first century temple system about which John is writing, is controlled by a corrupt, Messiah-denying, High Priesthood and has now become an idol linked with and likened to emperor worship.

Consequently, Christ begins moving his people away from the temple because with his coming it no longer serves any God-approved purpose. The reason Christians visit the temple in Acts is not to participate in its cult worship, but to gain access for a witness to the Jews (Ac 5:25, 42; cf. 3:11; 5:12, 20). In this, they were following the example of Jesus who had "spoken openly" in "synagogues, and

---

[27] I. Howard Marshall, *The Acts of the Apostles: An Introduction and Commentary* (Grand Rapids: Eerdmans, 1980), 146.
[28] Ben Witherington, *The Acts of the Apostles: A Socio-Rhetorical Commentary* (Grand Rapids: Eerdmans, 1998), 273. Emph. mine.

in the temple, where all the Jews come together" (Jn 18:20; cp. Mt
21:23; 26:55; Lk 19:47). The temple is "the meeting-point for the
disciples, and the natural place for the apostles to present their claim
to Jerusalem's religious leadership that Jesus, though crucified, is Israel's Messiah. It is a 'natural strategic objective.'"[29] Certain key passages in Acts

> indicate that the apostles were in the Temple mainly to spread the
> word about the fulfillment of history that they believed had begun
> with Jesus' actions .... The Temple courtyard was the principle public
> meeting place in Jerusalem, and the obvious place for such activities.[30]

Stephen's martyr sermon highlights Israel's radical spiritual and
moral failure, showing that "you who received the law as ordained
by angels ... did not keep it" (Ac 7:53): Israel is "stiff-necked," "uncircumcised in heart," "always resisting the Holy Spirit" (Ac 7:51).
They persecuted the prophets and are "betrayers and murderers" of
"the Righteous One (Ac 7:52). The people themselves are corrupt,
their temple is corrupt, irrelevant, and wrongly exalted. It therefore
detracts Israel from the proper worship of God, serving therefore as
an idol. The temple services

> no longer . . . represent the will of God so that that which it should
> have achieved is to be sought in quite different areas of religious ex-
> pression. Such an attitude could eventually result in the demand that
> the vain but seductive temple services should cease, even that the tem-
> ple should be destroyed.[31]

Because of this perspective "the early church was accused again
and again of opposition to the temple, in the case of Stephen (Ac
6:13f), Paul (Ac 21:28) and all the apostles (Evan. Pet vii, 26). It appears that this saying in Mk 14:58 was important in the anti-
Christian polemic of the time of Mark."[32] "The point of the speech
[of Stephen] is plainly directed against the over-estimation of the
temple in Jerusalem." As the second century Christian Barnabas de-
clared: "the wretched [Jews], wandering in error, trusted not in God
Himself, but in the temple, as being the house of God. For almost
after the manner of the Gentiles they worshiped Him in the temple"
(*Barn.* 16). The God-ordained cult, under the control of those crying

---

[29] Walker, *Jesus and the Holy City*, 65. He cites J. Munck, *Paul and the Salvation of Mankind* (London: SCM, 1959), 242.
[30] Horsley, *Jesus and the Spiral of Violence*, 292.
[31] Lloyd Gaston, *No Stone On Another: Studies in the Significance of the Fall of Jerusalem in the Synoptic Gospels* (Leiden: Brill, 1970), 103
[32] Gaston, *No Stone On Another*, 69.

"we have no king but Caesar," is tantamount to emperor worship which John is exposing.

Hare notes that "persecution occurred when Christians challenged the symbols of ethnic solidarity so sharply that they placed themselves beyond the tolerance-limits of the Jewish community."[33] The Jews, therefore, seek capital punishment for any who speak against or defile the temple, in Jeremiah's day (Jer 26:7-8, 11; *Ant.* 10:6:2) as well as in the first century (Ac 6:14; 21:26-30; 24:6; 25:7-8; *Sanh.* 13:5; *Ros. Has.* 17a; *Ber.* 9:13b). Josephus records the story of Jesus Ananias who preaches woe against Jerusalem and the temple the Jews finally kill him (*J.W.* 6:5:3).

Thus, "the charge leveled against Jesus at his trial that he would 'destroy the Temple,' though 'false' at one level, proves true at a deeper level. 'Jesus is the destroyer of the Temple in a figurative sense: its destruction is the result of his death, brought about by those in charge of the Temple worship.'"[34] Likewise the "false witnesses" brought against Stephen (Ac 7:13) "seem to have been false more in nuance and degree than in kind. From the accusations and frm his defense, it is clear that Stephen had begun to apply his Christian convictions regarding the centrality of Jesus of Nazareth in God's redemptive program."[35]

---

[33] Douglas R. A. Hare, *The Theme of Jewish Persecution of Christians in the Gospel according to St. Matthew* (Cambridge: University Press, 1967), 130.

[34] Walker citing Juel. Walker, *Jesus and the Holy City*, 12

[35] Frank E. Gaebelein, ed., *The Expositor's Bible Commentary* (Grand Rapids: Zondervan/Regency, 1976-79), 9:335-36.

8

HEBREW RIDDLES, 666, AND ASIAN CHRISTIANS

Here is wisdom. Let him who has understanding calculate the number of the beast, for the number is that of a man; and his number is six hundred and sixty-six. (Rev 13:18)

Introduction

In Revelation 13:18 we find the famous and perplexing gematria identifying the beast of Revelation (the first beast, i.e., the beast from the sea; cp. Rev 13:1):

> Here is wisdom. Let him who has understanding calculate the number of the beast, for the number is that of a man; and his number is six hundred and sixty-six.

Since the beast plays a prominent role in Revelation and since John presents his number to provide his reader "wisdom" and "understanding," interpreting the number is important to recognizing who the beast is.

In several of my works I argue that the man who is this relevant, contemporary, blasphemous, authoritative danger to the Church when John writes is Nero Caesar, the sixth Caesar of Rome (see: Suetonius, *Lives of the Twelve Caesars*, Book 6, *Nero*).[1] One line of argument in this direction points out that the number six hundred and sixty-six (*not* a series of three sixes, for the text actually reads: "six hundred, sixty, six") happens to be the numeric value of Nero Caesar's name when spelled in Hebrew characters. This discovery is simultaneously made in the late 1800s by several scholars working independently of each other: Heinrich Julius Holtzmann, Ferdinand Benary, Ferdinand Hitzig, and Eduard Wilhelm Eugen Reuss.[2] This is a remarkable discovery which pours a flood of new light on one of Revelation's deep mysteries.

Many, however, see this interpretation as ingenuous, but highly unlikely. They complain that this view is based on a misspelling of

---

[1] *Before Jerusalem Fell, The Beast of Revelation, Perilous Times, Four Views on the Book of Revelation,* and *The Book of Revelation Made Easy.*

[2] See discussion of this discovery in R. H. Charles, *The Revelation of St. John* (ICC) (Edinburgh: T & T Clark, 1920), 1:367.

"Nero Caesar" in that the normal Hebrew spelling lacks one letter necessary for resulting in the value of 666. For instance, Mounce complains: "A shift to Hebrew letters is unlikely in that Revelation is written in Greek and there is no indication that the riddle is to be solved by transposing it into another language."[3] Morris agrees: "To get this result we must use the Greek form of the Latin name, transliterate into Hebrew characters, and with a variant spelling at that."[4] They also argue that is very doubtful because John is writing to seven Gentile churches in Asia Minor (Rev 1:4, 11; 2:1–3:22). Perhaps if he were writing to a Hebrew-speaking community of Christians in Israel this might be possible. How do we respond to such reasonable complaints?

The Problem of Spelling

I will quickly respond to the spelling problem first, in that it can be dismissed quite easily. Archaeological finds document that a first century Hebrew spelling of Nero's name provides us with precisely the value of 666: "Neron Kaiser."[5] In fact, Jastrow's famous lexicon of the Talmud contains this very spelling.[6] That being so, we cannot summarily dismiss this possibility: it does in fact fit a spelling of Nero's name in the first century. Even if it is a relatively rare spelling, it nevertheless *is* an acceptable spelling.

What is more, we should be aware that variants of names are not uncommon in biblical days. We see that frequently in Scripture itself. Many debates have arisen over the spellings of the names of some of the prophets (such as "Elijah" which is sometimes spelled "Elijah" and sometimes "Eliah"). We also have the famous situation regarding the city of "Jerusalem": it has two distinct spellings in the New Testament Greek: *Ierosalem* and *Ierosolyma*. We today are more familiar with standardized spelling in modern, Western culture. So then, this variant spelling does not harm the argument that it refers to Nero Caesar.

---

[3] Robert H. Mounce, *The Book of Revelation* (2d. ed.: Grand Rapids: Eerdmans, 1998), 262.

[4] Leon Morris, *Revelation* (TNTC) (Grand Rapids: Eerdmans, 1987), 169.

[5] D. R. Hillers, "Revelation 13:18 and A Scroll from Murabba'at," *Bulletin of the American Schools of Oriental Research* 170 (April, 1963): 65. See also: P. Benoit, J. T. Milik, and R. deVaux, *Les Grottes de Muraba'at*, DJD 2 (Oxford: Clarendon, 1961).

[6] Marcus Jastrow, *A Dictionary of the Targumim, the Talmud Babli and Yerushalmi, and the Midrashic Literature* (London: Judaica, 1903). See R. H. Charles, *The Revelation of St. John* (Edinburgh: T & T Clark, 1920), 1:367.

The Problem of Location

But the other objection is really the more persuasive for some. How could John write to Gentile Christians in Greek-speaking Asia Minor and expect them to undertake the linguistic gymnastics necessary to convert the Greek number "six hundred, sixty-six" into the Hebrew name "Neron Kaiser"? But again, we can adequately answer this. Consider the following explanation.

First, John's ethnicity. John himself — the very author of Revelation — is a Hebrew Christian. His native language is Hebrew (or Aramaic) and his thought patterns are Hebraic. We see the strong Hebraic character of the author in his grammar. For instance, in his scholarly commentary R. H. Charles includes a major introductory section titled "A Short Grammar of the Apocalypse." Section 10 of this "Grammar" is entitled "The Hebraic Style of the Apocalypse."[7] There Charles notes of John's unusual syntax: "The reason clearly is that, *while he writes in Greek, he thinks in Hebrew.*"[8] David Aune agrees with Charles.[9]

As J. P. M. Sweet puts it: "The probability is that the writer, thinking in Hebrew or Aramaic, consciously or unconsciously carried over Semitic idioms into his Greek, and that his 'howlers' are deliberate attempts to reproduce the grammar of classical Hebrew at certain points."[10] The Hebraic character of the prophecy is so pronounced that some scholars have even suggested John originally wrote it in Aramaic, a cognate language to Hebrew.[11]

Thus, we must understand that Gentile readers are *always* confronted with Hebraic difficulties in Revelation. Hebrew is the very atmosphere of John's presentation.

Second, John's backcloth. Although John writes in Greek (Hebraicized Greek, we must remember) and to Gentiles, scholars have long recognized Revelation as the most "Jewish" book in the New Testament, surpassing both Matthew and Hebrews. John makes in-

---

[7] Charles, *Revelation*, 1:cxvii, cxlii.

[8] Charles, *Revelation*, 1:cxliii.

[9] David E. Aune, *Revelation 1–5* (Dallas: Word, 1997), clx–ccxi.

[10] J. P. M. Sweet, *Revelation* (Philadelphia: Westminster, 1979), 16. Beale virtually lifts Sweet's text into his own, when he writes: "It seems that his grammatical 'howlers' are deliberate attempts to express Semitisms and Septuagintalisms in his Greek." G. K. Beale, *The Book of Revelation* (NIGTC) (Grand Rapids: Eerdmans, 1999), 96.

[11] Charles C. Torrey, *The Apocalypse of John* (New Haven: Yale University Press, 1958), 27–58.

numerable allusions to the Old Testament: "The Apocalypse contains more Old Testament references than any other NT book."[12]

Sometimes John even alludes to very obscure Old Testament passages. But in all cases the Old Testament forms the backcloth of the work. For instance, in the letter to the church at Pergamum, he refers to Balaam and Balak. John is not accidentally using the Old Testament; he is using it for dramatic purposes. His Gentile readers would have to secure a clear knowledge of the Old Testament Scriptures to fully understand Revelation. The "problem" of the Hebraic spelling of "Neron Kaiser" is only one part of the problem facing Gentile readers.

Third, the local population. This objection against this analysis of the identity of six hundred, sixty-six overlooks the social context of the Asian churches. In the first century Asia Minor is heavily populated by diaspora Jews. The Jewish population in the empire at that time is no fewer that six to seven million,[13] ranging upwards to as much as 15 per cent of the population.[14] What is more, we find the "largest concentrations of Jewish settlements" in Egypt, Palestine, Syria, and Asia Minor (John's direct audience).[15] Jeffers notes that

> by the time of Christ, Jews were widely dispersed throughout the cities and countryside of the Empire and beyond.... The regions of Mesopotamia, Syria, Asia Minor and Egypt each had more than 1 million Jewish residents.... There was a substantial Jewish population in virtually every town of any decent size in the Mediterranean region.[16]

The first century Jewish philosopher Philo notes of his native race that "ten thousand of them are in every region of the habitable world, in Europe, *in Asia*, and in Africa, on the continent, in the islands, on the coasts, and in the inland parts" (*Embassy* 36 §283). This is why we see Jews from Asia in Jerusalem at Pentecost (Ac 2:9)

---

[12] Beale, *Revelation*, 77.

[13] Philip L. Mayo, *"Those Who Call Themselves Jews": The Church and Judaism in the Apocalypse of John* (Eugene, Ore.: Wipf and Stock, 2006), 30. See also: Mireille Hadas-Lebel, *Flavius Josephus: Eyewitness to Rome's First-Century Conquest of Judea.* Trans. by Richard Miller (New York: Macmillan, 1993) 53; Mary E. Smallwood, *The Jews Under Roman Rule: From Pompey to Diocletian.* (Boston: Brill, 2001), ch 6

[14] Paul Barnett, *Behind the Scenes of the New Testament* (Downer's Grove, Ill.: InterVarsity, 1990), 158.

[15] Mayo, *"Those Who Call Themselves Jews,"* 62.

[16] James S. Jeffers, *The Greco-Roman World of the New Testament Era: Exploring the Background of Early Christianity* (Downers Grove, Ill.: Inter-Varsity, 1999), 213. See also: Henry Barclay Swete, *Commentary on Revelation* (Grand Rapids: Kregel, rep. 1977 [1906]), lxvi.

and why we hear of Asian Jews elsewhere in Acts (Ac 6:9; 21:27; 24:18).

We know from Paul's practice that he often establishes churches in the context of synagogues. Interestingly, one of the seven churches in Revelation is Ephesus (Rev 1:11; 2:1), where Paul reasons with the Jews in their synagogue (Ac 18:19; see also Ac 20:17-18). This is also where Jewish converts eventually begin teaching false doctrine that Paul has to warn against (1Ti 1:3-7). In Acts 19:10 we read: "this took place for two years, so that all who lived in Asia heard the word of the Lord, both Jews and Greeks" (Ac 19:10). We should expect the same method to be employed in the churches of Asia Minor to whom John addresses his book, especially since the gospel is to the "Jew first" (Ro 1:16).

Consequently, we should expect a significant concentration of Hebrew Christians in the churches in Asia Minor. In fact, one of John's sub-purposes would be like that of the author of Hebrews: to warn Jewish converts against falling back into Judaism. After all, in two of the seven letters introducing Revelation asserts that Christians are the true Jews, whereas racial Jews just "say they are Jews" (Rev 2:9; 3:9). Thus, the gematric designation of Nero in Hebrew would not totally miss his target audience.

Fourth, the method of reception. John does not send multiple copies of Revelation to each church expecting all the members in each of the seven churches to peruse it on their own. Rather he sends Revelation to the leaders of the churches, the "angels" of the church (Rev 2:1, 8, 12, 18; 3:1, 7, 14). These would undoubtedly be leaders who were well-schooled interpreters.

Christianity is a religion of the book, and therefore requires a leadership trained in the book. In fact, two of Paul's requirements for elder in the Church are that they be: (1) "able to teach" (1Ti 3:2; cp. 2Ti 2:24) and (2) "not a new convert" (1Ti 3:6). He instructs Timothy to "pay close attention to yourself and to your teaching" (1Ti 4:16). Interestingly, Paul addresses this letter to Timothy while Timothy is in Ephesus (1Ti 1:3), which is one of the cities John addresses in Revelation (Rev 1:11; 2:1). Paul also directs him to train up leaders capable of teaching: "the things which you have heard from me in the presence of many witnesses, these entrust to faithful men, who will be able to teach others also" (2Ti 2:2).

The problem of any Gentile novice understanding Scripture is solved by instruction by a teacher, such as we see in the case of Philip and the Ethiopian eunuch: "And when Philip had run up, he heard him reading Isaiah the prophet, and said, 'Do you understand what you are reading?' And he said, 'Well, how could I, unless someone guides me?' And he invited Philip to come up and sit with him. . . . And Philip opened his mouth, and beginning from this Scripture he preached Jesus to him" (Ac 8:30-31, 35).

Furthermore, John writes Revelation with a view to being publicly *read* before the churches: "Blessed is he who reads and those who hear the words of the prophecy, and heed the things which are written in it" (Rev 1:3). The public readers in each of the churches (whoever they are) would certainly *explain* what they are reading. For instance, when Jesus enters the synagogue in Nazareth, he reads from the synagogue's scroll of Isaiah (Lk 4:16-18), then he explains it for his hearers (Lk 4:20-22). This is even a pattern we find in the Old Testament, as when Ezra and his assistants read the Law to Israel: "They read from the Book of the Law of God, making it clear and giving the meaning so that the people could understand what was being read" (Neh 8:8).

Unlike today, not everyone in the first century has personal Bibles, because books (scrolls) are expensive (in that they are hand-written) and the ability to read is limited. The Jews of that era depend upon hearing God's word through *public readings* at the local synagogue (cf. Ac 13:15, 27; 15:21; 2Co 3:14-15). The early Christians receive the New Testament epistles in the same manner (Col 4:16; 1Th 5:27). Thus, it is common practice for the leaders of the New Testament churches to read *and explain* Scriptures: "Until I come, give attention to the public reading of Scripture, to exhortation and teaching" (1Ti 4:13). The *"public* reading" of Scripture would include "exhortation and *teaching,"* that is, application and explanation.

Fifth, the nature of the book. Besides all of this, we must recognize the book is difficult to understand even apart from this Hebrew understanding of the beast's number. Who among us would say that Revelation is an easy read? Why should we be surprised if there is a difficulty such as this Hebrew reading at Revelation 13:18? Is not Revelation a book replete with numerous difficulties? Even John himself is confused on occasion. In fact, on one of those occasions an interpreting angel explains the matter to him: In Revelation 7:13 the angel asks John the meaning of those dressed in white robes. John has to ask the angel to tell him (Rev 7:14).

In Revelation 17:6 when John sees the drunken harlot he "wondered greatly." In the next verse we read: "And the angel said to me, 'Why do you *wonder?* I shall *tell you* the mystery of the woman and of the beast that carries her, which has the seven heads and the ten horns.'" Thus, John does not initially understand what he sees, so the angel comes to explain. We could expect that the local "angel" (leader, Rev 2:1, 8, 12, 18; 3:1, 5, 7, 14) at each of the seven churches might do the same regarding Revelation 13:18.

Sixth, similar Hebraicism's elsewhere. The use of Hebrew names is not unique in identifying the beast. In other places John uses Hebrew names. For instance, in Revelation 16:16 we read: "And they gathered them together to the place which in Hebrew is called Har-Magedon." Elsewhere we read: "They have as king over them, the angel of the abyss; his name in Hebrew is Abaddon, and in the Greek he has the name Apollyon" (Rev 9:11).

We also see the Hebrew word "Satan" used by John, which is interpreted into Greek as "the devil": "the great dragon was thrown down, the serpent of old who is called the devil and Satan" (Rev 12:9). Other Hebrew words appear, as well: "Amen" is said to mean "truthfully" (Rev 3:14). The Hebrew "hallelujah" occurs only in Revelation in the New Testament and is not even translated into its Greek equivalent (Rev 19:1, 3, 4, 6).

Thus, it would not be an unparalleled situation for John to be referring to a Hebrew name here in Revelation 13:18. His hearers would see this in other contexts, which might serve as a hint to that possibility in the text before us.

Seventh, the scholarly consensus. Many noteworthy New Testament scholars accept the Hebrew name "Neron Kaiser" as the solution to the mystery of 666. No one could dismiss these scholars as failing to note a misspelling or overlooking John's Asia Minor setting.

See for instance:

B. C. Birch, "Number," in Geoffrey W. Bromiley, ed., *The International Standard Bible Encyclopedia* (2d. ed.: Grand Rapids: Eerdmans, 1982), 3:561.

Ian Boxall, *The Revelation of St. John* (BNTC) (Peabody, Mass.: Hendrikson, 2006), 198.

Ralph P. Martin and Peter H. Davids, eds., *Dictionary of the Later New Testament & Its Developments* (Downers Grove, Ill.: InterVarsity Press, 1997), 909.

Bruce M. Metzger and Michael D. Coogan, eds., *The Oxford Companion to the Bible* (New York: Oxford University Press, 1993), 700.

Brent C. Butler, ed., *Holman Bible Dictionary* (Nashville: Holman, 1991), 1030–31.

Allen C. Myers, ed., *The Eerdmans Bible Dictionary* (Grand Rapids: Eerdmans, 1987), 956.

Ernst Dieter Schmitz in Colin Brown, ed., *New International Dictionary of New Testament Theology,* (Grand Rapids: Zondervan, 1986), 2:684.

Interestingly, a textual variant at Revelation 13:18 gives the number as "616," which happens to present the value of Nero's name when spelled in Latin. As renowned Greek scholar Bruce Metzger explains: "Perhaps the change was intentional, seeing that the Greek form Neron Caesar written in Hebrew characters (*nrwn qsr*) is equivalent to 666, whereas the Latin form Nero Caesar (*nrw qsr*) is equivalent to 616."[17]

Conclusion

Strong evidence suggests that John's number six hundred, sixty-six represents Nero Caesar. And that evidence derives from a first century Hebrew spelling of his name. Though some complain that this creates unnecessary problems for John's Gentile audience in Asia Minor, such a problem is not unique in Revelation. And the problem is solved by directing Revelation to knowledgeable public readers in the churches, who would explain the difficulties for the congregations.

---

[17] Bruce M. Metzger, *A Textual Commentary on the Greek New Testament* (New York: United Bible Socities,1971) , 752. See also: David E. Aune, *Revelation 6–16* (Nashville: Thomas Nelson, 1998), 2:770–71 and TDNT, 1:462–63.

9

THE LAND BEAST
AND THE HIGH PRIESTLY ARISTOCRACY

And I saw another beast coming up out of the earth; and he had two horns like a lamb, and he spoke as a dragon. (Rev. 13:11)

Introduction

In Revelation John presents two evil beasts as plaguing the world. In my previous chapter I focus on an issue that relates to the first beast, the beast from the sea (Rev 13:1). In this chapter I will be considering the second beast, the beast from the earth, which we may literally translate "land" (Rev 13:11).

Introducing the Beast

Here appears the third personage in Revelation's antithetical parody of the holy Trinity: "another beast," who is aligned with the dragon and the sea beast (Rev 13:1, 2, 11; cf. 16:13). The dragon comes from the sky (Rev 12:4, 7–9), the first beast from the sea (Rev 13:1), and now the second beast from the land (Rev13:11). This new beast is "coming up out of the earth" paralleling the first beast who was "coming up out of the sea" (Rev 13:1). Both of these beasts are directly linked to the dragon, Satan (Rev 13:2, 11), which appears to be a major rationale for this whole section.

This linkage with Satan reminds us of Christ's temptation just before he enters his public ministry to Israel. In Mark 1:12–13 Christ must face "Satan" (*satana*, cp. Rev 12:9) in the "wilderness" (*erēmon*, cp. Rev 12:14; 17:3) among wild "beasts" (*thērion*, cp. Rev 13:1, 11). Regarding this section's function, Ruiz notes that "we are not faced with discrete, separate motifs when we read what John tells us about the Dragon and the Beasts, but a complex of interrelated theriomorphic symbols that aims at identifying God's enemies in the language of Dan 7."[1]

This second beast appears *after* the first beast, indicating he is *subordinate to* him and *lesser in power*. Thus, he has only "two horns like a lamb" rather than ten horns set on a fearsome compound car-

---

[1] Jean-Pierre Ruiz, *Ezekiel in the Apocalypse: The Transformation of Prophetic Language in Revelation 16:17 – 19:10* (New York: Peter Lang, 1989), 319.

nivore (cp. Rev 13:1). This beast's authority derives from the first beast, for he "exercises all the authority of the first beast" (Rev 13:12a). And he does so under his watchful eye, i.e., "in his presence" (Rev 13:12b). His subordinate mission is further emphasized in that "he makes the earth and those who dwell in it to worship the first beast" (Rev 13:12c).

Like his mentor, the dragon also employs the second beast, for in Revelation 13:1c we read: "he spoke as a dragon" ("dragon" is anarthrous but surely "the" recently mentioned dragon). Since we never actually hear the dragon speak, how does he speak?[2] We must resolve this question contextually.

Earlier we learn that the dragon is cast out of God's heavenly court (Rev 12:7) where he *accused* the brethren before God's throne (Rev 12:10 [2x]). Note also that he has two names, both of which mean "slanderer": "devil" and "Satan" (Rev 12:9). This second beast is subordinate to the first beast (Rev 13:12) who has Satanic authority given to him by the dragon (Rev 13:2b) to war against the saints (Rev 13:5, 7). Consequently, the second beast's speaking "as a dragon" entails his deadly legal slander (Rev 2:9; 3:9; cp. 13:1, 5, 6; 17:3) while deceiving and lying (*plana*, Rev 13:14; cp. Ge 3:13; cf. 12:9; 20:3, 8, 10).

Interestingly, even the second beast's appearance is deceitful: He had two horns "like a lamb" but "he spoke as a dragon." He is like his father the devil who both "was a murderer from the beginning, and does not stand in the truth" (Jn 8:44). Jesus charges this against the Pharisees and others (Jn 8:13) in the context of their desire to kill him (Jn 8:37, 40, 59). The second beast's mission is to employ murderous slander in continuing the dragon's accusatory judicial work (Rev 12:10c), though he is no longer in heaven (Rev 12:10d).

Smalley summarizes the dominant understanding of this land beast. He discounts any particular local, contemporary referent, stating instead: "While these [first century] themes may be woven into the tapestry of John's visionary thought at this point, the picture is ultimately broader and deeper . . . . John is speaking of deceit and falsehood at any time and in any place."[3] But although the applicatory nature of all Scripture makes *any passage* "broader and deep-

---

[2] Carrington amusingly dismisses R. H. Charles' statement on the dragon: "Dr. Charles is distressed about this statement, because he says dragons do not speak [Charles 1:358]; I am too ignorant about the natural history of dragons to contradict him here." Philip Carrington, *The Meaning of the Revelation* (Eugene, Ore.: Wipf & Stock, 2007 [rep. 1931]), 231.

[3] Stephen S. Smalley, *The Revelation to John: A Commentary on the Greek Text of the Apocalypse* (Downers Grove, Ill.: InterVarsity, 2005), 345.

er" by way of *application*, surely Smalley's approach is exactly opposite of how we must understand the passage.

The second beast arises in a particular historical context (Rev 1:1,
3 — near term) and in a specific geographical setting (Rev 13:11 —
"the Land"). As with most of Scripture, Revelation is occasional
literature dealing with specific issues relating to historical people. Of
course, we may and should draw lessons from this beast's appearance in history; we must expect extended moral and spiritual application in all Scripture (e.g., 1Co 10:6, 11 in its context, vv 1–10). But
John writes about the second beast's concrete appearance in time
and on earth. He is *not* presenting moral lessons in symbolic form,
but prophesying historical events that embody moral principles
(e.g., these "things" must happen, Rev 1:1, 19; 4:1; 22:6). Could not
Christ declare that "thou shalt not kill" not only means what it
directly asserts, but *also* include *by extension* a prohibition of hatred
(Mt 5:21–22)? Were not the Old Testament case laws extensions of
and concrete applications of the fundamental moral law found in the
ten commandments? Does not any specific directive in Scripture
precede and *lay the foundation for* general, broader applications?

Identifying the Land Beast

Who, then, is this second beast in the proximate service of the
first beast and the ultimate ministry of Satan? We must notice his
historical origin which differs from the first beast: he is "coming up
out of the earth" (Rev 13:11, 12, 14), whereas the first beast arises
from the sea (Rev 13:1). This appears to portray the beast's association with "the Land," i.e., Israel. Milligan argues that "the 'earth,'
as here used, must be the symbol of the Jews."[4] Ford sees "the land"
here as referring to "Palestine" because "land" is "synonymous with
Israel in Jewish writings."[5] The phrase "the earth" may be literally
translated "the land."

John appears frequently to use the term of Israel. In fact, John's
theme verse (Rev 1:7) associates "the earth" with Israel's tribes, suggesting that it means "the Land." Revelation 6:10 presents the martyrs calling for God's judgment against those who dwell in the Land,
which strongly reflects the language of Matthew 23:34–36 and which
clearly refers to Israel. In several places John distinguishes the
"Land" dwellers from the peoples of the whole world (Rev 11:9–10;
13:7–8).

Redemptive-historical preterism is bound by exegetically derived time-frame indicators demanding that Revelation's events oc-

---

[4] William Milligan, *The Book of Revelation* (New York: Armstrong, 1903), 227.
[5] J. Massyngberde Ford, *Revelation* (Garden City, N.Y.: Anchor, 1975), 213.

cur shortly after Revelation is written (Rev 1:1, 3; 22:6, 10). This requires that the land beast be relevant to John's suffering first century audience. Preterist commentators present several options from this perspective for identifying the second beast.

The Optional Interpretations

First, the imperial priesthood. Conservative preterists Moses Stuart, David Clark, Nils Lund, Loren Brink, and Jay Adams see him as representing the imperial priesthood (often associated with provincial governors) throughout the empire.[6] This comports with a great number of scholars from other schools who "are almost unanimous"[7] regarding this interpretation. We have clear evidence from a little later in history (*ca.* A.D. 113) that Pliny requests advice from Trajan regarding how best to deal with Christians who would not worship the emperor's image.

Second, the Judean procurators. Others, such as Stuart Russell, Milton Terry, and James Ratton propose that this beast portrays the local imperial administrators overseeing Israel.[8] Terry suggests that the *two* horns may indicate the last two procurators who serve just before and cause the Jewish War: Lucceius Albinus (A.D. 62–64) and Gessius Florus (A.D. 64–66). Josephus mentions them together as the worst of the procurators and the goads to the war (*J.W.* 2:14–15; *Ant.* 20:11:1; cp. 18:1:6; *J.W.* 2:16:2; 2:17:4). Tacitus agrees with Josephus' assessment (*Hist.* 5:10).

---

[6] Moses Stuart, *Commentary on the Apocalypse* (Andover: Allen, Morrill, Wardwell, 1845), 2:283. David S. Clark, *The Message from Patmos* (Grand Rapids: Baker, rep. 1989 [1921]), 89. Nils Wilhelm Lund, *Studies in the Book of Revelation* (n.p.: Covenant, 1955), 149. Loren Brink, *Rethinking Revelation in the Light of the Old Testament Prophets* (Portland, Ore.: Northwest, 1986), 163. Jay E. Adams, *The Time Is At Hand* (Nutley, N.J. Presbyterian and Reformed, 1966), 73.

[7] BBC 12:315. Cp. G. R. Beasley-Murray, *The Book of Revelation* (NCBC) (Grand Rapids: Eerdmans, 1974), 216; Isbon T. Beckwith, *The Apocalypse of John: Studies in Introduction with a Critical and Exegetical Commentary* (Grand Rapids: Baker, rep. 1979 [1919]), 639; Louis A. Brighton, *Revelation* (Concordia Commentary) (St. Louis: Concordia, 1999), 359; Robert H. Mounce, *The Book of Revelation* (2d. ed.: Grand Rapids: Eerdmans, 1998), 255.

[8] J. Stuart Russell, *The Parousia: A Study of the New Testament Doctrine of Our Lord's Second Coming* (Grand Rapids: rep. Baker, 1983 [1887]), 467; Milton S. Terry, *Biblical Apocalyptics: A Study of the Most Notable Revelations of God and of Christ* (Grand Rapids: Zondervan, 1988 [1898]),398; James J. L. Ratton, *The Apocalypse of St. John: A Commentary on the Greek Text* (London: R & T Washbourne, 1915), 301.

Third, General Vespasian. F. W. Farrar, referencing Hildebrandt, presents a strong ten point argument for Vespasian.[9] Included among these are Vespasian's milder ways (imaged by his being a lamb, Rev 13:11), his being the commissioned delegate of Nero to put down the Jewish revolt (Rev 13:12; *J.W.* 3:1:1), his enforcing Nero's will (Rev 13:14), his being known as a miracle worker (Rev 13:13a; Dio 66:8; Suetonius *Vesp* 7; Tacitus *Hist.* 4:82), and more.

Fourth, political messianism. Rick Van De Water[10] offers a novel suggestion: the second beast represents "political messianism" in the Land while the first beast symbolizes diaspora Judaism spread throughout the empire. He notes that in the Gospels and Acts Rome shows no particular hostility to Christians, whereas the Gospels repeatedly warn about Jewish opposition (Mt 10:16–18; 23:34–37) and Acts records its unrelenting assaults (e.g., Ac 8:1; 21:27; 24:19). This fits well with Revelation's theme of Jewish judgment (Rev 1:7), specific Jewish concerns mentioned in two of the seven letters (Rev 2:9; 3:9), and the strongly Hebraic cast of the whole Revelation. Consequently, neither beast represents Imperial Rome, but rather the Church's first enemy, covenantal Israel.

Fifth, Flavius Josephus. Ford and Barker argue that the second beast symbolizes Josephus.[11] They point out that he is from the Land (Jos., *Life* 1); is a priest, thus appearing as a "lamb" (Jos., *Life* 1); exercises the authority of the first beast in his presence, while serving as Vespasian's and Titus' spokesman to the Jews (Jos., *J.W.* 5:9:2; 6:2:1); interprets oracles and prophesies as a false prophet (*J.W.* 3:8:3; 3:8:9; *Life* 9; cp. Rev 19:20); attempts to secure the surrender and submission of the Jews (*J.W.* 5:9:3) warning that if they do not bow before Rome, they will die (*J.W.* 5:9:3; cp. Rev 13:15); and warns of fire overwhelming the temple and Jerusalem (Jos., *J.W.* 5:9:4; 6:2:1; cp. Rev 13:13).

Sixth, apostate Judaism. Eugenio Corsini, Cornelis Vanderwaal, David Chilton, and J. E. Leonard surmise that this beast represents the Jewish religious establishment.[12] According to Arthur Wain-

---

[9] F. W. Farrar, *The Early Days of Christianity* (London: Cassell, 1884), 478–81.

[10] Rick Van De Water, "Reconsidering the Beast from the Sea (Rev 13.1)," *New Testament Studies* 46 (April, 2000) 245–46, 251, 255–56.

[11] Ford, *Revelation*, 227–38 and Margaret Barker, *The Revelation of Jesus Christ* (Edinburgh: T & T Clark, 2000), 236–41.

[12] Eugenio Corsini, *The Apocalypse: The Perennial Revelation of Jesus Christ*, trans. and ed. by: Francis J. Moloney. (Wilmington, Del.: Michael Glazier, 1983), 250–54. Cornelis Vanderwaal, *Search the Scriptures*, (St. Catherines, On.: Paideia, 1979), 10:100–01. David Chilton, *The Days of Vengeance: An Exposition of the Book of Revelation* (Fort Worth: Dominion, 1987), 336–37. J. E. Leonard, *Come Out of Her, My*

wright, Firmin Abauzit (1679–1767) holds that "the beast from the land stands for the Pharisees, and Babylon symbolizes Jerusalem. Its fall is the destruction of that city by the Romans."[13] The High Priestly aristocracy that governs Israel's religious and cultural life is headquartered in the Land; blasphemously employs the Roman judicial apparatus to crucify Christ (Mt 26:59‖; Jn 11:47–48; 19:5, 12); involves religious leaders associated with worship (Mt 26:3) and prophecy (Jn 11:51), who would thereby be wolves in sheep clothing (Mt 7:15; 24:5, 11; cp. Rev 13:11); work false miracles (Mt 24:24; Ac 8:9–24; 13:6–11; 19:13–16); and are a widespread cause of death for Christians (Ac 5:27ff; 9:1–2; 21:11; 22:5; 25:7; 26:10).

The Preferred Interpretation

We must discount the first view, for the beast's coming "out of the Land" (*ek tēs gēs*) is an emphasized and key datum identifying him. Again we must understand that "the 'land" is synonymous with Israel in Jewish writings."[14] Though distinct from and subordinate to the Roman beast, he is in league with him *in Judea*, "the Land." So then, just as the sea from whence the greater beast arises touches most of the Roman provinces, thereby presenting him on the "world" (the *oikoumenē*) stage, so the subordinate beast has a lesser realm, "the Land" (*hē gē*), Israel.

And though I long held the procurator view, it ultimately fails to satisfy Revelation's requirements. The Judean procurator appears in the Land and has indisputable links to imperial Rome and her emperor. However, the land beast has strong religious associations, whereas the procurators were mainly fiscal agents with police powers representing the emperor.[15] This lesser beast appears as a "lamb" reminding us of temple worship in that "the lamb is the dominant sacrificial victim."[16] Just as the first beast's image as a carnivore compound points to Rome and her bloody amusements, so it seems that the second beast's lamb image points to Israel's sacrificial system and religious claims. And later John identifies him as the "false *pro-*

People: A Study of the Revelation to John (Chicago: Laudemont, 1991), 97, 103.

[13] Johann Gottfried von Herder (1744–1803) understood the land beast to be Johanan ben Levi, one of the Jewish revolutionaries. See: Arthur W. Wainwright, *Mysterious Apocalypse: Interpreting the Book of Revelation* (Nashville: Abingdon, 1993), 126.

[14] Ford, *Revelation*, 212; cp. Russell, *Parousia*, 466; Terry, *Biblical Apocalyptics*, 398; Leonard, *Come Out of Her*, 97; Barker, *Revelation*, 237.

[15] Paul S. Harvey, *Oxford Companion to English Literature* (Oxford: Oxford University Press, 1967), 347. DNTB, 961, 980.

[16] George Arthur Buttrick, ed., *Interpreter's Dictionary of the Bible* (Nashville: Abingdon, 1962), 3:58.

phet" (Rev 19:20) who is directly associated with the devil and the first beast (Rev 16:13; 20:10). In that Revelation is a very Old Testament-oriented book, we should recognize that "in Scripture, false prophecy appears only within the covenant context"[17] and possesses a religious character. Thus, the land beast serves "primarily a religious role" here.[18]

Furthermore, the Judean procurators do not seem significant enough to bother with tracing their ultimate doom to the abyss. The second beast ought to have more presence elsewhere in Revelation (which the procurators do not), even if under different images. As I will show, he is closely associated with the harlot Jerusalem in later chapters, whereas the procurator's administrative seat is in Caesarea. In addition, like the Roman armies themselves, the procurators serve as God's chastening rods against Israel and are of no direct moral concern to John's drama, which highlights the afflictions intentionally aimed at the followers of the Lamb and presents Israel's judgments as necessary and just. We may argue the same way regarding the fourth suggestion, Vespasian. He may appear as the rider on the white horse bringing judgment on Israel from afar (Rev 6:2), thereby effecting the will of God. Furthermore, he never persecutes Christians.

The final three options meet the three fundamental requirements of Revelation: contemporary relevance, judgment on Israel, and focus on the Land. Indeed, these three options are so closely related in significance that we should combine them (except for the portion of Van De Water's interpretation regarding the *first* beast). Though Josephus alone is too narrow an interpretation, he is, however, a factor in the proper solution. After all, he is a priest and a Jewish aristocrat, who serves as a general during the Jewish War, and is a prominent member of the religious leadership headquartered in Israel (*Life* 1; *J.W.* 2:20:3). As I work through the material below, I will show how the second beast symbolizes apostate Judaism *as concentrated in its religious leadership in its High Priestly aristocracy.*

Explaining the Land Beast

We must recognize the historical significance of the temple and its leadership in Israel. Horsley observes:

> The Temple and high priesthood were the central and dominating political-economic institutions of ancient Judea, their religious dimen-

---

[17] Vanderwaal, *Search the Scriptures*, 10:89; cp. Chilton, *Days of Vengeance*, 336; Beale, *Revelation*, 707.

[18] Beale, *Revelation*, 707.

sion inseparable from their political-economic function. The Torah served, in effect, as the constitution and law-code of the temple-state centered in Jerusalem. The Pharisees and other scribes/sages served a mediating political-economic-religious function in that Judean temple-state.... Two brief passages from Josephus suffice to illustrate how we must proceed in order to understand the temple-state in Judea.[19]

The two Josephan passages Horsley cites are:

And where shall we find a better or more righteous constitution than ours, while this makes us esteem God to be the Governor of the universe, and permits the priests in general to be the administrators of the principal affairs, and withal intrusts the government over the other priests to the chief high priest himself? which priests our legislator, at their first appointment, did not advance to that dignity for their riches, or any abundance of other possessions, or any plenty they had as the gifts of fortune; but he intrusted the principal management of Divine worship to those that exceeded others in an ability to persuade men, and in prudence of conduct. These men had the main care of the law and of the other parts of the people's conduct committed to them; for they were the priests who were ordained to be the inspectors of all, and the judges in doubtful cases, and the punishers of those that were condemned to suffer punishment. (*Ap.* 2:21)

Josephus speaks of two important positions for controlling Israel:

the one belonging to the city itself, the other belonging to the temple; and those that could get them into their hands had the whole nation under their power, for without the command of them it was not possible to offer their sacrifices; and to think of leaving on those sacrifices is to every Jew plainly impossible. (*Ant.* 15:7:8)

Elsewhere Josephus explains the domineering political function of the High Priests in the first century after Herod Archelaus' rule: "the government became an aristocracy, and the high priests were intrusted with a dominion over the nation" (*Ant.* 20:10:1). As Horsley puts it: "the government itself was dominated by, if not composed exclusively of, high priests, other notables, and leading Pharisees."[20]

The position of Israel's religious leadership is such that in the apocrypha Ben Sira can write of the High Priest in his day:

---

[19] Richard A. Horsley, *Galilee: History, Politics, People* (Valley Forge, Penn.: Trinity, 1995), 129.

[20] Richard A. Horsley, "High Priests and the Politics of Roman Palestine: A Contextual Analysis of the Evidence in Josephus," *Journal for the Study of Judaism in the Persian, Hellenistic, and Roman Period,* 17 (1986):53.

How glorious he was, surrounded by the people, / as he came out of the house of the curtain. / Like the morning star among the clouds, / like the full moon at the festal season; / like the sun shining on the temple of the Most High, / like the rainbow gleaming in splendid clouds. . . . / When he received the portions from the hands of the priests, / as he stood by the hearth of the altar / with a garland of brothers around him, / he was like a young cedar on Lebanon / surrounded by the trunks of palm trees. / All the sons of Aaron in their splendor / held the Lord's offering in their hands / before the whole congregation of Israel. . . / Then the sons of Aaron shouted; / they blew their trumpets of hammered metal; / they sounded a mighty fanfare / as a reminder before the Most High. / Then all the people together quickly / fell to the ground on their faces / to worship their Lord, / the Almighty, God Most High. (Sir 50: 5–7, 12–13, 16–17)

But before I move further along I must note that John does not present the drama here diachronically but thematically. That is, John does not concern himself with the specific order of events; he is exposing the unholy trinity in its inherent character as illustrated in its antipathy to God and his people. In Revelation 12 he presents Satan being foiled by Christ's ascension (wholly overlooking his life, ministry, and death, except for his birth, Rev 12:2, 4), and the Christian flight to Pella. In Revelation 13:1–10 he brings forward the first beast and shows his evil character as exhibited in the Neronic persecution and in beast's resilience despite the Roman civil wars (Rev 13:3).

Returning to Revelation 13:11–18, John exposes the evil character of the Land beast's apostate worship and conduct, which have as a backdrop Christ's judicial trials in the Gospels, as well as the temple and synagogue persecution of Christians throughout Acts. John is here showing the *moral* linkage between the dragon (Satan), the sea beast (Rome), and the land beast (Israel's high-priestly aristocracy). Revelation 2:9 and 3:9 already link Satan and Israel.[21] John is now fleshing this out more directly and dramatically by showing Israel's moral and legal alignment with pagan Rome. Later we will witness the Jerusalem harlot sitting on the beast in Revelation 17:3, 6 which provides an even sharper moral focus.

The Activity of the Land Beast

Now we read that "he exercises all the authority of the first beast in his presence" (Rev 13:12a). This phrase and its following context

---

[21] Later Justin Martyr links Satan and the Jews: "Punishments even to death have been inflicted on us by demons, and by the hosts of the devil, through the aid ministered to them by you" (*Dial.* 131).

engage in *moral retrospective*, unconcerned with the Jewish War to which he alludes earlier when mentioning the church's sojourn in Pella (Rev 12:6, 13–16). Rather than introducing either beast with chronological indicators, we have a simple: "And I saw" (Rev 13:1, 11). His interest here lies in *character determination through summation* rather *than chronology development through sequencing*. Therefore John brings the lesser beast on stage after presenting the first beast's war with the saints (Rev 13:5, 7, the Neronic persecution in A.D. 64–68) and Rome's revival under Vespasian (Rev 13:3, A.D. 69) without incongruity.

Regarding the statement that "he exercises all the authority of the first beast," Beale points out that "the second beast is now explicitly said to be aligned with the first beast."[22] This is certainly true. But then Beale draws an erroneous implication: "further confirming its identification with the state." I will show instead that this presents us with an *"unholy alliance" between Rome and Jerusalem* rather than an accentuation of the imperial state's authority.

The "authority" of the Land beast is expressly rooted in that of the sea beast. This must contextually refer to the particular, relevant, dramatically-presented authority in view: the authority to continue what Satan seeks from his heavenly vantage point. That is, Satan's attempt to overthrow God's redemptive purpose by securing the death of Christ (Rev 12:4d) and accusing the brethren (Rev 12:10) to the point of "death" (Rev 12:11) by means of persecution (Rev 12:13, 17). Thus, the Land beast reflects the sea beast's "authority to act" (Rev 13:5) which "was given to him [by the dragon] to make war with the saints" (Rev 13:7). *This* is the authority in view, not literally "all [*pasan*]" of Rome's authority in *everything* (such as minting coins, appointing procurators, taxing provinces, governing trade, building roads, or commissioning legions), for the next phrase places constraints upon the Land beast's exercise of authority. The Land beast's highest court, the Sanhedrin, could not even legally convene without the consent of the Roman authorities (Jos., *Ant.* 20:9:1).

Hare summarizes the evidence in Acts regarding Jewish resistance to Christianity, showing that Jews employ Roman authority: The Jews were "(1) poisoning the minds of the populace, (2) stirring up the rabble to attack the Christians, (3) bringing Christians before Gentile tribunals on charges of having broken Gentile law, and (4) inciting Gentiles to hale Christians into court on such charges."[23]

---

[22] Beale, *Revelation*, 708.

[23] Douglas A. Hare, *The Theme of Jewish Persecution of Christians in the Gospel according to St. Matthew* (Cambridge: University Press, 1967), 75.

In John's introductory letters to Revelation he highlights the Jewish legal assault on Christians. In Revelation 2:9 he speaks of the "blasphemy" of the Jews who are a synagogue of "Satan." Bratcher and Hatton suggest translating *blasphēmian* as "slander," noting that "it probably consisted of false accusations made by their enemies for the purpose of getting them into trouble with the Roman authorities .... In translating this phrase it should be made clear that these false accusations were directed against the believers in Smyrna."[24] They point out also that the word "Satan" is "the Hebrew word for 'adversary,' 'opponent.'" This also highlights the legal issues (as emphasized in Rev 12:7-10). In Revelation 12 we see Satan's legal battle in heaven (Rev 12:7-12) and his consequent assault on the Judaean church (Rev 12:13-16).

In Revelation 13:12 the Land beast exercises the "authority" (*exousian*) of the sea beast — not *independently* from him, but rather "in his presence" (*enōpion*, "in the sight of").[25] That is, the Land beast is under the sea beast's oversight and therefore subject to his constraints. After all, the Land beast is a "false prophet" (Rev 19:20) aping the true prophets who operate "before [*enōpion*] the Lord of the earth" (Rev 11:4), and we know that the Lord's prophets do not *independently* possess the Lord's *full* power.

The issue of authority is of great concern to first century Israel (just as it is in Revelation's legal drama with its references to witnesses, thrones, and so forth). John's Christian audience would be aware of Judaic challenges to Christ regarding the question of authority (Mk 2:10‖; 11:27-33‖; Mt 7:29). While John writes, imperial procurators administer Israel (they govern in A.D. 6-41 and 44-66). Indeed, Christ teaches "that the rulers of the Gentiles lord it over them, and their great men exercise authority over them" (Mt 20:25) as a reminder that Israel is under Rome's dominion.[26]

God's law establishes a number of capital crimes, some of which the Jewish authorities falsely charge against Christ and the Christians (Jn 19:7; Ac 23:29; 25:24). The Jews confront Jesus regarding whether he accepts the legitimacy of this ultimate Mosaic penalty (Jn

---

[24] Robert G. Bratcher and Howard A. Hatton, *A Handbook on the Revelation to John* (New York: United Bible Societies, 1993), 46-47; cp. Nils Wilhelm Lund, *Studies in the Book of Revelation* (n.p.: Covenant, 1955), 80.

[25] BAGD, 342; A. T. Robertson, *Word Pictures in the New Testament* (Nashville: Broadman, 1930), 6:403.

[26] In that Matthew writes his gospel later during the controversy with the Jews, this probably is included as a slap against Israel for siding with Caesar: he will "lord down upon" (*katakurieuousin*) Israel because their leaders "press authority down upon" (*katexousiazousin*) them.

8:3–5). As we engage this section of Revelation 13 we must remember that Rome jealously reserves to herself the authority to exercise *ius gladii*, capital punishment (Jos., *Ant.* 20:9:5; cf. *J.W.* 2:13:2; 2:14:1). According to Josephus, the procurator Albinus informs the Jews "it was not lawful for Ananus to assemble a Sanhedrin without his consent" (*Ant.* 20:9:1). Josephus particularly mentions that when Rome reduces Judea to a province, Augustus grants the procurator Coponius "authority" (*exousian*) to inflict capital punishment (*J.W.* 2:8:1), that is, he intrusts death to the procurator (*kteinein labon para Kaisaros exousian*). We see this reflected in the Gospel record (Mt 27:2, 11, 27; Lk 20:20; Jn 19:10; Ac 23:24, 26; 24:37; 26:30).

This is significant for John's legal drama, just as it is in his record of Jesus' trial, where the Procurator Pontius Pilate menacingly declares to the Lord: "Do You not know that I have authority [*exousian*] to release you, and I have [*exousian*] authority to crucify you?" (Jn 19:10–11). The Palestinian Talmud reads: "A *baraitha* says, 'Forty years before the destruction of the temple they took from Israel the right to inflict capital punishment'" (Talmud, *j. Sanh.* 1:1; 7:2; cp. *p. Sanh.* 1:18a, 37).[27]

Thus, the Gospel record shows that for the Jews to secure the death of Christ (and later, Christians) *legally* and without severe repercussions, they must petition the Roman judicial authority to handle the matter. This is an important issue in Christ's judicial trials and is emphasized in John's Gospel: the Sanhedrin demands that the Romans put him to death because they themselves do not have the legal authority to do so while under Roman rule (Jn 18: 31).[28] And, of course, the Jewish role in Christ's trial and crucifixion serve as the very reason for John's judicial drama (Rev 1:7), with its central character being the "slain Lamb" (Rev 5:6, 12; 13:8; cp. 5:8,

---

[27] See Josef Blinzler, *The Trial of Jesus: The Jewish and Roman Proceedings Against Jesus Christ Described and Assessed from the Oldest Accounts*, trans from 2d ed. by Isabel and Florence McHugh (Westminster, Mary.: Newman, 1959), 157–63: Excursus 7: "Concerning the Competence of the Sanhedrin." See also Shemuel Safrai and Menahem Stern, eds., *The Jewish People in the First Century: Historical Geography, Political History, Social, Cultural and Religious Life and Institutions* (Philadelphia: Fortress, 1976), 337ff, 398.

[28] A. N. Sherwin-White, *Roman Society and Roman Law in the New Testament* (Grand Rapids: Baker, 196), 35–43. The "testing" of Christ in Jn 8:1–11 may be an attempt to arouse Rome's concerns in this regard if Christ confirms capital punishment for the woman caught in adultery. This sort of test appears in the Roman coinage question also (Mt 22:15ff). Herman Ridderbos, *The Gospel of John: A Theological Commentary*, trans. by John Vriend (Grand Rapids: Eerdmans, 1997), 288–89.

6:1, 16; 7:9–10, 14; 7:17; 12:11; 14:1, 4, 10). This is also an important issue in our current context: John is moving from the (presently engaged) Roman persecution in A.D. 64–68 (Rev 12:17; 13:5, 7) back to the longer running Jewish persecution of Christians since A.D. 30 (cf. Rev 12:15). This continues the martyr-vindication theme which is so important in Revelation (Rev 6:10–11; 16:16; 17:6; 18:24; 20:4).

That the Jewish religious establishment was constrained by Rome's authority is illustrated in several significant issues relating even to the temple system — *despite* Judaism enjoying *religio licita*[29] status and special worship freedoms (Philo, *Embassy* 27 §296, 298; Jos. *Ant.* 14:10:8).[30] On one occasion the Roman procurator Gessius Florus invades the temple and takes "seventeen talents out of the sacred treasure" to pay Jewish taxes to the emperor (*J.W.* 2:14:6). The Romans use the massive tower of Antonia to keep a watchful eye on the Jews as they worship in the temple environs, which intrusion is a great offense to the Jews (*J.W.* 5:5:8; cp. 2:12:1). From it also led an underground passage to allow the Romans to "guard against any sedition" (*Ant.* 15:11:7). The Romans (or their approved political subordinates) control the High Priest's vestments (*Ant.* 15:11:4; 18:4:3; 20:1:1).[31]

The secular authority designated by Rome even involves himself in appointing the Jewish High Priests (e.g., *Ant.* 14:8:5; 20:9:1; 20:10:1). We hear of High Priests appointed by Herod the Great, Valerius Gratus, Herod of Chalcis, Vitellius, Tiberius Alexander, Agrippa I and II and others (*Ant.* 20:2–4 213, 223).[32] For example, under Herod's rule "in thirty-three years no fewer than seven High Priests were appointed."[33] Even in the brief reign of Agrippa I (A.D. 37–44) we find him deposing and installing High Priests three times (*Ant.* 19:6:4). Speaking of the sixty year line of six priests issuing from Annanus b. Sethi (*Ant.* 18:26), Goodman observes that "in every case their right to lead the Jewish nation rested ... entirely on the whim of the Romans, or in later cases Herodian princes, who

---

[29] *Religio licita* is a phrase derived from Tertullian, *Apol.* 21: *insignissima religio, certe licita*. Roman law actually employed the phrase *collegia licita*. Herbert B. Workman, *Persecution in the Early Church: A Chapter in the History of Renunciation* (Cincinnati: Jennings and Graham, 1906), 56 n2.

[30] Cf. Harry J. Leon, *The Jews of Ancient Rome* (Rev. ed.: Peabody, Mass.: Hendrikson, 1995), 8–10.

[31] Even when the Jews have them in their possession, they do so only with Rome's express say so (*Ant.* 15:11:4).

[32] Safrai and Stern, *The Jewish People in the First Century*, 312, 349, 362, 370, 372.

[33] Martin Goodman, *The Ruling Class of Judaea: The Origins of the Jewish Revolt Against Rome A.D. 66–70* (Cambridge: Cambridge University Press, 1987), 41.

appointed them."[34] The Tosefta (*Kip.* 1:7) mentions unacceptable kings "ordained the practice of regularly appointing priests, and they appointed high priests every single year."

In fact, Horsley notes that "far from representing the Judean people's interests, the high-priestly aristocracy collaborated with the Roman authorities on whom their positions depended."[35] He continues:

> The decrees of Caesar quoted by Josephus clearly understand the tithes as having been paid to the Hasmonean high priests — 'they shall also pay tithes to Hyrcanus and his sons, just as they paid to their forefathers' (*Ant* 14:194, 203). . . . It seems likely that the Hasmoneans, having created a far more extensive and complex community tributary to the temple-state, also consolidated control of its revenues, including the tithes.[36]

Conclusion

In keeping with Revelation's main theme — judgment upon Israel for crucifying their Messiah (Rev 1:7) — John presents the Land beast as symbolizing apostate Judaism as concentrated in its religious leadership in its High Priestly aristocracy. He shows the leadership of Judaism functioning as a subordinate to pagan Rome, further demonstrating Israel's apostasy and the legitimacy of God's judgment upon her. All of this is in keeping with the trial and crucifixion of Christ under Jewish pressure upon the local Roman authority.

---

[34] Goodman, *Ruling Class*, 44.
[35] Horsley, *Galilee* 137.
[36] Horsley, *Galilee*, 141.

10

THE JEWISH TEMPLE AND THE BEAST'S THRONE

And the fifth angel poured out his bowl upon the throne of the beast; and his kingdom became darkened; and they gnawed their tongues because of pain. (Rev. 16:10)

Introduction

In Revelation John presents a court drama condemning Israel for rejecting her Messiah (Rev 1:7), who appears before God's judicial throne (Rev 4:2–5) as the slain Lamb (Rev 5:6, 9, 12).[1] The following evidence suggests that Revelation portrays the Jerusalem temple of apostate, Christ-condemning first century Israel as the "throne of the beast," which is judged under the fifth bowl. Let us consider the evidence for identifying "the throne of the beast" as the Herodian temple.

The Demand of Consistency

First, interpretive consistency compels us to look in Israel for this "throne of the beast." In my Revelation commentary I will argue that the two previous judgment cycles (the seals and the trumpets) focus on Israel.[2] In that the judgment series are evidently recapitulatory,[3] we would expect that John is continuing the pattern here in the third series, the bowl judgments. These three judgment cycles are in keeping with Revelation's overarching theme of divine wrath upon Israel (Rev 1:7) and with the strongly Judaic imagery John employs.

The Roman beast does not appear at all in the seal judgments, and is only very briefly mentioned in passing during an interlude in the trumpet judgments (Rev 11:7). And in that allusion he is not even the *recipient* of divine judgment but the background agent involved in slaying God's two witnesses — who are ministering in Jerusalem and around the temple (Rev 11:1–2, 8). His proleptic ap-

---

[1] See: Gentry, *The Book of Revelation Made Easy* (Powder Springs, Geo.: American Vision, 2008).

[2] For a succinct presentation of the evidence, see my chapter in C. Marvin Pate, ed., *Four Views on the Book of Revelation* (Grand Rapids: Zondervan, 1998).

[3] See: G. K. Beale, *The Book of Revelation* (NIGTC) (Grand Rapids: Eerdmans, 1999), 808–12.

pearance there provides an important and relevant link between the
beast and the Jewish temple.

The Religious Character of Authority

Second, in antiquity governmental authority, which is naturally
associated with a "throne" (cf. Rev 13:2) is religious in character and
often linked with a temple.[4] This fits the (almost universal) interpretation of Revelation 2:13, associating Satan's *throne* with the
presence of imperial *temples* in Pergamum.[5] We learn in Revelation
13 that the beast-emperor's throne was given by Satan (Rev 13:2) and
results in the worship of the emperor (Rev 13:4b; cp. vv 5-6, 8). We
know from Roman imperial socio-political history that emperor worship was a convenient instrument for insuring the distant emperor's
"presence" among and influence over subjugated peoples, especially
those in the eastern empire.[6]

Furthermore, in Scripture itself, God's authority is linked with
a temple, for his own throne is set in his heavenly temple: "The Lord
is in His holy temple; the Lord's throne is in heaven" (Ps 11:4). Even
the earthly temple is his throne on earth (Eze 43:6-7). And in Isaiah's
vision (which impacts John's throne vision in Rev 4), we read: "The
Lord is in His holy temple; the Lord's throne is in heaven; / His eyes
behold, His eyelids test the sons of men" (Isa 6:1, cf. v 4; cp. Eze 10:1,
3-4; Zec 6:13). This linkage of throne and temple also appears in
Revelation itself: "For this reason, they are *before the throne* of God;
and they *serve Him day and night in His temple*" (Rev 7:15). This is
why in Revelation we often see God being *worshiped* while he is on
his throne (Rev 4:10; 5:13; 7:9-11; 8:3; 11:16; 14:3; 19:4). This is even
clearly affirmed in our context of the bowl judgments: "The seventh
angel poured out his bowl upon the air; and a loud voice came out
of the *temple* from the *throne*" (Rev 16:17).

So then, it is not unlikely that the Jewish temple could serve in
John's judgment drama as the throne of the emperor "in the Land,"
for the priestly rulers of the temple serve as a relevant source of
Roman rule. This is underscored in the fatal cry of the priestly aris-

---

[4] "What is a god? Wielding of power. / What is a king? Like a god" (*Philologus*
80). See Isa 14:4, 13-14.

[5] See: Robert L. Thomas, *Revelation 1-7* (Chicago: Moody, 1992), 184-85. Ben
Witherington III, *Revelation* (NCBC) (Cambridge: Cambridge University Press,
2003), 102. Grant R. Osborne, *Revelation* (BECNT) (Grand Rapids: Baker, 2002), 141.
Stephen S. Smalley, *The Revelation to John: A Commentary on the Greek Text of the Apocalypse* (Downers Grove, Ill.: InterVarsity, 2005), 68.

[6] S. R. F. Price, *Rituals and Power: The Roman Imperial Cult in Asia Minor* (Cambridge: Cambridge University Press, 1984), chs 1, 7-9.

tocracy against Christ: "We have no king but Caesar" (Jn 19:15b, cp. v 12; Mt 27:20). The Jewish authorities use Rome's judicial power to crucify Christ (Jn 19:12, 15; Mt 27:1-2, 12; Ac 2:23) and later to harry his followers (e.g., Ac 13:50; 14:2; 16:20; 17:6-7; 18:12; 21:11).

Even Josephus admits that the Sanhedrin crucify Christ: "they who loved him at the first did not cease to do so even after Pilate had condemned him to crucifixion *at the suggestion of the principal men [proton andron] among us*" (*Ant.* 18:5:2).[7] Evans notes of Josephus' writings: "His portrait of the High Priesthood indicates corruption, avarice, collaboration with Rome, and on occasion violence (*Ant.* 20.8.8; 20.9.2), details which certainly cohere with the portrait in the Gospels and Acts. . . . Jesus' critical stance toward the ruling priests is thus clarified."[8]

Bruce observes regarding the Sanhedrin's demanding Christ's death: "No doubt they were honest in saying that Caesar was the only *basileus* they knew; their status and privileges depended on their collaboration with the imperial power."[9] They even complain to the procurator that Jesus was "misleading our nation and forbidding to pay taxes to Caesar" (Lk 23:2). In Acts this alignment of Roman power with Jewish authorities becomes virtually a creedal statement by the earliest Christian community: "*they* [plural] lifted their *voices* to God with *one accord* and said . . . "For truly in this city there were *gathered together* against Thy holy servant Jesus, whom Thou didst anoint, *both* Herod and Pontius Pilate, *along with* the Gentiles *and* the peoples of Israel" (Ac 4:24, 27).

The Focus of the Bowl Judgments

Third, John specifically states that the bowl judgments are directed at "the Land" of Israel, the heart of which is the temple: In the introduction to the seven bowl plagues we hear a "loud voice from the [heavenly] temple" declaring that all of these bowls will pour out "into the Land" (*eis ten gen*, i.e., Israel) (Rev 16:1). The first bowl is poured out on the "Land" (Rev 16:2). Those afflicted in the fifth bowl judgment (Rev 16:10-11) bewail their "sores" (*helkon*) which re-

---

[7] Joseph Klausner, *Jesus of Nazareth: His Life, Times, and Teaching*, trans. by Herbert Danby (New York: Macmillan, 1957), 57-58, argues very ably that this is not a Christian interpolation in Josephus. Louis H. Feldman states that "our text represents substantially what Josephus wrote, but that some alterations have been made by a Christian interpolator." *Josephus* (*Loeb Classical Library*) Cambridge, Mass.: Harvard University Press, 1931), 9:49n.

[8] Craig A. Evans, *Ancient Texts for New Testament Studies: Guide to the Background Literature* (Peabody, Mass.: Hendrikson, 2005), 174.

[9] F. F. Bruce, *The Gospel of John* (Grand Rapids: Eerdmans, 1983), 365.

sult from the outpouring of the first bowl upon those "in the Land" (Rev 16:2). And the sixth bowl judgment involves the Euphrates River (Rev 16:12) which is the well-known covenantal boundary marker for Israel (Ge 15:18; Ex 23:31; Dt 1:7; 11:24; Jos 1:4; 1Ch 18:3; 9:26; Isa 27:12; cp. Rev 9:14).

Since our attention is on the Land, we cannot help but look immediately to the Jewish temple since "the Temple and high priesthood were the central and dominating political-economic institutions of ancient Judea, their religious dimension inseparable from their political-economic function."[10] Philo notes that he "thinks it right that the man who is consecrated to God, as his high priest, should, during the time of his exercising his office be superior to all men, not only to all private individuals, but even to all kings" (Philo, *Moses* 2:26). Indeed, Josephus speaks of two important positions for controlling Israel:

> the one belonging to the city itself, the other belonging to the temple; and those that could get them into their hands had the whole nation under their power, for without the command of them it was not possible to offer their sacrifices; and to think of leaving off those sacrifices is to every Jew plainly impossible. (*Ant.* 15:7:8)

John's Denunciation of Israel

Fourth, John's presenting the Jerusalem temple as the throne of the Roman beast is in keeping with his strong denunciations of apostate Israel. Earlier in his work he calls the Jewish synagogue a "synagogue of Satan" (Rev 2:9; 3:9), prophesies the destruction of the temple by the Gentiles (Rev 11:2), and designates Jerusalem as Sodom and Egypt (Rev 11:8). Later he will present Jerusalem in the garb of Babylon (Rev 17:3ff). In portraying the temple as the throne of the beast, he is following the example of the Old Testament prophets who scathingly denounce Israel's corrupted temple worship. In Isaiah 66:3 the prophet charges that current temple worship is tantamount to sacrificing a dog, offering swine's blood, and engaging in idolatry (Isa 66:3). This is why God refuses to accept Israel's worship in his temple (Isa 1:11–17). This is why both Jesus and Stephen imply idol terminology when speaking of the temple "made without hands" (Mk 14:58; Ac 7:48; cp. Dt 4:28; Ps 115:4; Isa 2:8; Hab 2:18).[11]

---

[10] Richard A. Horsley, *Galilee: History, Politics, People* (Valley Forge, Penn.: Trinity, 1995), 139.

[11] See fuller argumentation in Ch. 7 above.

Roman Rule and the Jewish Temple

Fifth, the angel expressly pours out the first bowl upon those who worship the image of the beast: "And the first angel went and poured out his bowl into the earth; and it became a loathsome and malignant sore upon the men who had the mark of the beast and who worshiped his image" (Rev 16:2). In Revelation 13:11ff we see that the second beast (the apostate temple-priestly system[12]) exercises the authority of the first beast (Rome) in the "Land" (Rev 13:11, 14). In Revelation 13:14–15 John presents the *temple authorities* themselves as imposing beast worship upon men under the threat of death. Hence they appear corporately as "another beast" (*allo thērion*, Rev 13:11) portrayed under the image of the sea "*beast*" (*thērion*).

Horsley observes that the temple "stood at the vortex of the imperial relationship between Rome and the Palestinian Jewish people . . . . The Temple was thus functioning as an instrument of imperial legitimation and control of a subjected people."[13] So here in the fifth bowl the "throne of the beast" could easily portray the temple. Thus, for dramatic, redemptive-historical purposes John presents the beast's "throne" (the locus of his rule over the Land) as the all-important temple system. In this regard we should remember that Jesus (Mk 14:58), Stephen (Ac 6:13), and Paul (Ac 21:28) are all charged with defying the temple.

In fact, as I show elsewhere in this book the Roman beast so dominates the priesthood and temple in order to rule Israel that the temple system becomes an extension of imperial authority. The Roman authorities not only control the High Priest's vestments necessary for his sacerdotal function (*Ant.* 15:11:4; 18:4:3; 20:1:1) but they even appoint the High Priests themselves, to insure their control over the central local authority in Israel (e.g., *Ant.* 14:8:5; 20:9:1; 20:10:5). In the 100 years leading up to the Jewish War, there were twenty-eight High Priests appointed by the following Roman authorities: Herod the Great, Archelaeus, Quirinius, Valerius Gratus, Vitellius, Agrippa I, Herod of Chalkis, and Agrippa II. See the list in Shurer.[14]

Speaking of first century high-priestly appointments, Goodman observes that "in every case their right to lead the Jewish nation rested . . . entirely on the whim of the Romans, or in later cases

---

[12] See my comments in Ch. 9

[13] Horsley, *Galilee*, 137.

[14] Emil Schurer, *A History of the Jewish People in the Time of Jesus Christ*, trans. by John Macpherson (2d. ed.: Peabody, Mass.: Hendrickson, rep. 1994 [1890], 3:197 –202.

Herodian princes, who appointed them."[15] Josephus reports of Quirinius that "he deprived Joazar of the high priesthood, which dignity had been conferred on him by the multitude, and he appointed Ananus, the son of Seth, to be high priest" (*Ant.* 18:2:1). He comments regarding Herod of Chalcis:

> Herod also, the brother of the deceased Agrippa, who was then possessed of the royal authority over Chalcis, petitioned Claudius Caesar for the authority over the temple, and the money of the sacred treasure, and the choice of the high priests, and obtained all that he petitioned for. So that after that time this authority continued among all his descendants till the end of the war Accordingly, Herod removed the last high priest, called Cimtheras, and bestowed that dignity on his successor Joseph, the son of Cantos.[16] (*Ant.* 20:1:3)

Regarding this situation "the problem was not just that the High Priests appointed by Herod were his puppets . . . but that they were *blatantly* his puppets, just as the incumbents after A.D. 6 were blatantly the political choices of Roman procurators."[17] Indeed, "the high-priestly aristocracy collaborated with the Roman authorities on whom their positions depended"[18] for "the Jewish upper classes cultivated Roman friendship and the Roman way of life."[19] Rhoades agrees, noting that they were the class:

> which cooperated most directly with the Romans and which had the most to lose by a war with Rome. This ruling class was opposed during the war by Jewish revolutionaries who rebelled not only against Rome, but also the traditional high-priests (*War* 4:148, 152 [4:3:6]), the wealthy (*War* 2:427 [4:7:5]), and those of noble birth (*War* 4:139 [4:3:4]).[20]

---

[15] Martin *Goodman, The Ruling Class of Judaea: The Origins of the Jewish Revolt Against Rome A.D. 66–70* (Cambridge: Cambridge University Press, 1987), 44. Also: "It was normal Roman practice not only to trust existing local leaders but also, and just as importantly, whenever possible to leave established local institutions intact when a province was created" (Goodman, *Ruling Class* , 43).

[16] Josephus is mistaken regarding the identity of this High Priest, it was actually Elionaeus the son of Cantheras (cf. note b in LCL *Ant.* 20:1:15).

[17] Goodman, *Ruling Class* 111. Cp. Jonathan J. Price, *Jerusalem Under Siege: The Collapse of the Jewish State 66–70 C.E.* (New York: Brill, 1992), 86.

[18] Horsley, *Galilee*, 137.

[19] James Park, *The Conflict of the Church and the Synagogue* (New York: World, 1961), 22.

[20] David M. Rhoades, *Israel in Revolution: 6–74 C.E.: A Political History Based on the Writings of Josephus* (Philadelphia: Fortress, 1976), 5.

Price comments that "the high priest Ananias . . . enjoyed an especially close relationship with the Roman procurator (AJ 20.205, 209 [20:9:2])."[21] His section titled "Pro-Romans" is illuminating.[22] As Horsley puts it: "the Jewish aristocracy, despite occasional friction with Roman officials, had been consistently loyal to Rome and, despite their own lapses into predatory activities, had willingly collaborated in Roman imperial rule."[23]

Michaels well notes that "the temple under Sadducee operation was being used to support Rome and essentially maintain Roman control in a land given by God to Judaism."[24] He continues: Revelation 17 engages in "condemnation of the religious leaders of the temple under the title of harlot and under the name Babylon."[25] Chilton observes that "the most striking feature of consensus among the Gospels and Josephus in respect to Caiaphas is his close relationship with the Roman administration. Cordial relations are implicit in his long tenure (some eighteen years) as high priest."[26] He further adds that "a single, symbolic, and physical center provided the focus of Roman and high priestly cooperation — the temple."

Remarkably Josephus does not mention the high-priests or the temple aristocracy involving themselves when Pilate brings the hated images on the Roman standards into Jerusalem (*J.W.* 2:9:2), or when he uses the sacred funds to build an aqueduct (*J.W.* 2:9:4). In fact, they do not even engage the matter when Gaius (Caligula) initiates plans to erect his statue in the temple, even though as Smallwood observes: "this event should have been a deeper concern to the high-priests."[27]

Josephus shows the high-priestly rulers are pro-Roman, in that "leading men" in Jerusalem enlist him to try "to persuade the ill men there to lay down their arms" (*Life* 7) at the initial outbreak of revolt against Rome. "The chief priests and all the people . . . were in favour of peace" (*J.W.* 2:17:5). The High Priests' collaboration with the Romans is so great that it spurs the Jewish Sicarii to turn "to as-

---

[21] Jonathan J. Price, *Jerusalem Under Siege: The Collapse of the Jewish State 66–70 C.E.* (New York: Brill, 1992), 29.

[22] Price, *Jerusalem*, 38–40.

[23] Richard A. Horsley, "High Priests and the Politics of Roman Palestine: A Contextual Analysis of the Evidence in Josephus" *Journal for the Study of Judaism in the Persian, Hellenistic, and Roman Period* 17 (1986): 51–52.

[24] Lawrence R. Michaels, *Revelation in Its Original Meaning* (San Diego: Bovee, 1999), 97.

[25] Michaels, *Original Meaning*, 97.

[26] ABD 1:805.

[27] Cited by Horsley, "High Priests," 36.

sassinating key high-priestly figures" (see: *J.W.* 2:13:3).[28] In fact, "when the Roman troops under Cestius finally came to retake control of Jerusalem . . . the priestly aristocracy attempted to open the gates to them . . . (November 66; [*J.W.* 2:19:2])."[29]

In addition, Josephus notes that "leading citizens" besought the Romans "to come up to the city with troops and to crush the revolt before it became insuperable" (*J.W.* 2:17:4). They even "decided to feign concurrence with the revolutionaries in order to influence them to pursue a strictly nonaggressive policy toward the Romans, because Cestius would come to deliver them" (cf. *Life* 22).[30] Simon charges Jerusalem's aristocracy of wanting to "admit the Romans into" the city (*J.W.* 4:4:4).

Consequently, "the majority of revolutionaries saw the war as an opportunity not only to exclude the foreign power, but also to overthrow the traditional aristocratic Jewish government. . . . Freedom for them ultimately implied freedom from the traditional Jewish authorities who had been so closely aligned with the Romans."[31]

The False Prophet

Sixth, the very next bowl (the sixth) specifically presents "the false prophet" (i.e., the Land beast) as aligned with the Roman sea beast (and Satan, cf. Rev 13:2): "I saw coming out of the mouth of the dragon and out of the mouth of the beast and out of the mouth of the false prophet, three unclean spirits like frogs" (Rev 16:13).[32] In chapter 9 I show the Land Beast represents the Jewish high-priestly aristocracy. This indicates the sixth bowl has something to do with Israel working with Rome, further underscoring the temple's serving as a throne for the beast.

We should note further that this judgment even gathers men for the battle at "Har Magedon" (Rev 16:16). Megiddo is well known in the Old Testament as a place of great battles: it is the place where Deborah and Barak defeat a superior force from the Canaanites (Jdg 5:19; cp. Jdg 4:3; 5:8), where King Ahaziah dies during Jehu's revolt (2Ki 9:27), and where good King Josiah is killed by Pharaoh Neco (2Ki 23:29). Josiah's death is particularly significant in that Jeremiah and Israel long mourn him (2Ch 35:24-25; Zec 12:11) and in that it leads to Israel's decline, apostasy, and captivity (2Ch 36). These

---

[28] Horsley, *Galilee*, 73–74.
[29] Horsley, *Galilee*, 74.
[30] Rhoades, *Israel in Revolution*, 6.
[31] Rhoades, *Israel in Revolution*, 178.
[32] This alignment between Israel and Rome appears more fully in Revelation 17:3ff, under the imagery of the harlot riding the beast.

events at Megiddo in Israel are significant in Israel's history and underscore John's interest here in Israel, rather than Rome.

The "Great City"

Seventh, the seventh bowl judgment falls on "the great city" (Rev 16:19) which John earlier identifies as Jerusalem: "their dead bodies will lie in the street of *the great city* which mystically is called Sodom and Egypt, *where also their Lord was crucified*" (Rev 11:8). I will provide arguments supporting the great city = Jerusalem identity in the next chapter. All of this shows John's concern with "the Land," because it involves the capital of the Land where political power revolves around the temple.

Conclusion

From these several lines of evidence we see how appropriately John's drama presents the temple as the "throne of the beast" in Israel. In my full commentary I will present more comprehensive evidence, but these elements show the main gist of this interpretation. The temple system is thoroughly corrupt in the first century due to its high-priesthood (cp. Mt 21:12‖). Earlier than Christ's day the Qumran community withdraws from Jerusalem and denounces the temple hierarchy. A part of the problem with the temple is its dominance by the Romans.

11

JERUSALEM AND THE BABYLONIAN HARLOT

And another angel, a second one, followed, saying, "Fallen, fallen is Babylon the great, she who has made all the nations drink of the wine of the passion of her immorality." (Rev 14:8)

Introduction

The dominant scholarly view of "Babylon" in Revelation studies holds that it is as an image of imperial Rome. Corsini observes that "nowadays the identification with imperial Rome is largely taken for granted."[1] This view is so strongly ingrained that Boring even states that "there can be no doubt that the harlot city of John's vision is Rome."[2] Others argue that while "Babylon" represents ancient imperial Rome, John is pointing through her to "the entire anti-Christian world"[3] because of Babylon's "transtemporal nature."[4]

Despite the widespread conviction that "Babylon" represents Rome, however, a number of both older (e.g., F. Abauzit; J. G. von Herder; C. F. J. Züllig; P. S. Desprez; J. S. Russell; M. S. Terry; W. Milligan) and more recent commentators (e.g., J. M. Ford; C. Vanderwaal; A. J. Beagley; E. Corsini; D. Chilton; D. E. Holwerda; I. Provan; L. R. Michaels; M. Barker; B. J. Malina) argue that she portrays first century Jerusalem, the capital city of Israel and the home of the temple and the high-priesthood or, sometimes more broadly, she pictures the whole nation of Israel.

Terry calls this Babylon-image a "highly wrought apocalyptic picture of the apostate Church of the old covenant," which is headquartered in Jerusalem.[5] Milligan declares that "the city of 'the Jews,' is that of which the Apocalyptist thinks when he speaks of it

---

[1] Eugenio Corsini, *The Apocalypse: The Perennial Revelation of Jesus Christ*, trans. and ed. by: Francis J. Moloney (Wilmington, Del.: Michael Glazier, 1983), 322.

[2] M. Eugene Boring, *Revelation: Interpretation: A Bible Commentary for Teaching and Preaching* (Louisville: John Knox, 1989), 179.

[3] Simon J. Kistemaker, *Exposition of the Book of Revelation* (NTC) (Grand Rapids: Baker, 2001), 460.

[4] G. K. Beale, *The Book of Revelation* (NIGTC) (Grand Rapids: Eerdmans, 1999), 850.

[5] Milton S. Terry, *Biblical Hermeneutics: A Treatise on the Interpretation of the Old and New Testaments* (Grand Rapids: Zondervan, rep. 1974), 478.

as Babylon."[6] Provan engages a careful Old Testament analysis of the imagery of Revelation 18 and concludes: "The case for Babylon as Jerusalem, then, is in my view a compelling one."[7] Quite contrary to Boring, Malina and Pilch even go so far (too far!) as to state that "there is no hint at all in this document that the author is concerned with Rome."[8] They do not even view the beast from the sea as Rome.

Throughout Revelation John's recurring redemptive-historical lament is similar to Isaiah's: "How the faithful city has become a harlot, / She who was full of justice! / Righteousness once lodged in her, / But now murderers" (Isa 1:21). In Revelation Israel/Jerusalem is being judged for her infidelity to God and his covenant, particularly as indicated in her rejecting the Lamb and persecuting his faithful witnesses. Below I will *summarize* the evidence for this identification.

Revelation Setting
Contemporary Expectation

An issue to which we must continually return in Revelation is John's temporal expectation. In his introduction and conclusion John insists that the events in his prophecy "must shortly take place" (Rev 1:1; 22:6) because "the time is at hand" (Rev 1:3; 22:10). All the way through the book we keep hearing that the events are about to occur (Rev 3:10; 6:10–11; 10:6; 12:12; 22:12, 20).

In keeping with this contemporary expectation we read in Revelation 17 that the harlot currently "is sitting" (*kathemenes/kahmenen*, pres. ptcp.) on "many waters" (Rev 17:1) and on the beast (Rev 17:3, 7). It is this harlot who will soon be judged: "And the ten horns which you saw, and the beast, these will hate the harlot and will make her desolate and naked, and will eat her flesh and will burn her up with fire" (Rev 17:16).

The only great city to perish "shortly" after John writes is Jerusalem. Josephus records for us that in A.D. 70 Titus "gave orders that they should now demolish the entire city and temple" (*J.W.* 7:1:1) and that "it was so thoroughly laid even with the ground by those that dug it up to the foundation, that there was left nothing to make those that came thither believe it had ever been inhabited" (*J.W.* 7:1:1). This was anticipated in the New Testament (Mt 22:7; 23:36 –24:2; Lk 19:44).

---

[6] William Milligan, *The Book of Revelation* (New York: Armstrong, 1901), 293.

[7] Iain Provan, "Foul Spirits, Fornication and Finance: Revelation 18 from an Old Testament Perspective," *Journal for the Study of the New Testament* 64 (Dec., 1996): 96.

[8] Malina, Bruce J. and John J. Pilch, *Social-Science Commentary on the Book of Revelation* (Minneapolis: Fortress, 2000), 213.

Thematic Statement

John establishes his overarching theme in Revelation 1:7 where we learn that "He is coming with the clouds" against "those who pierced Him" so that "all the tribes of the earth [literally, the Land, i.e., the Promised Land] will mourn over Him." Revelation's theme highlights Israel's judgment because of her slaying the Lamb of God. Consequently, we note the dominant image of the Lamb before the throne of God in Revelation, a Lamb who has been cruelly slaughtered (Rev 5:6, 12; 12:11; 13:8).

That being so, we should note that the harlot's destruction is the major, climactic judgment in Revelation: surely it must relate to Revelation's theme. Her judgment is the result of the final bowl of wrath (Rev 16:17ff) and is given more space than any other judgment scene in Revelation. Indeed, "Revelation 17:1–19:10 is a larger interpretive review of the sixth and seventh bowls."[9] Indeed, "it represents the detailed climax to those bowls of judgment."[10] Since Revelation's theme is Israel's judgment, and since Jesus was slain in Jerusalem (Rev 11:8), and since Babylon's judgment is the dominant catastrophe in Revelation, Babylon must be Jerusalem.

Leading Concern

Though Revelation 1:7 contains John's main theme, a secondary theme is "like unto it." John repeatedly declares the vindication of the Lamb's followers as a special concern: "And they cried out with a loud voice, saying, 'How long, O Lord, holy and true, wilt Thou refrain from judging and avenging our blood on those who dwell on the earth?'" (Rev 6:10). Therefore, he urges their patience, for Christ promises that "he who overcomes, I will grant to him to sit down with Me on My throne, as I also overcame and sat down with My Father on His throne" (Rev 3:21).

This is especially relevant to God's judgment on the Babylonian harlot, for while detailing her destruction he mentions three times her role in persecuting the saints. In his initial vision of the harlot he "saw the woman drunk with the blood of the saints [including the Old Testament saints and prophets], and with the blood of the witnesses of Jesus" (Rev 17:6). As she burns (Rev 18:18) we hear the call to "rejoice over her, O heaven, and you saints and apostles and prophets, because God has pronounced judgment for you against

---

[9] G. K. Beale, *The Book of Revelation* (NIGTC) (Grand Rapids: Eerdmans, 1999), 847; cp. Robert G. Bratcher and Howard A. Hatton, *A Handbook on the Revelation to John* (New York: United Bible Societies, 1993), 242.

[10] Ian Boxall, *The Revelation of Saint John* (BNTC) (Peabody, Mass.: Hendrikson, 2006), 239.

her" (Rev 18:20). After the harlot is destroyed John writes that "in her was found the blood of prophets and of saints and of all who have been slain on the earth" (Rev 18:24). This is precisely what Christ prophesies his followers must endure from Jerusalem's leaders:

> Therefore, behold, I am sending you prophets and wise men and scribes; some of them you will kill and crucify, and some of them you will scourge in your synagogues, and persecute from city to city, that upon you may fall the guilt of all the righteous blood shed on earth, from the blood of righteous Abel to the blood of Zechariah, the son of Berechiah, whom you murdered between the temple and the altar. (Mt 23:34–35)

This is certainly the Christian experience with the Jews in the first century when John writes, as we can see in various New Testament texts (see especially: Ac 7:58–8:1; 9:29; 12:1–3; 26:21). Paul himself states that "I persecuted this Way to the death, binding and putting both men and women into prisons" (Ac 22:4).[11] Once again as in Isaiah's day, Jerusalem has become a harlot by bloodshed: "how the faithful city has become a harlot, / She who was full of justice! / Righteousness once lodged in her, / But now murderers" (Isa 1:21).

Previous Example

In Revelation the harlot-city Babylon is called "Babylon the great" (Rev 14:8; 16:19; 17:5; 18:2) and "the great city" (Rev 16:19; 17:18; 18:10, 16, 18, 19, 21). But the first time we hear of "the great city" is in Revelation 11:8 which is the place "where also their Lord was crucified." This, of course, must be Jerusalem (Mt 16:21; Mk 8:31; 10:32–34; Lk 9:22; 13:32; 17:11; 19:28). Thus, John establishes in our minds the idea of Jerusalem as "the great city." And again, John's casting fits the theme of his forensic drama, which focuses on Israel's judgment (Rev 1:7).

Furthermore, to the Jewish mind (and Revelation is deeply Jewish in content, grammar, sentiment, and style) Jerusalem is "the great city." Jeremiah writes: "And many nations will pass by this city; and they will say to one another, 'Why has the Lord done thus to this *great city*?'" (Jer 22:8). In Lamentations he writes:

> How lonely sits the city / That was full of people! / She has become like a widow / Who was once *great* among the nations! / She who was

---

[11] See Ch. 5 above.

a princess among the provinces / Has become a forced laborer! (Lam. 1:1)

Josephus bemoans Jerusalem's horrific fall: "Where is now that *great city* [*megalē polis*] the metropolis of the Jewish nation?" (*J.W.* 7:8:7). Also in the preceding chapter John distinguishes "the great city" / "Babylon the great" from "the cities of the nations" (Rev 16:19). In my final point below, I will note he also distinguishes her from Rome.

In addition, we have precedent in Revelation for labeling Jerusalem with a pagan name. In Revelation 11:8 she is called "Sodom and Egypt." John even goes so far as to declare the synagogue system (subject to Jerusalem, cf. Ac 9:2) a "synagogue of Satan" (Rev 2:9; 3:9). In this, John follows the Old Testament prophetic pattern, as when Jeremiah warns that "the iniquity of the daughter of my people / Is greater than the sin of Sodom" (Lam 4:6). Jeremiah even does so for the same reason as John: "because of the sins of her prophets / *And* the iniquities of her priests, / Who have shed in her midst / The blood of the righteous" (Lam 4:13; cp. Rev 17:6; 18:24). Isaiah also refers to her as "Sodom" for an identical reason (cp. Isa 1:9-10, 21). Thus, rather than conducting herself as the covenantal wife of God, she becomes a harlot acting more like her traditional enemies. Early in her experience she desires to be like the nations (1Sa 8:5, 20); she now becomes like them.

Furthermore, we should note that John presents this relationship between Jerusalem and Rome under other images. In Revelation 13:13-16 we see the Jewish aristocracy as the second (Land) beast who furthers the cause of the first (sea) beast, which is Rome (see Ch 9 above). In Revelation 16:10 we see the temple appearing as the "throne of the beast" which involves the projection of Roman rule into the heart of Israel (see ch. 10 above). Now we see Jerusalem (the aristocracy's capital city) sitting on the Roman beast. It all fits together nicely.

Present Context

The angels who pour out the bowls containing God's wrath come from the heavenly temple (Rev 15:5-6a), which is the archetype for the earthly temple (Heb 8:5; 9:23-24; cf. Ex 25:40). They even dress like priests (Rev 15:6b; cp. Ex 28:39, 42; Lev 16:4; 1Sa 2:18) and use ritual libation bowls to pour out the judgments (Rev 15:7). This fits well with their pouring judgment on the earthly temple and its "holy city" Jerusalem. In his dramatic irony John sees the harlot's gold cup containing "unclean things" (Rev 17:4) which suggests the Jewish ceremonial laws separating the clean and the unclean — Rome certainly would not concern herself with Israel's ceremonial

laws. This is especially significant in that "one of the seven angels
who had the seven bowls" grants him this vision (Rev 17:1).

In Revelation 17:14 we will see the Babylonian harlot herself
dressed in the distinctive colors of the temple (*J.W.* 5:5:4, 6) and the
High Priest (Ex 28:1–2, 5–12, 17–23, 33), both of which are located in
Jerusalem. She even has prominently displayed on her forehead the
opposite of what the High Priest has inscribed on his turban which
appears on his forehead. Whereas the High Priest wears on his
forehead "a plate of pure gold" with "the engravings of a seal, 'Holy
to the LORD'" (Ex 28:38; cf. Sir 45:12; *Ant.* 3:172–178), in Revelation
17:5 we see the harlot, "and upon her forehead a name was written,
a mystery, 'Babylon the Great, the Mother of Harlots and of the
Abominations of the Earth.'" Surely the faithful city has become a
harlot (Isa 1:21), proudly displaying "a harlot's forehead" (Jer 3:3).

Literary Structure

John draws an unmistakable literary contrast between the
drunken harlot and the chaste bride which underscores their important relationship to one another. Not only so but this strongly suggests that John is continuing the overall drama regarding God's
divorce of Israel. Particularly in Revelation 17 and 21 we discover
numerous remarkable antithetical parallels between the two wo-
men-cities. Consider the following few samples of the remarkable
correspondences:

His invitation. One of the bowl angels introduces John to both the
harlot and the bride in the same way:

> Rev 17:1a: "And one of the seven angels who had the seven bowls
> came and spoke with me, saying, 'Come here, I shall
> show you.'"

> Rev 21:9a: "And one of the seven angels who had the seven bowls
> full of the seven last plagues, came and spoke with me,
> saying, 'Come here, I shall show you.'"

His transport. In order to see the two cities, John is transported
"in the Spirit" in an identical fashion (*apēnegken me eis erēmon en
pneumati*):

> Rev 17:3:   "He carried me away in the Spirit."

> Rev 21:10   "He carried me away in the Spirit."

Their character. When John arrives on each of the scenes, he sees
women of exact opposite character, one disreputable, one honorable:

> Rev 17:1:   "Come here, I shall show you the judgment of *the great
> harlot* [*pornē*] who sits on many waters."

Rev 21:9: "Come here, I shall show you the bride [*numphēn*], *the wife of the Lamb.*"

Their environs. John is taken in the very same manner to the contrasting environments of the two women:

Rev 17:3a: "And he carried me away in the Spirit *into a wilderness.*"

Rev 21:10a: "And he carried me away in the Spirit *to a great and high mountain.*"

Their relationships. The two women contrast each other in terms of their primary relationships. The Babylonian harlot is carried about in an illicit relationship by the blasphemous beast (Rev 17:3, 7). The New Jerusalem is "the bride, the wife of the Lamb" (Rev 21:9), possessing the very "glory of God" (Rev 21:11a).

Their descriptions. The Babylonian harlot is eulogized in great detail regarding her violent collapse (Rev 18:2, 8, 10, 17, 19, 21). Whereas the new Jerusalem bride is described in glorious detail as an eternally enduring reality (Rev 21:4–6) with sure foundations (Rev 21:12–14), possessing the water and the tree of life (Rev 21:6; 22:1, 17).

We must remember that John specifically calls the bride the "*new* Jerusalem" from heaven (Rev 21:1–2), suggesting her contrast to the *old* Jerusalem (cp. new order/old order contrasts elsewhere, Mt 9:16 –17; 13:52; 2Co 3:7–14; Heb 1:1–2; 3:1–6; 8:1–13). Such juxtapositioning in this Old Testament-oriented prophecy presents an intentional contrast between the Jerusalem below (Rev 11:8) and the Jerusalem above (Rev 21:2), and should be familiar to New Testament students (cp. Gal 4:22–31; Heb 12:18–19, 22).

Climax Expectation

John's drama has as its central theme Christ's judgment-coming against Israel/Jerusalem for crucifying him (Rev 1:7). Consequently, we should expect the later, climactic judgment chapters to detail *Jerusalem's* punishment. Revelation 16–19, which are climactic chapters, strongly emphasize Babylon's destruction. They even provide lengthy and detailed lamentation over the city's fall (Rev 18).

We should note also that it is "one of the seven angels who had the seven bowls full of the seven last plagues" who introduces John to the vision of the new Jerusalem. This shows that John is intentionally linking the coming of the new Jerusalem with the demise of Babylon-Jerusalem.

Rome Impossibility

The identification of Babylon as Rome is the majority view today. But not only does Jerusalem perfectly fit the local context, general flow, and over-riding message of Revelation, but the Rome view presents us with serious incongruities

Awkward picture. In Revelation 17:3, 7 we learn that the Babylonian harlot sits on the beast. If the seven-headed beast is the seven-hilled city of Rome, and if the Babylonian harlot sits on the beast, then Rome is sitting on Rome. This presents an awkward picture, at best. Rather than such an awkward scheme, we have a picture of Jerusalem in an alliance with Rome who supports her (cp. Jn 19:15).

Incorrect image. Corsini notes that "it is important to see [the beast] as a reality distinct from the prostitute. They are so distinct that John will describe, at the end of ch. 17 an implacable and murderous hatred between the two of them."[12] In fact, regarding Revelation 17:16, Carrington notes that "in the very chapter which has led scholars to identify the Beast with Rome, it is the Beast that destroys Babylon; and if Babylon is Rome then it is very odd that Rome should destroy Rome."[13]

No attempt at applying this to the Roman civil wars of A.D. 68–69 will do. The text says that the beast (and the ten horns) "will *hate (misēsousin)* the harlot" (Rev 17:16). *Miseō* means "to have a strong aversion to, *hate, detest,*"[14] like those who "hate you, and ostracize you, and cast insults at you" (Lk 6:22). The Roman civil wars, however, involve generals attempting to rule Rome, to possess her glory for their own, not to destroy her from hatred.

In fact, one of the vying generals, Vespasian, eventually secures the emperorship. But Josephus reports of Vespasian's initial learning the news of the civil war in Rome: "And as this sorrow of his was violent, he was not able to support the torments he was under, nor to apply himself further in other wars when his native country was laid waste."[15] This is not the conduct of one who "hates" Rome.

Judgment pandemonium. Beagley argues that "another difficulty is pointed out by Minear, who notes that the judgment on Babylon is distinguished carefully from the judgment of the beast and the kings, which are not mentioned until Rev 19:19–21. He says, '[T]his would be nonsense if all three (Babylon, beast, the kings) stood for the same historical reality." But if Babylon is Jerusalem, then we have a clear rationale for distinguishing Jerusalem from the beast and the kings.

---

[12] Corsini, *The Apocalypse*, 328.

[13] Philip Carrington, *The Meaning of the Revelation* (Eugene, Ore.: Wipf & Stock, 2007 [rep. 1931]), 274.

[14] BAGD, 652.

[15] *J.W.* 4:10:2.

Conclusion

So then, "the harlot in the Book of Revelation was not Rome; she had been Jerusalem since the time of Ezekiel."[16] It seems quite clear that John intends for his audience to see Jerusalem as the new Babylon, a new destroyer of the temple. The city that rejects the Messiah and even crucifies him falls to the depths of Babylon of old, causing God to destroy her and remove her temple from her midst. In John's drama God must remove this corrupt Jerusalem so that the new Jerusalem (Christianity) can take her place finally and forever (cf. Jn 4:20–23; Heb 8:13).

Not long before they crucify him, Jesus weeps over Jerusalem and her temple:

> O Jerusalem, Jerusalem, who kills the prophets and stones those who are sent to her! How often I wanted to gather your children together, the way a hen gathers her chicks under her wings, and you were unwilling. Behold, your house is being left to you desolate! (Mt 23:37–38)

It is truly as he warns: "the kingdom of God will be taken away from you, and be given to a nation producing the fruit of it" (Mt 21:43). Sadly for Israel: "many shall come from east and west, and recline at the table with Abraham, and Isaac, and Jacob, in the kingdom of heaven; but the sons of the kingdom shall be cast out into the outer darkness; in that place there shall be weeping and gnashing of teeth" (Mt 8:11–12).

This parallels the message of Hebrews, where we read:

> But you have come to Mount Zion and to the city of the living God, the heavenly Jerusalem, and to myriads of angels. . . . See to it that you do not refuse Him who is speaking. For if those did not escape when they refused him who warned them on earth, much less shall we escape who turn away from Him who warns from heaven. And His voice shook the earth then, but now He has promised, saying, "Yet once more I will shake not only the earth, but also the heaven." And this expression, "Yet once more," denotes the removing of those things which can be shaken, as of created things, in order that those things which cannot be shaken may remain. Therefore, since we receive a kingdom which cannot be shaken, let us show gratitude, by which we may offer to God an acceptable service with reverence and awe." (Heb 12:22, 25–28)

---

[16] Margaret Barker, *The Revelation of Jesus Christ* (Edinburgh: T & T Clark, 2000), xii.

12

THE HARLOT'S DRESS AND JERUSALEM'S DECOR

And the woman was clothed in purple and scarlet, and adorned with gold and precious stones and pearls, having in her hand a gold cup full of abominations and of the unclean things of her immorality, and upon her forehead a name was written, a mystery, "Babylon the Great, the Mother of Harlots and of the Abominations of the Earth." (Rev 17:4–5)

Introduction
John lays significant emphasis on the Babylonian harlot's dress. He not only details her adornment, but emphasizes especially her gold by stating she is "adorned with gold": literally he states that she is "golded with gold" (*kechrusomene chrusio*).

And the woman was clothed in purple and scarlet, and adorned with gold and precious stones and pearls, having in her hand a gold cup full of abominations and of the unclean things of her immorality, and upon her forehead a name was written, a mystery, "Babylon the Great, the Mother of Harlots and of the Abominations of the Earth." (Rev 17:4–5)

Furthermore, the high-priest is the human face of the temple, and "Josephus plainly regards the High Priesthood and the temple service as the heart and soul of Judaism."[1] Consequently, both temple and high-priest are similarly adorned (as we shall see). We should note that Israel was a priestly nation (Ex 19:6; Isa 61:6) and Jerusalem is her capital, wherein stands the temple (Ps 68:29; Mk 11:15; Lk 4:9).

The High-Priest's Attire
The famous and fabulous Jewish temple and high-priest are arrayed with the same colors as the harlot. Not only does the temple dominate Jerusalem, but the high-priest's robes are very important as we see in Herod's locking them up and controlling their use (*Ant.* 18:92–93; 20:247–49); Vitellius returning them to the high-priesthood by the authority of the Roman emperor, Tiberius; and the dispute over them after the death of Herod Agrippa I. Indeed, "merely don-

---

[1] Steve Mason, *Josephus and the New Testament* (Peabody, Mass.: Hendrikson, 1992), 127.

ning the robes gave them [the high-priests] prestige and authority in the eyes of others."[2]

Philo extols the majesty of the high-priest's robe: It is "a marvelous work to be beheld or to be contemplated. For it has an appearance thoroughly calculated to excite astonishment, such as no embroidered work conceived by man ever was for variety and costly magnificence" (*Spec. Laws* 1:17). Josephus states regarding its making in the Old Testament: "The high priest's mitre was the same that we described before, and was wrought like that of all the other priests; above which there was another, with swathes of blue embroidered, and round it was a *golden* crown polished, of three rows, one above another" (*Ant.* 3:7:6; cp. 3:7:2; 8:3:3; see also: Philo, *Moses* 2:24; *Migration* 13; also Aristeas 96–97; Sir 45:10–11).

This is the same as in Josephus' own day, for the high-priest's:

> girdle that tied the garment to the breast was embroidered with five rows of various colors, of *gold*, and *purple*, and *scarlet*, as also of fine linen and blue, with *which colors we told you before the veils of the temple were embroidered also*. The like embroidery was upon the ephod; but the quantity of *gold* therein was greater. Its figure was that of a stomacher for the breast. There were upon it two *golden buttons* like small shields, which buttoned the ephod to the garment; in these buttons were enclosed two very large and very excellent *sardonyxes*, having the names of the tribes of that nation engraved upon them: on the other part there hung twelve stones, three in a row one way, and four in the other; a *sardius*, a *topaz*, and an *emerald*; a *carbuncle*, a *jasper*, and a *sapphire*; an *agate*, an *amethyst*, and a *ligure*; an *onyx*, a *beryl*, and a *chrysolite*; upon every one of which was again engraved one of the forementioned names of the tribes. A mitre also of fine linen encompassed his head, which was tied by a blue ribbon, about which there was another *golden* crown. (*J.W.* 5:5:7)

The Temple's Adornment

Josephus speaks of the color scheme of the tabernacle (the predecessor to the temple): "at the front, where the entrance was made, they placed pillars of gold, that stood on bases of brass, in number seven; but then they spread over the tabernacle veils of fine linen and purple, and blue, and scarlet colors, embroidered" (*Ant.* 6:3:4; cp. 3:7:7; 6:3:2). Irenaeus mentions the tabernacle's visual glory:

> So also, according to them, the courts of the tabernacle constructed by Moses, being composed of fine linen, and blue, and purple, and scarlet, pointed to the same image. Moreover, they maintain that the long robe

---

[2] E. P. Sanders, *Jesus and Judaism* (Philadelphia: Fortress, 1985), 270.

of the priest falling over his feet, as being adorned with four rows of precious stones. (*Ag. Her.* 1:18:2; 2:24:4)

See also: Clement of Alexandria (*Strom.* 5:5:6), Jerome (*Jov.* 2:34), Ambrose (*Christian Faith* 2:10–12), and Leo (*Past. Rule* 2:3).

Revelation's temple setting further suggests John is referring to the great quantities of gold associated with the sacred house. In Revelation we see the *heavenly* temple which is the eternal original for the temporal copy on earth. The heavenly temple has a "golden censer" (Rev 8:3) associated with the "golden altar" (Rev 8:3; 9:13). We also see "golden bowls full of incense, which are the prayers of the saints" (Rev 5:8). Those prayers are pleas for vindication (Rev 6:10–11) ultimately resulting in the judgment series (of which our current section is a part) which involve "golden bowls" brought out of the temple by priest-angels girded with gold (Rev 15:6).

Josephus describes Solomon's temple: "He also had veils of blue, and purple, and scarlet, and the brightest and softest linen, with the most curious flowers wrought upon them, which were to be drawn before those doors. He also dedicated for the most secret place, whose breadth was twenty cubits, and length the same, two cherubims of solid gold" (*Ant.* 8:3:3). He records Antiochus' pillaging of the temple:

So he left the temple bare, and took away the golden candlesticks, and the golden altar [of incense], and table [of shew-bread], and the altar [of burnt-offering]; and did not abstain from even the veils, which were made of fine linen and scarlet (*Ant.* 12:5:4).

Regarding the first century Herodian temple, Josephus writes of the implements stored in the temple's many rooms, for "the greatest part of the vessels that were put in them was of silver and gold" (*J.W.* 5:4:4 ; cp. Heb 9:4). He also describes the temple as having a

gate which was at this end of the first part of the house was, as we have already observed, *all over covered with gold*, as was its whole wall about it; it had also *golden* vines above it, from which clusters of grapes hung as tall as a man's height. But then this house, as it was divided into two parts, the inner part was lower than the appearance of the outer, and had *golden* doors of fifty-five cubits altitude, and sixteen in breadth; but before these doors there was a veil of equal largeness with the doors. It was a *Babylonian [Babulonios] curtain, embroidered with blue, and fine linen, and scarlet [porphuras], and purple [kokkou]*, and of a contexture that was truly wonderful. (*J.W.* 5:5:4).

Again Josephus refers to the great quantity of gold adorning the temple: "Now the outward face of the temple in its front wanted nothing that was likely to surprise either men's minds or their eyes; for it was *covered all over with plates of gold of great weight*, and, at the first rising of the sun, reflected back a very fiery splendor, and made those who forced themselves to look upon it to turn their eyes away, just as they would have done at the sun's own rays" (*J.W.* 5:5:6; cp. *J.W.* 5:5:4).

The Tosefta also mentions this: "the priests covered the face of the entire porch [of the temple] with golden trays, a hundred [handbreadths], with the thickness of a golden *denar* .... [and] there was no imperfection in them" (t. Men. 13:19). John probably alludes to this gold plating when he states that the harlot was (literally) "gilded with gold" (*kechrusōmenē chrusiō*). Swete points out similar language in Exodus 26:37 where, regarding the five pillars of the tabernacle's screen, the craftsmen must "overlay them with gold" (*chrusōseis autous chrusiō*).[3] Jesus also mentions the gold of the temple when he denounces the scribes and Pharisees for swearing "by the gold of the temple" (Mt 23:16-17).

We can find statements regarding the great quantity of gold on and throughout the temple in various Jewish contexts. The walls of the holy of holies are overlaid with gold (m. Midd. 6:1; t. Shek. 3:6, 178; m. Shek. 4:4). Various gold items include a mirror of gold (b. Yoma 37b), the two talent weight candelabra (*J.W.* 6:8:3; 7:5:5; b. Men. 98b), and much more (m. Sukk. 5:2; m. Yom. 4:4; m. Midd. 2:3; 3:8; 4:6; 6:1; m. Shek 4:4; t. Shek. 3:6; m. Men. 11:7; Philo, *Embassy* 31:216).

Josephus records some of the temple elements turned over to Titus when the temple falls: A priest "also delivered to him the veils and the garments, with the *precious stones* [*tois lithois*], and a great number of other precious vessels that belonged to their sacred worship. The treasurer of the temple also, whose name was Phineas, was seized on, and showed Titus the coats and girdles of the priests, with a *great quantity of purple and scarlet* [*porphuran te pollēn kai kokkon*], which were there reposited for the uses of the veil" (*J.W.* 6:8:3). According to Josephus "the soldiers had such vast quantities of the spoils which they had gotten by plunder [of the temple], that in Syria a pound of gold was sold for half its former value" (*J.W.* 6:6:1).

The High Priest and Temple Associated

So then, the colors marking out the High Priest correspond to those in the temple. As Josephus describes the High Priest's liturgical robe he relates it to the temple: "that girdle that tied the garment to the breast was embroidered with five rows of various colors,

---

[3] Henry Barclay Swete, *Commentary on Revelation* (Grand Rapids: Kregel, rep. 1977 [1906]), 216; cp. Philip Carrington, *The Meaning of the Revelation* (Eugene, Ore.: Wipf & Stock, 2007 [rep. 1931], 287.

of gold, and purple, and scarlet, as also of fine linen and blue, with which colors we told you before the veils of the temple were embroidered" (*J.W.* 5:5:7). In Revelation 18:12 we see the cargoes necessary for such wealth in Jerusalem, when God's judgment falls upon "cargoes of gold and silver and precious stones and pearls and fine linen and purple and silk and scarlet, and every kind of citron wood and every article of ivory and every article made from very costly wood and bronze and iron and marble."

Interestingly, during Jesus' trial before the Sanhedrin "the high priest tore his robes, saying, 'He has blasphemed!'" (Mt 26:65). Though the Romans would not allow the High Priest to wear his special robe at all meetings of the Sanhedrin (cf. Jos., *Ant.* 15:11:4), due to the approaching Passover "on this particular occasion the vestments may have been in possession of the high priest."[4] Consequently, his action of tearing his High Priestly garment may have been "an ironic foreshadowing of the rending of the veil of the temple he serves."[5] The parallel account in Mk 14:63 employs the word *chitōnas* which is the word used in the Septuagint at Exodus 28:4 and Leviticus 16:4. Thus, the Gospels mention both the tearing of the High Priest's robe and the temple's veil in the events surrounding Jesus' death — whose death justifies God's judgment on Israel (Rev 1:7).

Conclusion

Though the Babylon = Rome interpretation dominates in Revelation studies, a more compelling case can be made for Babylon = Jerusalem. This fits remarkably well with the Judaic character of Revelation as well as with its overarching theme of judgment on Israel for crucifying Christ (Rev 1:7).

One of the ironies of the Rome view is that in teaching God's judgment upon Rome, Rome does not fall until after it has converted to Christianity and ceased persecuting the Church. Yet in the Babylon = Jerusalem view, Jerusalem falls at the very height of her rebellion against Christ and its resistance to Christianity — and as a di-

---

[4] John Nolland, *The Gospel of Matthew* (NIGTC) (Grand Rapids: Eerdmans, 2005), 1133.

[5] W. D. Davies and Dale C. Allison, Jr., *The Gospel according to Saint Matthew* (ICC) (Edinburgh: T & T Clark, 1988), 3:533. Though Lev 21:10 forbad the High Priest doing so, we should remember at this stage the High Priest and Sanhedrin were already involved in sinful conduct in "trying to obtain false testimony against Jesus" (Mt 26:59). Leon Morris, *The Gospel according to Matthew* (Grand Rapids: Eerdmans, 1992), 685, suggests, however, that the high priest may not have thought of himself as breaching God's law in that this "was an action reserved for extreme cases."

rect consequence of Christ's prophetic denunciation (Mt 23:38 –24:2; Lk 19:41–45). And the Lord never refers to Rome's fall.

13

NERO AND THE BEAST THAT "WAS"

The beast that you saw was and is not, and is about to come up out of the abyss and to go to destruction. And those who dwell on the earth will wonder, whose name has not been written in the book of life from the foundation of the world, when they see the beast, that he was and is not and will come. (Rev 17:8)

Introduction
In chapter 2 I point out that the sixth head of the beast represents the currently reigning sixth king of Rome, the emperor Nero Caesar. But now we come upon a passage that seems to contradict this identification. In Revelation 17 the interpreting angel states that "the beast that you saw was and is not, and is about to come up out of the abyss and to go to destruction" (Rev 17:8a). Two important questions arise here: (1) What is the significance of the beast being the one who "was and is not, and is about to come"? Is this one of the many instances of the beast's divine pretensions, wherein he parodies divine eternity? (2) Does this description undercut the early-date position and preterist approach by declaring the beast (Nero) is *already dead* when John writes? After all, the angel states that he "was and is not [*ouk estin*]."

The Beast's Parody
Regarding the potential parody of God's eternality, the Roman beast exhibits blasphemous divine pretensions that lead to his worship (Rev 13:8, 12, 15). Revelation probably even alludes to this in our passage in that he is "full of blasphemous names" (Rev 17:3b). The phrase "was and is not, and is about to come" is widely held to present a "devilish antithesis" to the eternality of God as presented in Revelation 1:8; 4:8; 11:16; and 16:5.[1] For instance, in Revelation 1:8 we read that God is the one "who is and who was and who is to come." This divine pretension would certainly fit the preterist argument regarding the role of emperor worship in the first century and in Revelation.[2]

---

[1] Martin G. Kiddle, *The Revelation of St. John* (New York: Harper, 1940), 345.
[2] In my *The Beast of Revelation* I show this to be a particularly significant demonstration of Nero's megalomania.

I have no theoretical problem with this description providing an ironic reversal of the true God in the pretentious beast; after all, John does delight in parody and irony in his drama. Nevertheless, I do not believe the evidence here allows it. This is *not* mocking "the threefold description of God found already in Rev 1:8; 4:8; 11:16; and 16:5," the "threefold formula for divine eternity."[3] Rather it mocks the threefold historical experience of Christ emphasized in his initial appearance in Revelation at 1:18 (cp. Rev 2:8): he is "the living One; and I was dead, and behold, I am alive forevermore" (cf. Php 2:8-9). The dramatic irony, though, is that despite his pretensions the beast does not live forevermore, but goes "to destruction" (Rev 17:8a). I will summarily list my objections to this representing a mockery of God's *eternity*, then flesh them out:

(1) The ideas do not really match. Revelation's references to God expressly state his eternality, whereas the phrase here in Revelation 17:8 does not suggest the beast's eternality. Rather than "was, is, is to come" the beast "was, is *not*, and is coming." It would be very easy for John to declare the beast "was, is, and is to come" did he so desire. But he does not. And he would most certainly never refer to God as "is not" — for God lives "forever and ever" (Rev 4:9-10; 10:6).

(2) The basic element that is repeated and invariable in each of the idea's three appearances is: "was and is not" (*en kai ouk estin*) (Rev 17:8a, 8d, 11). This core phrase has nothing to do with parodying eternality; in fact, for someone to be "is not" is the opposite of eternal existence. In Genesis 42:36 we find the deceased Joseph and Simeon spoken of as "is not" (*ouk esti*). In antiquity *ouk esti* is a statement declaring one's death: "I was not, I became, I am not" (*hostis ouk emēn, kai egenomēn, ouk eimi*).

(3) In each of the phrase's three appearances, the third element varies both lexically and grammatically, despite being in close proximity syntactically:

The beast "is about to come up [*mellei anabanein,* pres. act. indic.] out of the abyss" (Rev 17:8a)

The beast "will come [*parestai,* fut. mid. indic.]" (Rev 17:8d)

The beast "is himself also an eighth [*autos ogdoos estin*]" (Rev 17:11a)

Again, John could easily lock in the phrasing did he so desire. But something else is going on here, as we shall see.

(4) The point John is emphasizing in this imagery is *death*. The beast's *inevitable* death is in view, for the beast *does* now exist. De-

---

[3] G. K. Beale, *The Book of Revelation* (NIGTC) (Grand Rapids: Eerdmans, 1999), 864.

spite the phraseology before us, John sees a woman currently sitting [*katoikountes*, pres. act. ptcp.] on the (apparently living) beast (Rev 17:3) and the angel expressly declares that the beast is now carrying [*bastazontos*, pres. act. ptcp.] the woman (Rev 17:7). (5) The fact that the beast "is about to *come up* out of the *abyss*" fits the idea of his *resurrection* from death, not *eternality*. It shows a mockery of *Christ's experience*, not *God's existence*. (6) The reference to the "book of life" alludes to the resurrection, for the book of life is consulted at the eschatological resurrection (Rev 20:12). (7) The third reference seems peculiar on the surface, but provides a vital clue to the intended meaning: the beast "is himself also an *eighth*," which signifies resurrection.

As most agree, the words of Revelation 17:8ff "are in the main reproductive of the imagery of ch. xiii. 1–4."[4] That being so, we must note that Revelation 13 mimics the historical death and resurrection of Christ (Rev 1:18; 2:8; 5:12; 11:17) rather than the eternal existence of God. This is significant for many dramatic reasons, not the least of which is Christ's dying at the hands of the Romans under pressure from the Jews (Mt 27:17–26; Lk 23:13–25; Ac 3:13) who manipulate Rome's power (Jn 19:12, 15): "this Man, delivered up by the predetermined plan and foreknowledge of God, you nailed to a cross *by* [*dia*] the hands of godless men and ["you" implied, *aneilate*, 2d pers. pl., aor. act. ind.] put Him to death" (Ac 2:23[5]). All of this comports with John's overarching theme of the Jewish culpability in Christ's death (Rev 1:7) in a book which has as its main figure the slain Lamb (Rev 5:6, 12; 12:11; 13:8[6]). The beast imagery *here in* 17:8 is not mimicking God but Christ; it is mimicking existing, dying, and living again, not eternality. Lazarus certainly does that without any divine pretension (Jn 11:21, 44; 12:1)!

The message which John's audience needs to hear during their trials is terribly important. True, the beast has great power (he is a carnivore with seven heads and ten horns, Rev 17:7c; cf. Rev 13:2) and remarkable resilience (he was, but is "about to come up," Rev 17:7a). Yes, he receives his great power from below, the "abyss" (Rev 17:8a; cf. Rev 9:1, 11; 13:1–2), that is, from Satan (Rev 13:2b) the

---

[4] Henry Alford, *Alford's Greek Testament: An Exegetical and Critical Commentary* (5th ed: Cambridge: University Press, 1875; Grand Rapids: Guardian, 1976), 4:709.

[5] Acts 2:23 literally reads: "this man by the fixed counsel and foreknowledge of God given up through the hand of lawless men fastening you killed [*prospexantes aneilate*]."

[6] Cp. Rev 5:8, 13; 6:1; 7:9, 14, 17; 14:1, 4, 10; 15:3; 17:14; 19:7, 9; 21:9, 14, 22; 22:1, 3.

destroyer (Rev 9:11).[7] Nevertheless, John's *driving point* is: he is going to "destruction [*apoleian*]" (Rev 17:8a, 11; cf. the Danielic back-drop, Da 7:11 LXX, *therion . . . . apoleto*). He is doomed to hell (Rev 19:20; 20:10) — his dreaded power and resilience notwithstanding.

The Beast's Presence

In Chapter 8 above I note that Nero is the personification of the beast. The evidence is quite clear and most compelling. But in Revelation 17:11 we read a statement which causes some difficulties with this interpretation. In fact, it "presents all interpreters with a real difficulty."[8]

> And the beast which was and is not, is himself also an eighth, and is one of the seven, and he goes to destruction. (Rev 17:11)

Of course, the main difficulties have been solved for I show above what he means by "the beast which was and is not" (cf. Rev 17:8). But now who is this "eighth"? How can there be an eighth in a series of seven? And how is he "one of the seven"?

In biblical numerics eight seems to be the number of resur-rection.[9] In the Old Testament the eighth day follows the day of rest and is the day on which man's labor begins anew, as a resurrection of sorts (cf. Ex 20:8–11). God saves eight people on the ark to "resur-rect" the human race (1Pe 3:20).[10] Leprosy is "regarded as a decomposition of the vital juices, and as putrefaction in a living body, [it] was an image of death."[11] Thus, in Israel the leper is not admitted back into the holy community as alive until his eighth day sacrifice (Lev 14:10, 23). The menstruous woman is unclean because

---

[7] Regarding the abyss: "the author's use throughout" Revelation shows that it "is the place of demons." Isbon T. Beckwith, *The Apocalypse of John: Studies in Intro-duction with a Critical and Exegetical Commentary* (Grand Rapids: Baker, rep. 1979 [1919]), 697.

[8] Alan F. Johnson, "Revelation" in Frank E. Gaebelein, ed., *The Expositor's Bible Commentary* (Grand Rapids: Zondervan/Regency, 1976–91), 12:560.

[9] Beale, 875; Austin Farrer, *A Rebirth of Images: The Making of St. John's Apoca-lypse* (Boston: Beacon, 1949), 70–72; Gaebelein, "Revelation,"560.

[10] "For righteous Noah, along with the other mortals at the deluge, i.e., with his own wife, his three sons and their wives, being eight in number, were a symbol of the eighth day, wherein Christ appeared when He rose from the dead, for ever the first in power" Justin Martyr, *Trypho*, 138:1 "The sacramental import of the 8th number, as signifying the resurrection" (Augustine, *Januarius*, 55). Cp. Augustine, *Faust.* 19; John of Damascus, *Orth. Faith* 23.

[11] C. F. Keil and Franz Delitzsch, *The Pentateuch*, vol. 1 in *Commentary on the Old Testament* (Edinburgh, T & T Clark, 1866–91; rep.: Peabody, Mass.: Hendrikson, 2001), 2:384.

of her blood flow for seven days, then she is cleansed on the eighth day (Lev 15:29). This cleansing is necessary "unless they die in their uncleanness" (Lev 15:31). Each of these issues is analogous to resurrection.

But most importantly, Christ arises from death on the first/ eighth day (Jn 20:1), which is the first day of a new week.[12] This begins a new creation (2Co 5:17). In Revelation he first appears as "the first-born of the dead" (Rev 1:5), establishes the book's theme as the "pierced" (slain) one who will return alive to avenge himself (Rev 1:7), appears in its initial vision dressed as a priest (Rev 1:13) proclaiming "I was dead, and behold, I am alive forevermore" (Rev 1:18; cp. 2:8), and dominates the whole drama as the slain but living Lamb (Rev 5:6, 12; 12:11; 13:8).

Thus, here in Revelation 17:11 the "eighth" points to the beast's mimicking Christ's death and resurrection (cf. Rev 13:3; 17:8). Our text reflects this through an inter-textual parallelism: his coming "up out of the abyss" in Revelation 17: 8a is a form of resurrection reflected in his being "an eighth" (the number of resurrection) in Revelation 17:11[13]:

Revelation 17:8a	Revelation 17:11
"the beast . . . . was and is not" (*hen kai ouk esti*)	"the beast . . . . was and is not" (*hen kai ouk esti*)
"is about to come up out of the abyss"	"is himself also an eighth"
"to go to destruction" (*eis apoleian hupagei*)	"he goes to destruction" (*eis apoleian hupagei*)

The heart of this parallel is between the phrases "come up out of the abyss" and "an eighth." In Scripture the "abyss" (*abussos*) is a part of the three-level cosmology of heaven, earth, and underworld (cf. Php 2:10; Rev 5:3, 13). "In the underworld (*abussos*) is not only the realm of the dead . . . but also Gehenna, the place of punishment" as well as "the prison of punished demons."[14] In Romans 10:7 *abussos*

---

[12] Barnabas writes: "We keep the eighth day with joyfulness, the day also on which Jesus arose from the dead" (Barn. 15).

[13] Moses Stuart, *Commentary on the Apocalypse* (Andover: Allen, Morrill, Wardwell, 1845), 2:326; Beale 875–76; Simon J. Kistemaker, *Exposition of the Book of Revelation* (NTC) (Grand Rapids: Baker, 2001), 473.

[14] EDNT, 1:4.

appears in the context of resurrection: "'Who will descend into the abyss?' (that is, to bring Christ up from the dead)" (cp. Ps 71:20).

But now who is this "eighth," this resurrection of the beast? As I show regarding the seven heads (Rev 17:9–10) in Chapter 2 above, the "five" are Julius, Augustus, Tiberius, Gaius, and Claudius who have already "fallen" (i.e., are dead).[15] We know, therefore, that the sixth one "is" (*estin*) the reigning emperor, Nero. And "the other who has not yet come" is the seventh, Galba, who will only "remain a little while." And we know that the Roman Civil Wars during the Year of the Four Emperors pictures the beast's corporate death throes. Now the "eighth" must represent Rome's revival, its resurrection to new life and strength. But the next emperor after Galba is Otho, one of the inter-regnum emperors who is a part of Rome's death throes. How can he picture the beast's resurrection? He is continuing those death throes. Besides, he is the "seventh," not the "eighth."

To resolve this difficulty we should note a couple of factors in the passage. (1) The number of heads on the beast is seven, *not* eight (Rev 13:1; 17:3, 7, 9). The eighth is a surprising addition, unaccounted for by the beast John sees. This should alert us to some sort of disruption in the counting. (2) In fact, John conspicuously drops the definite article when mentioning the eighth: *to therion ho en kai ouk estin kai autos ogdoos estin* is translated as "the beast which was and is not, is himself also *an* eighth." The definite article clearly and repeatedly defines the chronological series of the first six heads / kings: *hoi pente epesan ho eis estin ho allos oupo elthen* ("*the* five have fallen, *the* one is, *the* other has not yet come"). Thus, this eighth king is "*an* eighth," not "*the* eighth." But now what does this signify? Two interpretations seem quite plausible.

It could be that this "eighth" is the emperor who causes the revival of the Empire, though he is outside of the originally specified seven kings. In an important sense the revival of the Empire under *Vespasian* is a "resurrection" under "an eighth" king who is, nevertheless, "of the seven." Vespasian's victory in the Roman Civil Wars causes the *same* Roman Empire to come back to life from the death of the civil wars — not some new empire.[16]

---

[15] For more detail, see my *The Book of Revelation Made Easy*, (Powder Springs, Geo.: American Vision, 2008), 57–58.

[16] Interestingly, according to Levick, Suetonius credits Vespasian with at least eleven miracles, "supporting Vespasian's claims to power." And "to the world at large the miracles were a metaphor of the new régime's healing powers" (*Vespasian*, 67–68).

Contrary to the NASB, the angel does *not* state that "he is *one* [which would require: *heis*] of the seven" (cf. NRSV, NIV, NKJB), for Vespasian is not: the Julio-Claudian line of emperors ceases in Nero (Suet., *Gal.* 1; Tac., *Hist.* 1:16). Rather: "he is *out of* [*ek*] the seven" which indicates he is "the successor and result of the seven, following and springing out of them."[17]

The phrase *ek ton hepta* functions as a "genitive of relationship"[18] signifying that he is not an outsider (*e.g.*, a Parthian conqueror as when "the Parthians were almost roused to arms" in those times, Tac., *Hist.* 1:2). Vespasian is not only a Roman citizen but has a political (though Plebian) standing (Suet., *Vesp.* 1), even though as an emperor he was "made elsewhere than at Rome" (Tac., *Hist*). He "became consul in 51" and was later "governor of Africa, and in 67 was appointed commander-in-chief against the insurgent Jews by Nero"[19] (cp. Tac., *Hist.* 1:10; *J.W.*, Pref. 8; 3:1:3). He was even later deified by the Roman senate. As Josephus expresses it:

> upon this confirmation of Vespasian's entire government, which was now settled, and upon the unexpected *deliverance of the public affairs of the Romans from ruin*, Vespasian turned his thoughts to what remained unsubdued in Judea. (*J.W.* 4:11:5; cp. Pref. 9)

Yet another interpretation of this "eighth" seems stronger and has caused me to change my former position (the one just stated above). Though it is very similar to the one above, it shifts attention from the specific emperor (Vespasian) to the general emperorship. John appears to be stating that the *corporate* beast himself is "an eighth," i.e., is a resurrected entity (remember the parallel with Rev 17:8).

Note that John writes: "the beast which was and is not, is himself [*autos*, reflexive] also an eighth." The beast that he is speaking of is the one "which was and is not," that is, the empire which dies in the Civil Wars. No emperor dies and is himself resurrected — not even metaphorically, as in being banished and then returning (cf. Eze 37:11–12 Lk 15:24, 32; Ro 11:15). Rather, it is the beast which "you saw" (Rev 17:8), that is the corporate beast with all of his seven heads (Rev 17:3). He does not say (as in Daniel's case with the little horn, Da 7:8): "While I was contemplating the heads, behold, another head, came up among them" (cf. Da 7:20, 24). Again we must note that the NASB is incorrect in adding the word "one," when it

---

[17] Alford, *Alford's Greek Testament*, 4:711.
[18] Beale, *Revelation*, 876.
[19] Catherine B. Avery, ed., *The New Century Handbook of Leaders of the Classical World* (New York: Appleton-Century-Crofts, 1972), 385.

translates the phrase as "and is one of the seven." Rather, the corporate beast, the Roman imperial government, is renewed in Vespasian's ascendency; it is "of the seven," that is, continues imperial rule
anew.

In this sense the corporate beast's being *ek ton hepta* ("out of the
seven") reflects resurrection language. Jesus prophesies of himself
that he "should suffer and rise again *from* [*ek*] of the dead" (Lk 24:46;
cp. Php 2:11; Eph 1:20). In John's Gospel Jesus arises on the
first/eighth day (Jn 20:1) because he "must rise again *from* [*ek*] the
dead" (Jn 20:9). The *Empire* arises, as it were, out of the dead.

Though Vespasian's ascension brings a reprieve for Christians
in that he does not persecute them (Euseb., *Eccl. Hist.* 3:17[20]) as does
Nero (Rev 13:7; Tac. *Ann.* 15:44; Suet., *Nero* 16), nevertheless he does
resurrect the blasphemous Roman beastly system. He directs "the
reconstruction of the temple of the Capitoline Jupiter . . . . and a
temple to Peace."[21] Even while alive the Egyptians proclaim him a
god; and the Roman Senate eventually deifies him.[22] Such a
blasphemous system cannot help but eventually return to persecuting, as it does thirty years later under Trajan, A.D. 98–117 and later
emperors. Therefore, the (corporate) beast is destined "to destruction" (Rev 17:11c); eventually "Eternal Rome" must be destroyed (cf.
Da 2:35, 44).[23]

Conclusion

The evidence for the specific identity of the beast being Nero,
with the generic identity being Rome, is strong. Though initially the
problem of the past tense statement ("the beast which was") seems
to create a problem for the argument, when we more carefully consider it, it does not. Nero is the specific emperor living when John
writes. His death in A.D. 68 puts the Roman Empire in death throes,

---

[20] Vespasian did not persecute Christians. Eusebius states regarding Domitian
that he "was in fact the second that stirred up a persecution against us, although his
father Vespasian had undertaken nothing prejudicial to us" (*Eccl. Hist.* 3:17; cp.
4:26). Tertullian skips from Nero to Domitian as a persecuting emperor, omitting
any reference to Vespasian (*Apol.* 5). Augustine calls Vespasian "a most agreeable
emperor" (*City* 413–26).

[21] Sir Paul Harvey, ed., *The Oxford Companion to Classical Literature* (Oxford:
Clarendon, 1940), 445.

[22] Barbara Levick, *Vespasian* (London: Routledge, 1999), 67–71.

[23] The Roman Empire is viewed in antiquity as eternal. Otho speaks of "the
eternity of our power" [*aeternitas rerum*]" (Tacitus, *Hist.* 1:84). Rome is called *aeterna
urbs* in various places, including in the Latin Poet Albius Tibullus (54–19 BC) at 2,
5, 23; Ovid (43 BC–A.D. 17), *The Festivals*, 3.72. See Frank G. Moore, "Corrections
and Additions to Lewis and Shorst," *American Journal of Philology* 15:13 (1894): 349.

from which it arises after the Roman Civil Wars (AD 68–69). The beast generically considered is in John's view — not the beast specifically considered. This corporate beast mimics the life, death, and resurrection of Christ.

14

THE MARTYRS' MILLENNIUM

And I saw thrones, and they sat upon them, and judgment was given to them. And I saw the souls of those who had been beheaded because of the testimony of Jesus and because of the word of God, and those who had not worshiped the beast or his image, and had not received the mark upon their forehead and upon their hand; and they came to life and reigned with Christ for a thousand years. (Rev 20:4)

Introduction

In Revelation 20 we come upon the passage that has created the millennial debate in the field of theology. The full passage on the millennium reads:

> And I saw an angel coming down from heaven, having the key of the abyss and a great chain in his hand. And he laid hold of the dragon, the serpent of old, who is the devil and Satan, and bound him for a thousand years, and threw him into the abyss, and shut it and sealed it over him, so that he should not deceive the nations any longer, until the thousand years were completed; after these things he must be released for a short time.

> And I saw thrones, and they sat upon them, and judgment was given to them. And I saw the souls of those who had been beheaded because of the testimony of Jesus and because of the word of God, and those who had not worshiped the beast or his image, and had not received the mark upon their forehead and upon their hand; and they came to life and reigned with Christ for a thousand years. The rest of the dead did not come to life until the thousand years were completed. This is the first resurrection. Blessed and holy is the one who has a part in the first resurrection; over these the second death has no power, but they will be priests of God and of Christ and will reign with Him for a thousand years. (Rev. 20:1–6)

In Revelation 20:1–3 we witness the binding of Satan for a thousand years. This immediately raises the millennial debate. I maintain the Augustinian view on *this* portion of the chapter. That is, I believe that the thousand years is a symbolic time frame covering Christian history from the first century down to the end. And I also believe that it teaches that Satan is bound in his mission to "deceive the nations" (Rev 20:3). In other words, Satan has been bound since the first century (cp. Mt 12:28–29).

However, I am no longer a Revelation 20 Augustinian *across the board*. In fact, an enormous change has recently occurred in my views regarding the next three verses, Revelation 20:4-6.[1] The changes have resulted from my deeper analysis of Revelation as I work on my full commentary. Consider the following three major changes in my understanding. These three issues are important in the millennial debate, as well as in the flow and meaning of Revelation.

The Issues Impacted

First, I originally held that two groups were in view Revelation 20:4. I held the common Augustinian view that the martyrs represent deceased Christians in heaven (the Church Triumphant) and the confessors represent living saints on the earth (the Church Militant). And together these two groups picture all Christians throughout Church history. I no longer accept this interpretation.

Second, I also previously held that the fact that they "came to life and reigned with Christ" (Rev 20:4c) portrayed the new birth experience, where the Christian arises from spiritual death to sit with Christ in heavenly places. I still believe this *doctrinal* position, for it is taught in various places in Scripture (see especially Eph 2). But I do not believe this is a proper *exegetical* position *here* in Revelation 20. In other words, I now believe that this view is good theology but bad exegesis — if we try to draw it from Revelation 20.

Third, I previously held that "the rest of the dead" who "did not come to life until the thousand years were completed" (Rev 20:5) pointed to the bodily resurrection of all the unsaved at the end of history, as a part of the general resurrection of all men. As an orthodox Christian I do, of course, believe that John teaches a general resurrection of all men. He even teaches it in Revelation 20. But I now believe he holds off on that until verses 11–15.

The Problem Created

In Revelation John takes images from the Old Testament Scriptures — often *reworking, restructuring,* and *reapplying them.* He is effectively mining the Scriptures for material that he can use to construct his own symbolic world. His symbolic world primarily dramatically presents the first century Judeo-Christian historical experience leading up to and including the destruction of the temple in A.D. 70.

---

[1] See my previous view in C. Marvin Pate, *Four Views on the Book of Revelation* (Grand Rapids: Zondervan, 1998), 82–86. See also my first edition of *The Book of Revelation Made Easy* (Powder Springs, Geo.: American Vision, 2008), 99–124.

As Revelation teaches, A.D. 70 changes everything in redemptive-history: it ends *biblical* Judaism (after 1500 years Israel can no longer offer sacrifices as required by her Scriptures; Judaism becomes *rabbinic* Judaism, a mutated form of biblical religion; see Ch. 1), stops animal sacrifices (Heb 8:6; 9:11–28), universalizes the true religion (Jn 4:20–24; Eph 2:11–19), enlarges the people of God (Ro 11:17; Gal 3:29), and initiates the new creation (2Co 5:17; Gal 6:15; see Ch. 15 below). In A.D. 70 Christianity finally separates from her parent religion, never to return.[2] As dispensationalist theologian David K. Lowery observes: "It is generally accepted that Jewish Christians maintained connections with Judaism to one degree or another before the revolt and subsequent destruction of Jerusalem and the Temple in A.D. 70."[3] But after that event Christians no longer conceive of themselves as a sect of the Jews, but understand that in Christ "the old things passed away; behold, new things have come" (2Co 5:17). This effectively parallels the message of Hebrews, where the writer warns Jewish Christians against apostatizing back into Judaism (Heb 2:1–4; 4:1–11; 10:19–39) because the old covenant is ending (Heb 8:13) as Christ introduces the final stage of redemptive-history (Heb 1:1–13). Old covenant Israel is nearing the time of God's judgment as the new covenant is dramatically secured in the destruction of Jerusalem (Heb 12:18–29; Matt 3:11–12; 8:11–12; 21:43 –45; 23:34 – 24:2).

One distinguishing characteristic of Revelation involves its awkward grammar, which does not follow standard Greek structure and patterns. John self-consciously takes on the mantel of the classical prophets (much like John the Baptist), and in doing so he structures his grammar to mimic the Hebrew of the old covenant prophets, whose material he abundantly adopts, often reapplying them.

---

[2] Early Christians see in A.D. 70 the final conclusion to biblical Judaism and the permanent separation of Christianity from Judaism. For instance, Ignatius (*Magn.* 10) states: "Let us learn to live according to the principles of Christianity. For whosoever is called by any other name besides this, is not of God. Lay aside, therefore, the evil, the old, the sour leaven, and be ye changed into the new leaven, which is Jesus Christ. . . . It is absurd to profess Christ Jesus, and to Judaize. For Christianity did not embrace [*episteusen*, believe in , merge into] Judaism, but Judaism Christianity . . . . It is absurd to speak of Jesus Christ with the tongue, and to cherish in the mind a Judaism which has now come to an end. For where there is Christianity there cannot be Judaism."

[3] David K. Lowery in Donald K. Campbell and Jeffrey L. Townsend, *A Case for Premillennialism: A New Consensus* (Chicago: Moody, 1992), 169.

;cholars note that John's awkward Hebraicisms tend to oc-
s visionary material rather than in his other sections.[4]

is all by design; it is not due to John's inability to write Greek (see the Greek of his Gospel and Epistles for more standard Greek form). He is "becoming" an Old Testament prophet to take up his Old Testament-like challenge to Israel. Thus, John approaches Israel like Isaiah (see especially Isa 1), Jeremiah (see especially Jer 2–3), and Ezekiel (see especially Eze 2–6, 16).[5] In fact, he organizes his material around Ezekiel's structure — which explains so many specific parallels to Ezekiel:

Eze 1 = Rev 1
Eze 2 = Rev 5 (10)
Eze 9–10 = Rev 7–8
Eze 16, 23 = Rev 17
Eze 26–28 = Rev 18
Eze 38–39 = Rev 19–20
Eze 40–48 = Rev 21–22 (11)

But now, what are my changes? And how are they significant?

The Explanation Offered

My three changes appear in two places in the text. Though seemingly small, they carry radical implications. In my view, the eschatological debate (the "millennial" views) does not need to come to Revelation 20 at all.[6] It is better waged elsewhere in Scripture — *almost* everywhere else in Scripture (hence the size of my *He Shall Have Dominion: A Postmillennial Eschatology*, which builds up the postmillennial eschatology from a wide range of Old Testament and New Testament Scriptures). Postmillennialism and amillennialism certainly do not depend on Revelation 20, though dispensationalism and premillennialism absolutely do. In fact, Revelation 20, though serving as *the* foundational passage for premillennialism and dis-

---

[4] For instance, Vern S. Poythress, "Johannine Authorship and the Use of Inter-sentence Conjunctions in the Book of Revelation," *Westminster Theological Journal* 47 (1985): 329–36. See also J. P. M. Sweet, *Revelation* (Philadelphia: Westminster, 1979), 16.

[5] This realization effectively mutes the charge of anti-Semitism, which is often hurled against preterism. If this is anti-Semitic, then the views of Isaiah, Jeremiah, and Ezekiel are anti-Semitic! See my Appendix below.

[6] Craig Blaising rebukes me for playing down Rev 20 in the eschatological debate. See Blaising in Darrell L. Bock, ed., *Three Views of the Millennium and Beyond* (Grand Rapids: Zondervan, 1999), 161.

pensationalism, actually creates irresoluble problems that undermine those systems.

The Two Shall Be One

John writes in Rev 20:4b: "I saw the souls of those who had been beheaded because of the testimony of Jesus and because of the word of God, and those who had not worshiped the beast or his image, and had not received the mark upon their forehead and upon their hand." Previously I held that this presents two separate groups, martyrs and confessors, which themselves represent all Christians in history, dead or living. As such I originally thought these groups portray the whole Christian Church throughout the Christian era.

I now believe that John envisions only *one* group: deceased martyrs who did not worship the beast. The phrase "and those" in the Greek is: *kai oitines*. This is a relative pronoun clause: *kai* = "and" and *hostis* derives from the root of *hoitines* ("which, who"). This relative pronoun clause *can go either way*: It can sometimes *separate* two ideas; at other times it can further *explicate* one idea. That is, grammatically it can refer either to one group or to two. Which is it here? Scholars are divided.[7]

I believe it functions as an analeptic interpolation (a back reference) referring to the preceding group, while adding some additional explanatory information. That is, it is epexegetical, providing significant expansion for the preceding. I began to notice that everywhere else in Revelation, John uses *hostis* to further explain the preceding. For instance, in Revelation 1:12 he turns to see the voice, the one *which* (*hetis*) was speaking with him. In Revelation 11:8 the bodies of the two prophets lie in the great city, the city *which* (*hetis*) is mystically called Sodom and Egypt. In Revelation 12:13 the dragon persecutes the woman, the one *who* (*hetis*) gives birth to the child. In Revelation 19:2 God judges the great harlot, the one *who* (*hetis*) is corrupting the Land.

Then I realized that after stating that he "saw thrones, and they sat upon them, and judgment was given to them" (Rev 20:4a), then "he saw the souls of those who had been beheaded." Since he saw

---

[7] Those holding that two groups are in view include: Moses Stuart, Friedrich Düesterdieck, Milton Terry, William Hendriksen, J. P. M. Swete, R. C. H. Lenski, J. Ramsey Michaels, G. K. Beale; Vern Poythress, and Stephen S. Smalley. Those arguing for one group include: R. H. Charles, G. B. Caird, Isbon T. Beckwith, John F. Walvoord, Leon Morris, Charles Homer Giblin, Bruce M. Metzger, G. A. Krodel, Wilfred J. Harrington, G. R. Beasley-Murray, Robert Mounce, Richard Bauckham, Alan F. Johnson, J. Webb Mealy, Robert L. Thomas, David E. Aune, Simon J. Kistemaker, Grant R. Osborne, Iain Boxall, and James L. Resseguie.

souls on the thrones, and since he specifically mentions *beheaded* persons, and since in the context "they came to life," he seems quite clearly to be referring *only* to deceased believers in heaven. But this is not all.

Not only are these enthroned ones deceased, but they are deceased under specific circumstances. They have been judicially killed: "beheaded" is a standard form of capital punishment well-known in the Roman Empire (cf. Mt 14:10). These did not die from plantar faciitis (very few people do!) or old age. Furthermore, this imagery fits all the preceding story of Revelation, where the Jewish aristocracy is drunk on the blood of the saints (Rev 17:6), as is the Roman beast (Rev 13:7). This further confirms my redemptive-historical preterism and continues John's concern for his audience, which is facing the very real prospect of death for their faith.

What is more, I now realize that structurally Revelation 20:4 is really the answer to the prayer of Revelation 6:9–11. In fact, it clearly repeats some of the same thoughts and words. Revelation 6:9–11 speaks of "the souls of those who *had been slain*." These did not just fall over and die; they were *slaughtered* (*esphagmenōn*, Rev 6:9). They are crying out for God to avenge [*ekdikeis*] their blood on those who "dwell in the Land [*tēs gēs*]" (Rev 6:10). Revelation 20:4 and 6:9 are doublets, based on replicated wording and strong parallels. Note:

Revelation 20:4	Revelation 6:9
And *I saw* the *souls* of those who had been *beheaded* because of the *testimony* of Jesus and because of the *word of God*.	I saw underneath the altar the *souls* of those who had been *slain* because of the *word of God*, and because of the *testimony* which they had maintained.

Exact wording parallels include *eidon* ("I saw"), *tas psuchas* ("the souls"), and *dia* ("because"). Additionally, the clear allusions are: *ton esphagmenōn* ("of those slain"[8]) / *ton pepelekismenōn* ("of those beheaded") and *ton logon tou theou* ("the word of God") / *tēn marturian* ("the witness" or "testimony").

I would argue that these two passages represent promise and fulfillment. In Revelation 6:9 the souls are beneath heaven's altar praying for vindication and receiving the *promise* of such in due time. But in Revelation 20:4 they actually *receive* their vindication by being given the right to sit in judgment over their enemies (cp. Rev 19:2). To those caught up in the earthly terror, the martyrs would seem to be tragically destroyed and altogether lost in the struggle

---

[8] *Esphagmenon* implies a violent death, which the image of beheading well matches. / This is the same Greek word describing the Lamb "who had been slain."

(cp. Rev 11:9–10; 13:7, 15). It would also seem to the world round about that the martyrs have lost the battle and that the living persecutors have won the victory. But John characteristically provides a heavenly insight, showing that these are actually living and enthroned with Christ. These are the "blessed" ones who are *dead* (*hoi nekroi*, Rev 14:13).

The "souls" at the altar in Revelation 6:11 are told to "rest for a little while longer," until others join them in a *martyr's death*, being "killed even as they had been." Since Christ's judgment-coming against Israel in Revelation 19:11ff (cp. Rev 6:12–17) results in the glory of Revelation 20:1–4, John appears to be stating that by A.D. 70 the martyrs will be vindicated within the promised time frame of "a little while" (*chronon mikron*, Rev 6:11; cp. Lk 18:7–8). Thus, their "coming to life" as fulfillment of the promise given to them (which is given to them *while they already are in heaven*, Rev 6:11), appears to be an image of their *vindication* in the *death* of their opponents in A.D. 70 rather than at the very moment of their entering heaven. This is unique to John — whose work is unique in many respects.

In the New Testament John is the only writer to use *chronon mikron* (Jn 7:33; 12:35; Rev 6:11; 20:3), and in both instances in the Gospel, it covers a very short period — less than three years. As Jesus (elsewhere) explains to those who will be caught up in the war that leads to the temple's destruction: "the one who endures to the end, he shall be saved" (Mt 24:13). This, of course, fits well with Revelation's overarching theme (Rev 1:7), within its specific time frame ("shortly" and "near"; Rev 1:1, 3; 22:6, 10), and with its recurring concern for judging the slayers of the saints (Rev 12:10–11; 13:7–10; 14:9–13; 15:2–4; 16:5–7; 17:1–6, 14; 18:20, 24; 19:2).

We must remember the alignment of the Roman beast with the Jewish high-priestly aristocracy ("We have no king but Caesar. Crucify him"). This vision fulfills the promise that Christ "will cause those of the synagogue of Satan, who say that they are Jews, and are not, but lie — behold, I will make them to come and bow down at your feet, and to know that I have loved you" (Rev 3:9). That fulfillment was "about to come [*mellouses erchesthai*]" soon in the first century experience, for he is "coming quickly" to judge (Rev 3:10, 11). And though they initially must wait that "little while" (Rev 6:11) for vindication, the *consequences* of their soon-coming vindication will span an enormous period of time: "the thousand years" (Rev 20:4) The events transpiring during the Jewish War (from A.D. 67–70), especially the destruction of the temple, represent "their reward" (Rev 11:18; cp. 18:20; 19:1–3), as their enemies are destroyed and their long-lasting, triumphant reign begins in earnest.

Now all of this means that those who are on the thrones in the millennium are not *living* Christians. Nor are they simply *deceased*

Christians. Nor are they Christians from all ages. They are *deceased* Christians *in heaven*, who are *martyred* in the *first century*. This is John's point: Keep the faith! Withstand your oppressors! You will be greatly rewarded in heaven even if you die! Indeed, that is effectively how he introduces his book: "I, John, your brother and fellow partaker in the tribulation and *kingdom* and *perseverance* which are in Jesus" (Rev 1:9).

Of course, heavenly reward awaits all Christians in all ages. But that is not *John's* point *here*. We learn this extended truth from other Scriptures. Here in Revelation 20 he is speaking from a particular context in completing a long-running call to accept martyrdom rather than succumbing to the beast or the false prophet. Remember how Hebrews warns Jewish converts to Christ not to apostatize — especially since the old covenant is "obsolete and growing old" and "ready to disappear" (Heb 8:13)? John is doing the same in Revelation, only more dramatically.

So then, my first two changes in my understanding of Revelation 20 are: I now see only one group in the vision; and that one group involves only the first century martyrs. Revelation 20:4–6 does *not* speak of the reign of the Church in history, nor does it prophesy a still-future political reign on earth. Though again: I *do* believe the Church reigns in history (1Co 3:21–23; Eph 1:19–23), and that we are seated with Christ in heavenly places (e.g., Eph 2:6; Col 3:1). But John is writing an *occasional* epistle dealing with *specific historical matters*. We may take principles from Revelation and apply them in other contexts (just as we apply, for instance, principles from Paul's congregation-specific directives to the church at Corinth). But John's *express teaching* regards the first century persecuted Church and her two persecutors, Rome and Israel.

The Rest of the Dead

Now having changed my view regarding the occupants on the thrones of Revelation 20:4, another issues arises: Who are "the rest [*hoi lopoi*] of the dead" (Rev 20:5) that are being set over against the enthroned ones? Since Revelation 20:1–6 is linked with Revelation 19:11–21,[9] John's context offers a clue to understanding "the rest of the dead" who "did not come to life until the thousand years are completed" (Rev 20:5). We should interpret this group *contextually* in terms of John's literary flow and dramatic story-line.

---

[9] In my commentary I will demonstrate that Rev 20 does not recapitulate Rev 19:11ff. Rev 20 *results from* Christ's judgment action in Rev 19:11ff (which deals with A.D. 70).

It does not seem that "the rest of the dead" are the unbelievers of all of history who stand before God on Judgment Day. They have not been mentioned yet. I do hold that all unbelievers will stand before God on Judgment Day. And, as I stated above, I believe John teaches that — in Revelation 20:11–15. But he does not teach this here in Revelation 20:5. Who are these "the rest of the dead" then? How are they related to John's overarching story-line?

"The rest of the dead" are the other dead just mentioned in the preceding context. Who did we last hear had died *in John's narrative*? Revelation 19:19–21 answers this:

> And I saw the beast and the kings of the earth and their armies, assembled to make war against Him who sat upon the horse, and against His army. And the beast was seized, and with him the false prophet who performed the signs in his presence, by which he deceived those who had received the mark of the beast and those who worshiped his image; these two were thrown alive into the lake of fire which burns with brimstone. And *the rest* [*hoi lopoi*] were killed with the sword which came from the mouth of Him who sat upon the horse, and all the birds were filled with their flesh.

"The rest" of the dead are the ones allied with the first-century beast and his false prophet, the ones responsible for executing the martyrs. In Revelation 19:20 the beast and the false prophet are thrown directly and immediately into the lake of fire, which accents their leadership role in opposing God and his people. But "the rest [*ho lopi*] were killed with the sword which came from the mouth of Him who sat upon the horse." Remember: the beast is Nero (particularly), the false prophet is the Jewish High Priestly aristocracy; thus, their armies are their supporters in the persecution and the war against the Lamb.

John is encouraging his first century audience to withstand their assailants. Those enemies have a hollow victory: they will die and lie in the chains of darkness until the resurrection at the end of history. But the martyrs will not only enter heaven and eternal bliss, but after entering into heaven will be elevated and "come to life" and begin reigning in the presence of God and Christ.

Remember: Christ dies and is resurrected, then ascends into heaven and sits at God's right hand in victory. And he is publically vindicated against his tormentors in A.D. 70. As Jesus warns the High Priest and the Sanhedrin during his trial: "You have said it yourself; nevertheless I tell you, hereafter you shall see the Son of Man sitting at the right hand of Power, and coming on the clouds of heaven" (Mt 26:64; cp. Mk 9:1). Likewise, his faithful martyrs will also die, arise to new life, and experience heavenly vindication. Thus, they actually will live in the glory of triumph and heavenly vindication while their persecutors die in ignominy. This is *John's* point. This fits everything *he has been saying* previously.

Conclusion
Though my understanding of Revelation 20 has been considerably altered, this alteration arose from purely exegetical and contextual considerations. What is more, Revelation 20 demonstrates the integrity of the preterist interpretive scheme in a remarkable way. Although I am able only to skim the material above, I hope two conclusions are evident: (1) Revelation 20:4–6 fits beautifully with redemptive-historical preterism. (2) This passage is really not useful to the "millennial" debate.

15

THE NEW CREATION AS NEW COVENANT

And I saw a new heaven and a new earth; for the first heaven and the first earth passed away, and there is no longer any sea. And I saw the holy city, new Jerusalem, coming down out of heaven from God, made ready as a bride adorned for her husband. (Rev 21:1-2)

Introduction

Despite initial appearances, Revelation 21-22 does not speak of the consummate new creation order. Rather, it provides an ideal conception of new covenant Christianity, presenting it as the spiritual new creation and the new Jerusalem. Though the ultimate, consummate, eternal new creation is *implied* in these verses (via the now/not yet schema of New Testament revelation), John's actual focus is on *the current, unfolding, redemptive new creation principle in Christ.*

John is encouraging the beleaguered first century saints to hold on through their trials: Once Jerusalem falls, they will complete their entry into the final redemptive-historical order which has been gradually dawning since the time of Christ (Jn 4:21-23). As the writer of Hebrews puts it: "since we are receiving a kingdom that cannot be shaken, let us be thankful, and so worship God acceptably with reverence and awe" (Heb 12:28 NIV; cf. Heb 8:13). Or as Paul expresses it in the mid-50s: "And this do, knowing the time, that it is already the hour for you to awaken from sleep; for now salvation is nearer to us than when we believed. The night is almost gone, and the day is at hand. Let us therefore lay aside the deeds of darkness and put on the armor of light" (Rom 13:11-12) — a reality worthy of enduring persecution.

Jesus promises his disciples that some of them will live to see the kingdom's final establishment in power: "Truly I say to you, there are some of those who are standing here who shall not taste death until they see the kingdom of God after it has come with power" (Mk 9:1). Thus in Revelation 21 John paints nascent, post-A.D. 70 Christianity — now finally separated from Judaism — in glowing terms, as a firmly established, glorious reality.

But why does John's new creation revelation differ from Peter's which speaks of the consummate order in similar terms (2Pe 3:10-13)? Why should we believe that John focuses on *temporal redemption* in Christ as the new creation whereas Peter highlights the *eternal result* of that redemption?[1] I believe Revelation 21–22 provides several clues to this end. Here is a summary of my reasons for understanding Revelation 21–22 as referring to the spiritual new creation unfolding in present history since the first century.

Revelation's Contextual Setting

The placement of this material in Revelation strongly suggests it. Though Revelation earlier provides glimpses of the ultimate glory awaiting saints in heaven above, here John presents an extended exhibition of the latent glory experienced in time and on earth in the present new covenant order. Though the pre-A.D.70 saints suffer much for the cause of Christ, their suffering is not in vain. They are suffering for a glorious faith with long-term implications.

First, John seems to settle the new creation's inaugurated, first century existence for us. *Immediately* upon ending this vision set describing the new creation/new Jerusalem at Revelation 22:5, the very next verse (Rev 22:6) records the words of the angel showing him all of this:

> And he said to me, "These words are faithful and true"; and the Lord, the God of the spirits of the prophets, sent His angel to show to His bond-servants the things which *must shortly take place.*

Second, we must remember that John employs bold symbolism in Revelation rather than descriptive literalism. He prepares us for such in his introduction, where he states that God "sent and signified [*esemanen*] it" (Rev 1:1 NKJV). Revelation is replete with symbols, such as the seven-horned Lamb, bizarre locusts, fire-breathing prophets, a woman standing on the moon, a seven-headed beast, and so forth.[2] If John can present historical realities and redemptive truths by such dramatic symbolism, surely he may present Christ's Church ideally in glorious symbols. The case for redemptive-historical preterism is not special pleading: it fits the whole character of Revelation.

Third, the alleged indication of chronological sequence between Revelation 20:11 (where the "earth and heaven fled away" at the final judgment) and Revelation 21:1 (where "first heaven and earth passed away") is more apparent than real. As Smalley observes: "The association is probably not deliberate, particularly since the

---

[1] See my discussion of Peter's new creation passage (2 Pet 3:10ff) in *He Shall Have Dominion* (3d ed.: Draper, Vir.: ApologeticsGroup, 2009), 302–03. Peter presents the *ultimate, consummate* new creation *conclusion* to the current, developing spiritual new creation.

[2] See: Gentry, *The Book of Revelation Made Easy* (Powder Springs, Geo.: American Vision, 19–26.

setting and mood contrast so markedly."[3] Actually the fleeing away of earth and heaven in Revelation 20:11 does not even speak of an actual physical occurrence, rather it symbolically portrays God's majesty — *as if* the (personified) earth flees away from God. After all, the sea still exists after Revelation 20:11, for it gives up the dead from its depths (Rev 20:13).

Fourth, the flow of Revelation's drama expects the immediate appearance of the New Jerusalem bride (Rev 21:2). John's theme involves Christ's judging Israel (Rev 1:7; cp. Rev 3:10; 11:1-2, 8), which leads to the destruction of old, historical Jerusalem. Once the old city is destroyed in A.D. 70 we should expect the New Jerusalem to take its place. Indeed, the New Testament declares the heavenly Jerusalem is already present in Christianity, as over against Judaism (Gal 4:26; Heb 12:22; cp. vv 18-21).

John's Source Material

Per the "unanimous agreement among scholars,"[4] John's immediate source material in Revelation 21:1 is surely Isaiah 65:17-20 (cf. LXX). And Isaiah's prophecy clearly portrays the coming new covenant order established by Christ, which Paul calls a "new creation" (2Co 5:17; Gal 6:15; cp. Eph 2:10; 4:24). As Young explains Isaiah's statement: "Heaven and earth are employed as figures to indicate a complete renovation or revolution in the existing course of affairs. With the advent of the Messiah the blessing to be revealed will in every sense be so great that it can be described as the creation of a new heaven and a new earth." By the very nature of the case, this inaugurated fulfillment will include "the *entire reign of Christ, including the second advent and the eternal state.*"[5]

We know that Isaiah was not speaking of the consummate order, for he includes aspects of the present fallen order in his description:

No longer will there be in it an infant who lives but a few days, / Or an old man who does not live out his days; / For the youth will die at the age of one hundred / And the one who does not reach the age of one hundred / Shall be thought accursed. (Isa 65:20)

[3] Stephen S. Smalley, *The Revelation to John: A Commentary on the Greek Text of the Apocalypse* (Downers Grove, Ill.: InterVarsity, 2005), 522.

[4] David Mathewson, *A New Heaven and a New Earth: The Meaning and Function of the Old Testament in Revelation 21.1–22.5* (London: Sheffield Academic Press, 2003), 33; cf. G. K. Beale, *The Book of Revelation* (NIGTC) (Grand Rapids: Eerdmans, 1999), 1041.

[5] E. J. Young, The Book of Isaiah (Grand Rapids: Eerdmans, 1965), 3:514; cp. John Calvin, *Commentaries on the Book of the Prophet Isaiah*, transl. by William Pringle (Grand Rapids: Eerdmans, 1948), 2:399.

The eternal order will not include infants, death, aging, and curse.

The First Century Reality

As demanded in the view I am presenting, we can detect implications of the first century experience of John's original audience.

First, the coming of the new Jerusalem (Rev 21:2) leads to the proclamation from God's throne: "Behold, the tabernacle of God is among men, and He shall dwell among them, and they shall be His people, and God Himself shall be among them." This transpires in the first century, as a result of Christ's work and the outpouring of God's Spirit to inaugurate the new age (Jn 7:39; Ac 1:4; 2:16–21, 33). Are we note *now* God's people, indwelled by his Spirit (Rom 8:9). Paul writes in 2 Corinthians 6:16: "We are the temple of the living God; just as God said, 'I will dwell in them and walk among them; / and I will be their God, and they shall be My people.'"

Second, at Revelation 21:5 God speaks from his heavenly throne declaring: "I am *making* all things new." The present tense here ("making" [*poi*]) suggests this divine activity is occurring in John's day as he writes, not centuries in the future. He seems to emphasize the present reality in that he also sees the new Jerusalem "coming down" [*katabainousan*, pres. act. ptcp.] out of heaven (Rev 21:2).[6]

Reflected Redemptive Truths

In his grand vision John also presents redemptive truths embodied in the gospel of Jesus Christ and its ultimate effect on the world.

First, the promise of the water of life without cost echoes Isaiah 55:1 — which extends God's offer of salvation. This of course is related to the redemptive-historical order established by Christ in the first century. In his Gospel John speaks of the water of life flowing from Christ during his incarnation (Jn 4:10–14), as when he urges men to "come to Me and drink" (Jn 7:37). He also records Christ's promises of its fuller flow at his exaltation (Jn 7:38–39; cp. Ac 1:4; 2:16–21, 33).

Second, the twelve foundation stones of the city in Revelation 21:14 picture the historical church, which Paul presents as already "having been built upon the foundation of the apostles and prophets" (Eph 2:20; cp. Mt 16:18; 1Co 3:10). (John tends to re-align redemptive truths by associating them with the A.D. 70 victory, which is the final confirmation of Christianity as it finally separates from Israel.)

---

[6] M. Robert Mulholland, Jr., *Revelation: Holy Living in an Unholy World* (Grand Rapids: Zondervan, 1990), 316.

Third, in Revelation 21:16 we learn that the city appears as a cube of 12,000 stadia (1400+ miles) on each side. This also suggests a first century setting for the new Jerusalem. Mulholland writes:

> The vision has a practical purpose in the dimensions of the city. If one takes a map of the Mediterranean area and draws a square of 1,400 miles to the scale of the map, then places the center of the square on Patmos, the western edge of the square extends to Rome, the eastern edge to Jerusalem, and northern and southern edges approximate the northern and southern boundaries of the Roman Empire in the first century. At the time of John's revelation, whether it took place in the 60s or the 90s, all the Christian communities known to exist were located within those boundaries.[7]

Fourth, John writes in Revelation 21:22: "And I saw no temple in it, for the Lord God, the Almighty, and the Lamb, are its temple." This suggests a first century reality, for with Christ's coming and death the temple is rendered unnecessary (Mk 15:38∥; Jn 4:21; Ac 17:24; Heb 8:13), for he is the temple (Jn 2:19–21; Eph 2:19–20) and is greater than the physical temple (Mt 12:6). Both the High Priest's tearing his sacerdotal robes (Mt 26:65) and the temple's veil being rent (Mt 27:51) signify the coming removal of the temple system and the opening of heaven to the faithful (Heb 10:19–22). Because Christ indwells us, we spiritually reflect the glorious truth of the temple (1Co 3:16; 6:17; 2Co 6:16; 1Pe 2:5, 9).

Fifth, that "the nations shall walk by its light" (Rev 21:24a) suggests that the nations as separate national entities still exist. Furthermore, not only is Christ the light of the world (Jn 8:12; 9:5) but he establishes his Church to be "the light of the world" (Mt 5:14), which is "already shining" (1Jn 2:8b; cp. Ro 13:12). Thus, historical conditions still prevail, rather than radically new, eternal conditions of perfect union and the fading of all national divisions.

Sixth, the declaration that "its gates shall never be closed" (Rev 21:25b) pictures the city's openness to new converts. This shows the ongoing work of evangelism operating in the pre-consummate order. As Christ exhorts: "Come to Me, all who are weary and heavy -laden, and I will give you rest" (Mt 11:28).

Seventh, the city is not a purely consummational phenomenon, for the "unclean" and he "who practices abomination and lying" are not allowed in (Rev 21:27). This implies a pre-Judgment setting, where sinners still exist. The unconverted are the unclean, as we see in Scripture's image of Gentiles outside of Christ (as per Peter's vi-

---

[7] Mulholland, *Revelation*, 122.

sion of the sheet filled with unclean animals, Ac 10:14–15, 28; 15:19; cp. 2Co 6:17).

Eighth, in fact, the city contains the "tree of life," which produces leaves "for the healing of the nations" (Rev 22:1–2). This also requires conditions existing prior to the eternal order. John's Old Testament backdrop appears to be Ezekiel's vision of the river of life flowing from God's altar, which speaks of salvation-healing:

> And by the river on its bank, on one side and on the other, will grow all kinds of trees for food. Their leaves will not wither, and their fruit will not fail. They will bear every month because their water flows from the sanctuary, and their fruit will be for food and their leaves for healing." (Eze 47:12)

Revelation's healing of the nations strongly suggests conversion. Note another Old Testament backdrop: "Thus the Lord will make Himself known to Egypt, and the Egyptians will know the Lord in that day. They will even worship with sacrifice and offering, and will make a vow to the Lord and perform it. And the Lord will strike Egypt, striking but healing; so they will return to the Lord, and He will respond to them and will heal them." (Isa 19:21–22; cp. Ro 16:25–26)

Ninth, John even declares the continued existence of "dogs and the sorcerers and the immoral persons and the murderers and the idolaters, and everyone who loves and practices lying" (Rev 22:15), though they are "outside" of the city. Presumably they are the targets of evangelism, for whom the healing leaves of the tree of life and the water of life exist.[8]

New Creation Gradualism

The principle of gradualism is important to understand as we look into the idea of the present new creation process. Gradualism recognizes that God *generally* works his will *incrementally over time* rather than *catastrophically* all *at once*. We see this in God's method in the progress of redemption in time (Ge 3:15; Gal 4:4), in Israel's gradual conquest of the Promised Land (Ex 23:29–30; Dt 7:22), in God's unfolding of his revelation in history (Isa 28:10; Heb 1:1–2), and in the expansion of Christ's kingdom to the end (Mk 4:26–32; Isa 9:6–7).

---

[8] These images *may* especially reflect apostate Judaism, like Paul's referring to "the false circumcision" as "dogs" and "evil workers" (Php 3:2). See Israel's sins in Ro 2:17–29 (cp. Jn 8:44). Remember John's designating the Jewish synagogues as a "synagogue of Satan" (Rev 2:9; 3:9) and his presenting the temple as an idol for Israel (see my Ch. 7 above).

This gradualism principle fits well with the "now but not yet" principle in redemptive eschatology. For instance, our Lord establishes his kingdom in the first century. Not only does he declare "the time *is fulfilled*, and the kingdom of God is *at hand*" (Mk 1:15) but later he states that "if it is by the Spirit of God that I cast out demons, then the kingdom of God *has come* upon you" (Mt 12:28). Yet he also teaches us to pray: "Your kingdom come" (Mt 6:10). So then, the kingdom is present, yet it also is to come; it is now (in one sense), but not yet (in the full sense).

The same is true of our own resurrection. Christ teaches us about a spiritual resurrection that is present ("now") and which is directly linked to a physical resurrection to come ("not yet"):

> Truly, truly, I say to you, an hour is coming, and is *now here*, when the dead will hear the voice of the Son of God, and those who hear will live. . . . Do not marvel at this, for an hour *is coming* when all who are in the tombs will hear his voice and come out, those who have done good to the resurrection of life, and those who have done evil to the resurrection of judgment. (Jn 5:25, 28–29)

We also can see this principle at work in Christ's subduing his enemies, which in one sense is accomplished now (1Pe 3:22) but in its ultimate sense is not yet (Heb 10:13).

In the same way, God unfolds the new creation in stages. The new creation is *now* with us for: "if anyone is in Christ, he is a new creation. The old has passed away; behold, the new *has come*" (2Co 5:17; cp. Gal 6:15; Eph 2:10; 4:24; Col 3:10). Yet *we are awaiting* its final, full, corporeal establishment: "But according to his promise *we are waiting* for new heavens and a new earth in which righteousness dwells" (2Pe 3:13). And this waiting may consume thousands of years in that "with the Lord one day is as a thousand years, and a thousand years as one day" (2Pe 3:8).

Isaiah prophesies the Church age by using dramatic new creation language: "For behold, I create new heavens and a new earth, / And the former things shall not be remembered or come into mind" (Isa 65:17). This clearly is not speaking *directly* of the consummate, eternal order, for as I note above, it still experiences birth, death, and sin at work (Isa 65:20).

Thus, in the kingdom that Christ establishes in the first century we find the new creation order in spiritual form, anticipating its growth through time, and its ultimate climax at the end of history. Consequently, the new heavens and new earth presently exist within the bosom of the Church. Just as Scripture links the present spiritual and future physical resurrections, so also it links the present spiritual and the future physical new creation. Therefore, we can learn what the consummated order will be like by reflecting on the implications of the present spiritual realities already at work, realities which anticipate the perfected consummate order.

Conclusion

In Revelation John details Christ's judgment upon Israel (Rev 1:7; cp. 3:10) and the collapse of the temple and the old covenant order (Rev 11:1–2, 19). Christianity is born out of Judaism, and for its first forty years functions as a sect of Judaism. But once the temple collapses (Heb 8:13; 12:20–28), Christianity is finally and forever freed from its mother and the constraints involved in that previous association (cf. Mk 2:21–22‖; Jn 4:20–24). John is picturing the glory of new covenant Christianity, which arises from the ashes of collapsed Judaism (cp. Mt 8:11–12; 21:43; 22:1–10). Christ promises victory over Israel and her resistance: "Truly I say to you, that you who have followed Me, in the regeneration when the Son of Man will sit on His glorious throne, you also shall sit upon twelve thrones, judging the twelve tribes of Israel" (Mt 19:28).

APPENDIX
ANTI-SEMITISM AND PRETERISM

Behold, I will cause those of the synagogue of Satan, who say that they are Jews, and are not, but lie — behold, I will make them to come and bow down at your feet, and to know that I have loved you. (Rev 3:9)

Introduction

Some Christians deem preterism's applying Revelation's judgments to Israel in A.D. 70 as anti-Semitic. Almost invariably dispensationalists do so, because their system is so heavily invested in a dominant, special future for Israel. But many other evangelicals also have difficulty applying Revelation's catastrophic, rhetorically-framed judgment language against first century Israel without complaining that it is inherently anti-Semitic. In this Appendix I will consider the charge of anti-Semitism.

The Charge

The Backdrop

Three issues merge today in forming the anti-Semitism charge against preterism: The first is the recent Nazi holocaust that ruthlessly slaughtered so many Jews in our lifetime. This enormous evil has rightly impacted our collective psyche regarding both the suffering of the Jews and the sinfulness of man. Its impact is widely felt in biblical and theological studies, just as it is in historical, sociological, political, psychological, and other fields of academic endeavor.

The second is political correctness, with all of its hyper-sensitivity. We are all familiar with this mindset and its heightened sensitivity to any sort of perceived slight to any people group. Combined with an extreme relativism so rampant in modern culture, the very facts of history are either totally suppressed or radically reinterpreted in order to promote the new values inherent in this perspective.

In this environment any promotion or defense of *Christianity*, especially regarding its truth claims, salvific exclusivism, and its history-altering impact, is fair game for public derision and academic assault. The modern mind recoils at the notion that Jesus Christ is "*the* way, *the* truth, and *the* life" and that "no one comes to the Father, but through Me" (Jn 14:6). The notion of Jesus as the only

Savior is an anathema that is resolutely condemned.[1] We see this even in the academic practice of changing the long-standing practice of using B.C. ("Before" Christ") and A.D. (*Anno Domini*, "in the year of our Lord") by adopting the nomenclature "C.E." (Common Era) and B.C.E. ("Before the Common Era").

The third issue involves the dominant evangelical perspective in America: dispensationalism. Dispensationalism has as its chief cornerstone a special future for Israel. In fact, dispensationalism teaches that we must treat the Jews with a special deference today, recognizing that they are God's special people.[2] They also hold to a political millennium wherein Jews will be exalted over the nations. Consider the following comments:

Charles Ryrie: "Israel, regathered and turned to the Lord in salvation, will be exalted, blessed, and favored through this period."[3]

J. Dwight Pentecost: "The Gentiles will be Israel's servants during that age. . . . The nations which usurped authority over Israel in past ages find that downtrodden people exalted and themselves in subjection in their kingdom. And these are not unsaved Gentiles: The Gentiles that are in the millennium will have experienced conversion prior to admission."[4]

Herman Hoyt: "The redeemed living nation of Israel, regenerated and regathered to the land will be head over all the nations of the earth . . . . So he exalts them above the Gentile nations. . . . On the lowest level there are the saved, living, Gentile nations."[5]

---

[1] See the helpful study by Ronald H. Nash: *Is Jesus the Only Savior?* (Grand Rapids: Zondervan, 1994).

[2] Ironically, this very day as I am writing this Appendix I received an appeal for funds in the mail. It is from the International Fellowship of Christians and Jews™. The front of the envelope stated: "You can feed an elderly Jewish widow in Israel for only $2.40. Enclosed: An important message from Christian leaders." On the back of the envelope is a quote from Pat Robertson: "I believe a blessing has been ordained by God for those who bless Abraham and the descendants of Abraham." The letter within includes photos of and statements from Pat Robertson, Paige Patterson, and Jerry Rose.

[3] Charles C. Ryrie, *The Basis of the Premillennial Faith* (Neptune, N.J.: Loizeaux, 1953), 149.

[4] J. Dwight Pentecost, *Things to Come: A Study in Biblical Eschatology* (Grand Rapids: Zondervan, 1958), 508.

[5] Herman Hoyt, "Dispensational Premillennialism," in Robert G. Clouse, *The Meaning of the Millennium: Four Views* (Downers Grove, Ill.: InterVarsity, 1977), 81.

H. Wayne House and Thomas D. Ice: "God will keep his original promises to the fathers and will one day convert and place Israel as the head of the nations."[6]

John F. Walvoord: "Israel will be a glorious nation, protected from her enemies, exalted above the Gentiles. . . . In contrast to the present church age in which Jew and Gentile are on an equal plane of privilege, the millennium is clearly a period of time in which Israel is in prominence and blessing. . . . Israel as a nation will be exalted."[7]

Arnold G. Fruchtenbaum: "In the millennium Israel as a nation will rule over the Gentiles."[8]

Hal Lindsey: "The whole point of this passage [Ro 11] revolves around Israel's being restored to a position of preeminence as a believing nation."[9]

Dave Hunt: "The biblical teaching [is] that the coming millennial kingdom will have its headquarters in Jerusalem with the Messiah ruling the world from the throne of David and with national Israel restored to its place of supremacy over the nations."[10]

Dispensationalists even publish books warning of this perspective. Hal Lindsey's *The Road to Holocaust* (1990) is perhaps the most significant of these charges.

The Preterist "Sin"

The preterist approach to New Testament prophecy makes the matter even "worse" by (allegedly) adding the additional baggage of anti-Semitism. This is because preterists believe that two series of events from the first century are foundational to New Testament prophecy and the future development of human history. The first set of events involve the birth, life, work, death, resurrection, and ascension of Christ. The second includes the destruction of Jerusalem, the collapse of the Jewish temple, and the permanent cessation of the sacrificial system.

In the preterist system these two series vividly demonstrate the wrath of God against Israel, combining to:

---

[6] H. Wayne House and Thomas D. Ice, *Dominion Theology: Blessing or Curse?* (Portland, Ore.: Multnomah, 1988), 175.

[7] John F. Walvoord, *The Millennial Kingdom* (Findlay, Ohio: Dunham, 1959), 136, 302-03.

[8] Arnold G. Fruchtenbaum, "Israelology, Doctrine of," in *Dictionary of Premillennial Theology* (Grand Rapids: Kregel, 1996), 201.

[9] Lindsey, *Road to Holocaust*, 176. He also notes that "Israel's Restoration Will be National and *Eternal*" (p. 97; emph. mine).

[10] Hunt, *Whatever Happened to Heaven?*, 246.

- dramatically end the old covenant which was God's means for governing Israel;

- permanently disestablish Israel from its central role in redemptive-history; and

- establish forever the new covenant and its final reorganization of the people of God in the Church of Jesus Christ.

This is anathema. Such a theology is sorely *denounced* in the public square. How can we even think that God judges first century Israel for rejecting and crucifying the Son of God and persecuting his followers to death? The postmodern mind complains: "Aren't all religions equal?" "Isn't truth relative?" "Wasn't Jesus just a first century itinerant preacher and mystic?"

So then, evangelical, historical-redemptive preterism exalts Christ as the only Savior, affirms Christianity as the only approach to God, promotes the Bible as the unique, infallible, inerrant, authoritative revelation of God. And — God forbid! — we see the judgment of first century Israel as the will of God and the fulfillment of much biblical prophecy in clearing the way for the ascendency of Christianity. This, according to the modern mindset, is anti-Semitism in all of its ugliness and simplicity.

Our Defense

But is the preterist scheme anti-Semitic? I myself have been criticized for promoting this "anti-Semitic" theology. Before I even start with the general defense of preterism against this charge, I will clearly and forthrightly state: *anti-Semitism is evil and should not be tolerated by any Christian.* You cannot be anti-Semitic and follow Jesus' command: "Do unto others as you would have them do unto you." I will also declare that I myself am opposed to anti-Semitism and have never held to it or any form of racism.

But this issue is not about me. So I must speak to the broader issue regarding whether or not preterism as such is anti-Semitic. My answer to this question should be surmised from all that I have said before: *No.* Preterism as a theological construct is *not* anti-Semitic. Let me explain why I believe this is so.

Definitional Defense

First, I would point out that we need to define our terms. What is "anti-Semitism"? A basic and sufficient definition is found in *Webster's New Twentieth Century Unabridged Dictionary.* There we learn that "anti-Semitism" is:

1. prejudice against Jews; dislike or fear of Jews and Jewish things.

2. discrimination against or persecution of Jews.

This is the only legitimate definition of anti-Semitism. No plank in the preterist system suggests that preterists dislike Jews, fear them, or want to discriminate against or persecute them. Even the *Dictionary of Premillennial Theology* notes: "Anti-Semitism is defined as hatred toward the Jew only because the person is a Jew."[11]

The belief that God will *not* once again exalt Israel above all other nations (as in the Old Testament, e.g., Dt 7:6–8; Psa 147:19–20) is not anti-Semitic. It may be contra-*Judaic*, but it is not *anti*-Semitic. That is, preterism may contradict religious Judaism *theologically*, but it does not denounce or persecute racial Jews *socially*.

Second, I would point out another necessary definition. Preterism teaches that (1) *God* punished Israel; and (2) he did so conclusively in the events of *the first century*. Preterism holds *neither* that Christians are ever called upon to persecute Jews (in either the first century or today) *nor* that God's judgment wrath is to *continue* against them today. The prophetically-determined, biblically-defined judgment of God comes against them in the concrete, historical, non-repeatable events of the first century. *That* is the generation that rejects Christ; *that* temple is the focus of his wrath. And the particular individuals forming that generation and that temple institution have long since perished.

We need to distinguish between an *interpretation* of a book written 2000 years ago in the context of great struggle for the life of the Church and the *engagement* of racism and persecution. I am interpreting a book regarding events that occurred twenty centuries ago; I am not calling for a continuing pogrom against the Jews. In fact, my evangelical Christian theology forbids it: "blessed are the peacemakers" (Mt 5:9); "however you want people to treat you, so treat them" (Mt 7:12); "love your neighbor as yourself" (Lk 10:27); "if possible, so far as it depends on you, be at peace with all men" (Ro 12:18). It also contradicts my postmillennial expectations, which teach that all people-groups will be saved, including Jews.[12]

Theological Defense

To criticize the preterist interpretation of Revelation as anti-Semitic because of its strong teaching against the first century Jews requires that we also criticize the Gospels and Acts on the same basis. In fact, those liberals who charge that Revelation's denunciations of Israel are anti-Semitic *also* charge the Gospels and Acts as such. In fact, *virtually every contemporary academic study dealing with the history*

---

[11] Arnold G. Fruchtenbaum, "Israelology, Doctrine of," 202.

[12] See my *He Shall Have Dominion: A Postmillennial Eschatology* (3d. ed.: Draper, Vir.: ApologeticsGroup Media, 2008), ch. 11.

of anti-Semitism traces the roots of modern anti-Semitism to the New Testament books.

As evidence of this, see the following scholarly works:

• John Dominic Crossan, *Who Killed Jesus? Exposing the Roots of Anti -Semitism in the Gospel Story* (San Francisco: HarperSanFrancisco, 1995).

• Dan Cohn-Sherbok, *The Crucified Jew: Twenty Centuries of Anti-Semitism* (Grand Rapids: Eerdmans, 1992).

• T. A. Burkill, "Anti-Semitism in St. Mark's Gospel," New Testament 3 (1959): 34–52.

• W. R. Farmer, *Anti-Judaism and the Gospels* (Harrisburg, Penn.: Trinity, 1999).

• Riemund Bieringer, Didier Pollefeyt, and Frederique Vandecasteele, eds., *Anti-Judaism and the Fourth Gospel* (Louisville, Kent.: Westminster John Knox, 2001).

• L. T. Johnson, "The New Testament's Anti-Jewish Slander and the Conventions of Ancient Polemic," *Journal of Biblical Literature* 108 (1989):419–41.

I will now quickly sample a few other lines of evidence in this regard.

The New Testament in general. Jack T. Sanders writes that "whether or not Christian writers cringe at applying the term 'anti-semitism' to part of the New Testament, we must realize that it is that hostility that we are describing."[13]

The Gospel of Matthew. Some scholars view Matthew as the "most severely 'anti-Jewish" Gospel.[14] For instance, Jewish scholar David Flusser comments on Matthew 8:11–12 regarding the "sons of the kingdom" being cast out: "This is a vulgar anti-Judaism of many members of the early Gentile church."[15] Regarding Matthew 27:25,

---

[13] Jack T. Sanders, *The Jews in Luke-Acts* (Philadelphia: Fortress, 1987), xvi.

[14] Peter W. L. Walker, *Jesus and the Holy City: New Testament Perspectives on Jerusalem* (Grand Rapids: Eerdmans, 1996) 26. See: S. McKnight, "A Loyal Critic: Matthew's Polemic with Judaism in Theological Perspective," in C. A. Evans and D.A. Hagner, eds. *Anti-Semitism and Early Christianity: Issues of Polemic and Faith* (Minneapolis: Fortress, 1993), 199. Lloyd Gaston, "The Messiah of Israel as Teacher of the Gentiles: The Setting of Matthew's Christology," in James L. Mays, ed., *Interpreting the Gospels* (Philadelphia: Fortress, 1981), 78–96. C. Leslie Mitton, "Matthew's Disservice to Jesus," *Epworth Review* 6 (1979):47–54. Francis W. Beare, *The Gospel according to Matthew: Translation, Introduction, and Commentary* (San Francisco: Harper and Row, 1981), 461.

[15] David Flusser, *Judaism and the Origins of Christianity* (Jerusalem: Magness, 1988), xxiii.

Julie Galambush (an apostate Christian) laments: "It is hard to imagine a more *anti*-Jewish account than this 'most Jewish' gospel." She also states that 1Thessalonians 2:14–16 "was slanderous in its original context and, in later years, disastrous in its consequences."[16] In fact, David K. Lowery, a dispensationalist, can even speak of "the strong denunciation of Israel that pervades the gospel" employing a "strong polemic against Israel."[17]

Matthew 27:25 is of such concern that it plays prominently in the following news story. A May 21, 2000 Associated Press article comments on the re-writing of the decennial Passion Play in Oberammergau, Germany — which play performance dates back to 1634. It was re-written so as to remove (alleged) "anti-Semitic" aspects of the crucifixion account:

> When enraged Temple leaders shouted "Crucify him! Crucify him!" during a climactic scene at the premiere Sunday of the world's most famous Passion play, dissenters defended Jesus for the first time: "Set him free!" The revision is among a series of thoughtfully scripted changes introduced for the millennial production of the Oberammergau Passion play, acted roughly every decade since 1634. Many of the story's most ardent critics now declare this version a milestone in decades-long efforts to expunge negative images of Jews. "I can say positively that it is a turning point," said Irving Levine, an interfaith expert for the American Jewish Committee, which has been working with the Anti-Defamation League since the 1960s to remove Jewish stereotypes from the Oberammergau play.

In his article "Mel Gibson and the Gospel of Anti-Semitism" Charles Patterson (JewishVirtualLibrary.Org) writes:

> The trouble with Mel Gibson's film "The Passion" is not the film itself, but the gospel story on which it's based. The gospel story, which has generated more anti-Semitism than the sum of all the other anti-Semitic writings ever written, created the climate in Christian Europe that led to the Holocaust. Long before the rise of Adolf Hitler, the gospel story about the life and death of Jesus had poisoned the bloodstream of European civilization.[18]

To ameliorate the situation, Gibson edited the film to drop the language from Matthew 27.

---

[16] Julie Galambush, *The Reluctant Parting: How the New Testament's Jewish Writers Created a Christian Book* (San Francisco: HarperSanFrancisco, 2005), 125; cf. p. 59.

[17] David K. Lowery, in Donald K. Campbell and Jeffrey L. Townsend, eds., *A Case for Premillennialism: A New Consensus* (Chicago: Moody, 1992), 166, 171.

[18] Charles Patterson, "Mel Gibson and the Gospel of Anti-Semitism" (2009), www.jewishvirtuallibrary.org/jsource/anti-semitism/gibson.html

In February 4, 2004, the *New York Times* published an article by Sharon Waxman titled: "Gibson To Delete A Scene In 'Passion.'" That article also charged that Matthew 27:25 was anti-Semitic and dangerous. She writes:

> Mel Gibson, responding to focus groups as much as to protests by Jewish critics, has decided to delete a controversial scene about Jews from his film, "The Passion of the Christ," a close associate said today. A scene in the film, in which the Jewish high priest Caiaphas calls down a kind of curse on the Jewish people by declaring of the Crucifixion, 'His blood be on us and on our children,' will not be in the movie's final version, said the Gibson associate, who spoke on condition of anonymity. . . . Jewish leaders had warned that the passage from Matthew 27:25 was the historic source for many of the charges of deicide and Jews' collective guilt in the death of Jesus.

The Gospel of Luke. Weatherly opens his important defense of the historicity and moral character of Luke's writings with these words: "Is the New Testament anti-Semitic?. . . As the question has been posed and answers sought, the Lukan corpus has become a particular focus of investigation."[19] This is because Luke repeatedly blames the Jews for Christ's death: Luke 24:20; Acts 2:22–23, 36; 3:13–15a; 4:10; 5:28, 30; 7:52; 10:39; 13:27–29; 26:10. Josef Blinzler deems this the seed for full blown anti-Semitism, when he writes: "It was repeatedly stated on the part of the Jews that, when all was said and done, modern antiSemitism was nothing else than the logical result of the Christian thesis that the Jews were guilty of the death of Jesus."[20]

The Gospel of John. Many critical scholars argue that John is the most anti-Semitic of the Gospels. For example:

- Rosemary Ruether, *Faith and Fratricide: The Theological Roots of Anti-Semitism* (New York: Seabury, 1974), 111–16.

- R. Fuller, "The 'Jews' in the Fourth Gospel," *Dialog* 16 (1977): 35.

- E. J. Epp, "Anti-Semitism and the Popularity of the Fourth Gospel in Christianity," *CCAR Journal*, 22:4 (Fall, 1975), 35–52.

- M. A. Getty, "The Jews and John's Passion Narrative," *Liturgy* 22:3 (March 1977): 6ff.

---

[19] Jon A. Weatherly, *Jewish Responsibility for the Death of Jesus in Luke-Acts* (Sheffield: *Journal for the Study of the New Testament Supplemental Series 106*, 1994), 13.

[20] Josef Blinzler, *The Trial of Jesus: The Jewish and Roman Proceedings Against Jesus Christ Described and Assessed from the Oldest Account*, trans from 2d ed. by Isabel and Florence McHugh (Westminster, Mary.: Newman, 1959).

Unless we are willing to edit the Gospels by removing large portions of them, evangelicals need to be careful in accepting the charge of anti-Semitism against the redemptive-historical preterist approach to Revelation. For in the final analysis, Christianity would have to rid itself of the Gospels themselves if it is to successfully avoid the charge of anti-Semitism in the current climate.

Biblical Defense

Revelation has John speaking strong words against apostate Judaism. He clearly writes about Jewish synagogues calling them a "synagogue of Satan" (Rev 2:9; 3:9; cp. Jn 8:44) and he calls Jerusalem "Sodom and Egypt" (Rev 11:8). And more. The preterist approach to the book finds even more evidence of strong language against Israel. In Bratcher and Hatton's *Handbook on the Revelation to John*, which "concentrates on exegetical information important for translators, and . . . attempts to indicate possible solutions for translational problems related to language or culture."[21] When they get to Revelation 2:9 they well note that "it is probable that these are Jews" to whom John is negatively referring. But then they write: "If translators feel that translating **Jews** literally will give the wrong impression to readers, it will be helpful to say 'those who say (claim) to be God's people, but are not.'"[22] This avoids language many deem anti-Semitic. But this also alters the text of Scripture and distorts its meaning. But even still the problem remains — for we cannot deny that the original text stated these things.

But now a serious problem arises — a problem which creates a fundamental absurdity in the debate. Such strong language against Jews that we find in the New Testament is *no different from the way the classical prophets of the Old Testament spoke against Israel*. In the Old Testament — the Bible of Judaism — the prophets sorely denounce Israel, as we see for example in: Jeremiah 2–3; 23:1ff; Ezekiel 16:1ff; 34:10; and Isaiah 1:10ff; 56:8–11.

Isaiah castigates Israel: "Alas, sinful nation, / People weighed down with iniquity, / Offspring of evildoers, / Sons who act corruptly! / They have abandoned the Lord, / They have despised the Holy One of Israel, / They have turned away from Him" (Isa 1:4). He calls her leaders "rulers of Sodom" and her people "people of Gomorrah" (Isa 1:10; cp. Rev 11:8). In Isaiah 10:5–6 God sends Assyria against a "godless nation" (Israel). In fact, he scathingly derides the temple in his day:

---

[21] Robert G. Bratcher and Howard A. Hatton, *A Handbook on the Revelation to John* (New York: United Bible Societies, 1993), vii.
[22] Bratcher and Hatton, *Handbook*, 47.

he who kills an ox is like one who slays a man; / He who sacrifices a lamb is like the one who breaks a dog's neck; / He who offers a grain offering is like one who offers swine's blood; / *He who burns incense is like the one who blesses an idol.* / As they have chosen their own ways, / And their soul delights in their abominations. (Isaiah 66:3)

Was Isaiah the Jew, writing in Judaism's Bible, anti-Semitic? Must we remove Isaiah from Scripture so that true anti-Semites will not use it?

Jeremiah calls Jerusalem a harlot (like John does in Revelation!): "You are a harlot with many lovers. . . . You have a polluted land" (Jer 3:1, 2). "I saw that for all the adulteries of faithless Israel, I had sent her away and given her a writ of divorce, yet her treacherous sister Judah did not fear; but she went and was a harlot also" (Jer 3:8). Was Jeremiah the Jew, a contributor to Jewish Scripture, and a beloved prophet speaking in a way that we would condemn as anti-Semitic? But such is the logical implication of the modern charge of anti-Semitism in our relativist environment.

Does not Israel's own Scripture, the Tanak[23] (Christianity's Old Testament), warn Israel of God's wrath if they turn against him (as evangelicals believe they do in rejecting Jesus and demanding his crucifixion, Mt 23:37–38)? Deuteronomy 28:15ff and Leviticus 26 are just two Mosaic warnings to this effect. Thus, Walker well notes that:

> this threat-tradition cannot be dismissed as inherently anti-Semitic. Once again Jesus was standing four-square within an accepted tradition seen throughout the canonical prophets, whereby God's people and their institutions could be denounced in the name of Israel's God. Indeed within the Jewish sectarianism of Jesus' day the pronouncing of judgement upon the present regime in Jerusalem was not unusual.[24]

Historical Defense

Even outside of the Jewish Scriptures we find other Jews reviling Jerusalem, the temple, and the High Priesthood while calling for God's judgments on their own brothers. We see this very clearly in the Dead Sea Scrolls (DSS).

The DSS are written by a sect of Jews who separate from Israel to live in the area of Qumran sometime around 100 B.C. They write many documents justifying their leaving Jerusalem and the temple system. They long for the destruction of the high-priestly aristocracy

---

[23] Tanakh is an acronym based on the initial letters of the three main divisions of the OT: T (Torah, the Mosaic law), N (*Neviim*, the Prophets), *Ketuvim* (the Writings).

[24] Peter W. L. Walker, *Jesus and the Holy City* (Grand Rapids: Eerdmans, 1996), 274; see also 224.

so that Jerusalem may be purified. Their writings scathingly vilify Jerusalem, the temple and the inhabitants of Jerusalem. Are these devout Jews anti-Semitic in attacking their own culture and ethnic brethren? Consider their writings:

In 4QpNah the Qumranian Jews "accommodated the whole text of Nahum to Jerusalem ('Nineveh'), indicating the way in which even texts that did not originally concern faithless Israel could be read as if they did."[25] There they even declare of their fellow Jews that Jerusalem was the "dwelling place" of the wicked of the nations.

The Qumranians scorn the temple priests. The High Priest "robbed God and amassed the riches of the men of violence who rebelled against God, and they took the wealth of the peoples, heaping sinful iniquity upon himself" (1Qp Hab 8:11–12). 1QpHab 7 speaks of the "Wicked Priest" so that when he "ruled over Israel his heart became proud, and he forsook God, and betrayed the precepts for the sake of riches. He robbed and amassed the riches of men of violence who rebelled against God, and he took the wealth of the peoples, heaping sinful iniquity upon himself." They interpret Habakkuk 2:8 thus: "this concerns the last priests of Jerusalem, who shall amass money and wealth by plundering the peoples. But in the last days, their riches and booty shall be delivered into the hands of the army of the Kittim [Romans]" (1QpHab 9). They write: "The city is Jerusalem where the Wicked Priest committed abominable deeds and defiled the temple of God. The violence done to the land: these are the cities of Judah where he robbed the poor of their possession" (1QpHab 12). Thus, in the Tosefta (*t. Men.* 13:22) we find the reason for the destruction of the first century temple: "On what account did they go into exile? Because they love money and hate one another."

The Qumranians withdraw from Jerusalem partly due to Jerusalem's leaders being "the Spouter of Lies who led many astray that he might build his city of vanity with blood and raise a congregation on deceit" (1QpHab 10:12). The separatist Qumran community deem Jerusalem "a place of vanity built with blood" (CDC 12:2), a "fortress of wickedness" (4QTestimonia).

Johnson notes that "anyone who has read the Dead Sea Scrolls knows that the community that wrote them had an extreme hostility to all outsiders."[26] They call fellow Jews outside of their community

---

[25] Iain Provan, "Foul Spirits, Fornication and Finance: Revelation 18 from an Old Testament Perspective." *Journal for the Study of the New Testament* 64 (Dec., 1996):92-93.

[26] Luke T. Johnson, "The New Testament's Anti-Jewish Slander and the Conventions of Ancient Polemic," *Journal of Biblical Literature* 108 [1989]: 439.

"sons of the pit" (1QS 9:16; CD 6:15; 13:14), who are ruled by the angel of darkness (1Q3: 19-21; 5:2, 10), and who are "the ungodly of the covenant" (1QM 1:2). Of those fellow Jews they write in 1QS 2:4-10: "Be cursed of all your guilty wickedness! May he deliver you up to torture at the hands of all the wreakers of revenge."

Thus, the Qumran community judges Jerusalem to be defiled and worthy of divine curse (CDC 1:3; 4:18; 5:6; 6:16; 12:1-2) — as does much of the apocalyptic literature beginning in 200 B.C., as we see in 1 Enoch 83-89; The Apocalypse of Weeks; T. Levi 17:10; and Jubilees 23:21.

Conclusion
If we believe that the New Testament is the inspired word of God..., and if we believe that it records actual historical events and statements..., then we have to interpret it according to its original intent. It is certainly true that some small-minded racists have used the statements of the New Testament to justify ill-treatment of Jews. But this is an *abuse* of historical documents. These people should be rebutted on moral and theological grounds, not by throwing out the New Testament. Nor by suppressing the meaning of what John writes in Revelation. Besides, they could even take up the Jewish Tanak and use it for anti-Semitic ends.

SUBJECT INDEX

— born within Israel, 9, 22, 89, 184
— separates from Israel, 9, 10, 15, 169, 177, 181
circumcision, 22, 23, 52, 105, 107, 182n
Circus Maximus, 81
Claudius Caesar, 21, 84, 87, 136, 162
Clement of Alexandria, 27, 153
Clement (of Rome), 86, 88, 90
covenant, 22, 50f, 55f, 61, 145, 197
— old, 1, 4, 38, 48, 70, 73, 96, 134, 141, 169, 174, 188
— new, 1, 4, 6, 11, 42, 53, 63, 96, ch 15, 188

DAY of the Lord, 5
Dedication, Feast of, 183
demon(s), 5, 95, 125n, 160, 161
diaspora, 78, 79, 112, 121n, 160, 161
divorce, 6, 24, ch 4, 93, 94–96, 146, 195
Domitian, 14, 27, 28, 30, 86, 164n
dragon, 5, 91, 98, 115, 117–18, 125, 138, 167, 171

EGYPT,7, 51, 55, 98, 112, 134, 139, 145
— Jerusalem called, 5
eight/eighth, ch 13
Elijah, 5, 110
Eusebius, 26, 40, 80, 82, 83, 164n
excommunicate (-tion), 79, 82, 83, 94–96

FALSE prophet (see: prophet: false).
Fig tree, 6, 65, 66n, 100, 102

futurism, 15, ch 3

GAIUS Caesar, 137, 162
Galba Caesar, 21, 22, 162
generation, 23, 29
— adulterous, 5, 64, 106
— this, 5, 7, 19, 189, 190
Gentiles, 8, 19, 41, 81, 84, 107, 110f, 126, 133, 134, 181, 186, 191
— accept Christ, 3, 4, 10, 69, 75f
— times of, 10, 19
Gessius Florus, 120, 129
gradualism, 3, 177, 182–83
great city, 139, 142, 144, 176

HARLOT (-ry), 53–55, 57–59,70
— Jerusalem as, 5, 13n, 48–49, 68, 69, 75, 97, 114, 123, 125, 137, ch. 11, ch. 12, 171, 195
HarMagedon, 115, 138
hell, 79
Hermas, 25–26
Herod, 17, 18, 19, 59, 75–77,93, 102, 124, 129, 131, 133, 135, 136, 151, 153
High Priest (see: priest: high).
historicism, 15, 31–34, 36
holy city, 17, 19, 20, 48, 66n, 70, 77, 93, 100, 145, 177
horn(s), 114, 117, 118, 120, 142, 148, 159, 163
house, 95, 96, 101, 106, 107, 125, 153,
— God's, 48, 51, 52n, 58–59, 65, 66, 67, 101, 103, 105
— holy, 18
— of Israel, 77, 95
— spiritual, 23

SELECT SCRIPTURE INDEX

GOODBIRTH MINISTRIES, INC.

www.GoodBirthMinistries.com
P.O. Box 1722
Fountain Inn, SC 29644

MISSION STATEMENT

"Preaching the kingdom of God, and teaching concerning
the Lord Jesus Christ with all openness."
(Acts 28:31)

GoodBirth Ministries was established by Kenneth L. Gentry, Jr., Th.D.,
our Executive Director, in order to expound, apply, advance, and defend
conservative, evangelical Reformed theology in the modern world. To those
ends we offer the following Mission Statement:

Our Aims

As a religious educational ministry, GoodBirth Ministries, Inc., a 501 (c)
(3) corporation located in Fountain Inn, South Carolina, is committed to
sponsoring, subsidizing, and advancing serious Christian scholarship and
education in order to:

(1) Assist individual Christians, local congregations, and other
bodies of believers in understanding, applying, and promoting
a full-orbed Christian worldview, so that Christians might be
committed to the call of Scripture that "whether, then, you eat
or drink or whatever you do, do all to the glory of God" (1 Cor.
10:31; and

(2) Defend against and challenge the various expressions of
unbelief in our modern culture, by demonstrating "that the
weapons of our warfare are not of the flesh, but divinely
powerful for the destruction of fortresses" with a view to "destroying speculations and every lofty thing raised up against
the knowledge of God [by] taking every thought captive to the
obedience of Christ" (2 Cor. 10:4-5).

Our Doctrine

This ministry is founded upon the inspired, infallible, inerrant, and
authoritative Word of God and is committed to the biblically-based evangelical and Reformed doctrinal system outlined in the historic Westminster
Standards, including the Confession of Faith and the Larger and Shorter
Catechisms. As such this ministry affirms a Trinitarian, covenantal, opti-
mistic theology of sovereign grace.

Our Methods

GoodBirth Ministries seeks to promote these goals through various means of educational outreach, including: full-length books, published articles, video-taped studies, audio recordings, Internet newsletters, position papers, radio and television interviews, and conference lectures. In all of this it is engaged in "preaching the kingdom of God, and teaching concerning the Lord Jesus Christ with all confidence" (Acts 28:31).

Our Desire

We see GoodBirth Ministries as possessing the potential for impacting both the theological understanding and the spiritual commitment of Christians for a more vibrant, fuller and stronger service of the Triune God of Scripture. We are committed to researching, expounding, applying, advancing, and defending conservative, evangelical Reformed theology in the modern world.

Our Name

Our name "GoodBirth" is a play on the meaning of the name of our founder and Scholar-in-residence, Kenneth L. Gentry, Jr. Etymologically, "Gentry" means "a person of good birth and breeding." In referring to the "good birth," our name reflects the biblical hope for spiritual living and God-honoring service of God the Son, which is rooted in the new birth by the sovereign grace of God the Father through the internal operation of God the Spirit (John 3:1-8; 1 Peter 1:3, 23). GoodBirth Ministries wants Christians to understand their "good birth" so that they may faithfully "walk in newness of life" in Christ (Rom. 6:4).

Our Incorporation

The general purposes for which GoodBirth Ministries has been incorporated are to operate exclusively for such spiritual and educational purposes as qualify it as an exempt organization under Internal Revenue Code Section 501 (c) (3), including for such purposes, the making of distributions to organizations that qualify as tax exempt organizations under the Code. Consequently, all gifts made to our ministry are approved for a federal tax deductible status.

www.GoodBirthMinistries.com

CPSIA information can be obtained
at www.ICGtesting.com
Printed in the USA
LVHW011923120521
687208LV00003B/166

9 780984 322039